The

BROA
BO
COMMON
ERRORS *in*
ENGLISH

D0762872

WITHDRAWN
UTSA LIBRARIES

The

BROADVIEW
BOOK *of*
COMMON
ERRORS *in*
ENGLISH

A Guide to Righting Wrongs
Fifth Edition

Don LePan

broadview press

© 2003 Don LePan

All rights reserved. The use of any part of this publication reproduced, transmitted in any form or by any means, electronic, mechanical, photocopying, recording, or otherwise, or stored in a retrieval system, without prior written consent of the publisher—or in the case of photocopying, a licence from Access Copyright (Canadian Copyright Licensing Agency), One Yonge Street, Suite 1900, Toronto, ON M5E 1E5—is an infringement of the copyright law.

National Library of Canada Cataloguing in Publication
LePan, Don, 1954-
The Broadview book of common errors in English: a guide to righting wrongs / Don LePan. — 5th ed.
Includes index.
ISBN 1-55111-586-7
1. English language—Errors of usage.
2. English language—Errors of usage—Problems, exercises, etc.
3. English language—Grammar.
I. Title. II. Title: Common errors in English.
PE1460.B76 2003   428.2   C2003-901036-8

Broadview Press Ltd. is an independent, international publishing house, incorporated in 1985. Broadview believes in shared ownership, both with its employees and with the general public; since the year 2000 Broadview shares have traded publicly on the Toronto Venture Exchange under the symbol BDP.

We welcome comments and suggestions regarding any aspect of our publications—please feel free to contact us at the addresses below or at: **broadview@broadviewpress.com**

North America
Canada: PO Box 1243, Peterborough, Ontario, Canada K9J 7H5
USA: 3576 California Road, Orchard Park, NY, USA 14127
Tel: (705) 743-8990; Fax: (705) 743-8353
e-mail: customerservice@broadviewpress.com

UK, Ireland, and Continental Europe
Plymbridge Distributors Ltd.
Estover Road
Plymouth UK   PL6 7PZ
Tel: (01752) 202300; Fax: (01752) 202330
e-mail: orders@plymbridge.com

Australia and New Zealand
UNIREPS, University of New South Wales
Sydney, NSW, 2052
Tel: 61 2 9664 0999; Fax: 61 2 9664 5420
e-mail: info.press@unsw.edu.au

www.broadviewpress.com

Broadview Press Ltd. gratefully acknowledges the financial support of the Government of Canada through the Book Publishing Industry Development Program for our publishing activities.

Text composition, page and cover design by BookWorks, Calgary.

PRINTED IN CANADA

Library
University of Texas
at San Antonio

Contents

Acknowledgements

The list of those who have been helpful in the preparation of all editions of this book, and/or who have provided useful comments and suggestions, includes the following: Andrew Bailey, Sheila Bean, Ingrid Berzins, Molly Blyth, Ian Cameron, Robert Chambers, Barbara Conolly, R.W. Cooley, Eileen Eckert, Marjorie Holmes, Beth Humphries, Julia Gaunce, Reid Gilbert, Tom Hurka, George Kirkpatrick, Ann Levey, Robert Lovejoy, Tom Marshall, Mical Moser, Fraser Seely, Heidi Standell, and Terry Teskey. Their assistance is gratefully acknowledged.

Preface

In what sense are errors in grammar and usage wrong? Are they in fact wrong in any meaningful sense? Should "wrong" in this context be read as always having inverted commas around it?

Too often this sort of question becomes so infused with assumed political content that it is not taken seriously. On the one hand the conservative is likely to regard the question of whether *you* is a formation inherently superior to the vulgar *y'all* or *youse* as unworthy of debate. Of course the form established as correct is superior; of course the colloquialism is debased. On the other side are those who regard it as an article of faith that there are no universal or objectively verifiable truths, and that consequently there can be no rational justification for preferring *you* to *youse* or *y'all*.

Is *Would you like anything else?* correct and *Would youse like anything else?* incorrect in the same way that "12 x 3 = 36" is correct and "12 x 3 = 35" incorrect? Or in the same way that *The capital of Burkina Faso is Ouagadougou* is correct and *The capital of Burkina Faso is Harare* is wrong? Surely not, as we must recognize as soon as we recognize how odd it would be to say that *Would youse like anything else?* is false. "12 x 3 = 35" and *The capital of Burkina Faso is Harare* are false; they do not correctly make connections between symbolic systems of numbers or of language and a structure of reality that (albeit with certain qualifications) all of us assume to exist. But *youse* <u>does</u> connect with a structure of reality. In fact, as the cognitive scientist Stephen Pinker points out, it makes such a connection with a greater degree of precision than does currently correct usage:

> The mavens lament the loss of conjugal distinction in *he don't* and *we was*. But this has been the trend in standard English for centuries. No one minds that we have abandoned the second-person singular form of verbs, as in *thou sayest*. And by this criterion it is the non-standard

dialects that are superior, because they provide their speakers with sec-ond-person plural pronouns such as *y'all* and *youse*.

Returning for a moment to Burkina Faso may help us to sense the way in which *youse* and *y'all* may fairly if in a limited sense be thought of as wrong. The sentence *The capital of Upper Volta is Ouagadougou* is wrong in something like the same sense that *Would youse like anything else?* is wrong. Both use the symbolic system of language to corre-spond to an understood reality. But in both cases the signs used are not those used under currently accepted conventions; though a few may still cling to the old usage, almost everyone has now adopted the late 1980s change of name (from Upper Volta to Burkina Faso) for the area surrounding the headwaters of the Volta River. *Upper Volta* cer-tainly still corresponds to reality; it is not false. But nor is it right.

Similarly, if one were to transplant from Alberta to Massachusetts one of the Alberta highway signs that read "Speed Limit 110," it would not be in any way false. Given that the convention in all Canadian provinces is to measure speed in kilometres and the convention in the United States is to measure it in miles, however, the sign would in an important sense be wrong (much more wrong, indeed, than would be the use of *youse*, even in the most formal of essays).

But why stick to the conventional where the essay or the business report is concerned? Is there any legitimate argument in favour of standard English? On pedagogical grounds it seems to me that the acquiring of a knowledge of English grammar and syntax is an enor-mously helpful way of strengthening habits of abstract thought. But that speaks to the value of a byproduct, not of the thing itself. There may be only two <u>essential</u> justifications for standard English: ease of communication, and elegance of expression. The first of these is to a large extent obvious, but it is worth stressing that the ease of commu-nication that standard forms or conventions of usage make possible extends not only from individual to individual but also from one cul-ture to another, and over very long periods of time. It has been often noted but bears repeating that the ordinarily literate person in our own time is able to respond to the language of Shakespeare in a way that the ordinarily literate person in Shakespeare's day was quite un-able to respond to *Beowulf*, simply because the conventional codification of grammar and usage that print made possible has drastically slowed down the rate of linguistic change. (Cullen Murphy has interestingly suggested that the development beginning in the late nineteenth cen-tury of electric and then of electronic methods of reproducing sound has given the sloppy and unruly nature of the spoken word a much greater influence on the shaping of the language and on the speed of change than it had in the sixteenth through nineteenth centuries.)

The second legitimate argument in favour of standard English is by far the weaker, and I will readily concede that elegance of expression is often achievable outside the confines of standard English. But complex syntactical and grammatical pathways will inevitably tend to have been worn smoother in a greater variety of ways in long-established conventions of formal expression. Colloquial or non-standard usages may have a freshness to them or in other syntactical ways may appeal strongly in ways that standard English cannot compete with. But they are unlikely to consistently lend themselves to long and elegantly balanced combinations of clauses and phrases in the way that the mainstream of our culture has been training standard English to do for centuries.

*   *   *

If this book is prescriptive, then, it should be understood that it is prescriptive only in a context that recognizes correct English as a matter of convention, not as one in which one form is understood to be necessarily or absolutely better than another. Sentences such as *use aggravate to mean make worse, not to mean annoy or irritate* should always be taken as a convenient short form for *in formal written English, if you wish to conform to the most commonly accepted conventions of usage, use....* And, to return to the example with which I began, *y'all* and *youse* are alternative, arguably superior forms, that we may legitimately reject only on the grounds of convention.

On other specific issues, though, the case for standard usage is sometimes considerably stronger. The confusion of *uninterested* and *disinterested*, for example, will if *disinterested* is driven from the field represent a measurable loss of the communicative capacity of the English language. If we lose *disinterested* it will be more difficult and more cumbersome to express a variety of meanings. Yet there can be no question that many who are unperturbed by *disinterested* having largely been swamped by *uninterested*—indeed, many who do not even recognize the distinction—cringe at the supposed abomination of *youse* or *y'all*. Indeed, I must confess to having been among them until I read and was entirely persuaded by Pinker's argument. What such cases drive home to us is the degree to which the ways in which we use standard English and the assumptions we make about standard English may be linked to irrational sentiments such as social snobbery, or class or gender-based prejudice. (How many there still are who ludicrously claim *fisher* and *chair* to be "more awkward" than the longer and cumbersome forms *fisherman* and *chairman*.) There are good reasons for not abandoning standard English–but good reasons as well to keep questioning our own assumptions about it.

* * *

One of the ways in which this book differs from many other guides to grammar and usage is in its approach to change in language, and in the degree to which it attempts to resist the assumption that where the English language is concerned, change implies debasement. Thus in the chapter on part of speech conversions such previous entries as *liaise* and *mandate* have been dropped. I am not at all sure that the back formation of a verb from the noun *liaison* is a pretty thing. But nor am I sure that my own bias against it reflects anything more than habit; certainly I find it difficult in many cases to find more economical replacements. I cannot convince myself that the prejudice against such words is any better grounded than was the bias a generation or two ago against using *contact* as a verb. *Finalize* still grates slightly on my ear too. But sometimes *finish* just does not capture the sense, and *finalize* is more concise than *make final* or *put into final form*. A comparison of the current state of *finalize* with attitudes of the mid twentieth century may be instructive as to whether or not there are any good grounds today for objecting to *finalize*:

> *Finalize* is not standard: it is special, and it is a peculiarly fuzzy and silly word. Does it mean *terminate*, or does it mean *put into final form*? One can't be sure, really, what it means, and one gets the impression that the person using it doesn't know, either, and doesn't want to know. (Strunk and White, *The Elements of Style*, [New York, Macmillan: 2/e, 1972] 75–76)

That may have been true in 1957, when the first edition of *The Elements of Style* appeared, or even in 1972, when the second edition was published. But no one today uses *finalize* to mean *terminate*; that denotation has dropped away, and the word's meaning has stabilized as *put into final form*.

If Strunk and White are out of date on the particulars, this remains a good example of the wisdom of their advice to writers that one danger of "adopting new coinages too quickly is that they will bedevil one by insinuating themselves where they do not belong" (75–6). What was a fuzzy and confusing coinage in the 1950s has found a clearly defined place in the language of today. And even conservative arbiters such as Strunk and White recognize that language must change, and that this is not in itself a bad thing. In the end guides such as this one should continually strive for a balance between the value of continuity in language and in usage, and the value of language as a living thing; without change there can be no life.

* * *

In one area in particular this guide is not only unresistant to change but embraces change: the move towards bias-free language. In this one area a different sort of "correctness" than the correctness I have thus far been speaking of is involved. Call it political correctness if you will, but however it is referred to it concerns things that are right and wrong in a sense that goes far beyond questions of what is conventional or convenient. The point involved here is that language can have an important part to play in helping us to do the right thing. To treat men and women on an equal footing; to avoid discrimination on the basis of religion, or race, or class—language can be used to help accomplish all of these goals. An increased emphasis on the ways in which language can help or hinder social change of this sort is thus an important part of this book; a discussion of bias-free language forms one of the longer chapters in the book, and provides a much more thoroughgoing treatment of these issues than did the early editions of this book—or than do most other concise guides to usage.

* * *

I had rather assumed in preparing previous editions that if university instructors were to assign this book (as a great many have done), they would do so in conjunction with another book on essay style and structure. An increasing number of university professors and writing instructors, however, seem to prefer to expose their students to relatively little writing about writing in the abstract, and to look for books about writing that will function more as reference guides to the nuts and bolts of the thing than as full scale textbooks. Some say that discussions of writing process and of essay structure have more impact with their students if done in class or in individual meetings. Some simply say that their students respond better to books in a concise format. Some argue that even books renowned for the wisdom of their advice about writing process and style (*The Elements of Style* perhaps foremost among them) in fact often focus far more on style at the word-by-word and sentence-by-sentence level than on the large issues of essay construction. They argue too that the same habits of thought which need training and practice in order to structure clauses, sentences, and paragraphs coherently also operate in the structuring of the essay, the report, even the dissertation. And some simply suggest that the only truly effective way to learn how to construct longer pieces of writing most effectively is by doing it, paying attention to the comments made about it, and doing it again. Whatever the rights or wrongs of these views, it seems clear that concise guides such as this one are now widely regarded as strong candidates for use as university-level reference texts, and I have thus tried to do more here than in the earlier editions to accommodate the concerns of instructors at the university level.

That said, however, this also remains very much a book designed to be of interest and of use to writers and lovers of language outside the academic community. Such readers may find of particular interest features such as the inclusion of a mini-dictionary of variants in the largest traditional areas of English usage: Australia, Canada, England, and the United States. Quite aside from its inherent interest and usefulness I hope that little section of the book may help to underscore the sense in which particular usages are correct or incorrect. To refer to the body of water behind a dam as being itself a *dam* is certainly wrong to a North American, but not to an Australian, or for that matter to a Zimbabwean. Such examples should act as a reminder that a guide such as this one is inevitably a book as much about difference as it is about right and wrong.

Works Cited

Murphy, Cullen. "The Lay of the Language: The Decline of Semantic Distinction, and What It Suggests About Linguistic Evolution." *Atlantic Monthly* May 1995: 20-22.

Pinker, Steven. "Grammar Puss: The Fallacies of the Language Mavens." *New Republic* 31 Jan. 1994: 19-24.

Strunk, William Jr., and E.B. White, *The Elements of Style.* 2nd ed. New York: Macmillan, 1972.

VERBS AND VERB TENSE DIFFICULTIES

THE INFINITIVE

Although not properly speaking a verb tense, the infinitive is the starting point for building a knowledge of verb tenses; the infinitive is the most basic form of the verb. Some examples of infinitives are *to go, to be, to do, to begin, to come, to investigate*. The infinitive form remains the same, of course, whether the action referred to happens in the past, the present, or the future.

1. **split infinitives**: The most commonly made mistake involving infinitives is undoubtedly the slang substitution of *and* for *to*, especially in the expression *try and do it* for *try to do it* (see under Usage for a fuller treatment). The great issue in this area among grammarians, however, is the split infinitive—the infinitive which has another word or words inserted between *to* and the verb:

> *wrong* The time has come to once again go to the polls. Economic conditions are likely to greatly influence the outcome, and the Prime Minister has promised to forcefully speak out in defence of the government's fiscal record.

With re-united infinitives, the same passage looks like this:

> *right* The time has come to go once again to the polls. Economic conditions are likely to influence greatly the outcome, and the Prime Minister has promised to speak out forcefully in defence of the government's fiscal record.

On what grounds can the second passage be considered better? It comes down to a matter of sound and rhythm. To most ears *to go once again* and *to speak out forcefully* are preferable to the split alternatives, but *to influence greatly* seems more awkward than *to greatly influence*. Happily, most authorities are now agreed that it is not a grievous sin to split an infinitive; Philip Howard, editor of *The Times of London*, calls the split infinitive "the great shibboleth of English syntax," and even the traditionalist H.W. Fowler allows that while "the split infinitive is an ugly thing, we must warn the novice against the curious superstition that splitting or not splitting makes the difference between a good and a bad writer." This is not to say that the splitting of infinitives should be encouraged. In many cases a split infinitive is a sign of wordiness; in cases such as the following it is better to drop the adverb entirely:

poor	The Chair said it was important to really investigate the matter thoroughly.
better	The Chair said it was important to investigate the matter thoroughly.

Like all verb forms, most infinitives have both an *active* and a *passive* voice. The active, which is more common, is used when the subject of the verb is doing the action, whereas the passive is used when the subject of the verb is receiving the action, or being acted <u>on</u>. *To do, to hit, to write* are examples of infinitives in the active voice, while *to be done, to be hit, to be written* are examples of infinitives in the passive voice.

THE SIMPLE PRESENT TENSE

	singular	*plural*
1st person	I say	we say
2nd person	you say	you say
3rd person	he, she, it says	they say

2. **subject-verb agreement**: The simple present tense seems entirely straightforward, and usually it is. Most of us have no difficulty with the first person or the second person. But almost all of us occasionally have problems in writing the third person correctly. All too often the letter *s* at the end of the third person singular is left out. The simple rule to remember is that whenever you use a verb in the third person singular of the simple present tense, it <u>must</u> end in *s*.

wrong	He go to Vancouver at least once a month.
right	He goes to Vancouver at least once a month.
wrong	The litmus paper change immediately when the solution is poured into the beaker.
right	The litmus paper changes immediately when the solution is poured into the beaker.
	(*Paper*, which is the subject, is an *it* and therefore third person singular.)

It is not particularly difficult to ensure that the subject agrees with the verb in the above examples, but even professional writers often have trouble with more complex sentences. Here are two common causes of subject-verb agreement errors:

(a) The subject and verb are separated by a long phrase or clause.

wrong   The state of Afghanistan's roads reflect the chaotic situation.
right   The state of Afghanistan's roads reflects the chaotic situation.

Here the writer has made the mental error of thinking of *roads* as the subject of the verb *reflect*, whereas in fact the subject is the singular noun *state*. *The state reflect* ... would immediately strike most people as wrong, but the intervening words have in this case caused grammatical confusion.

wrong   As the statement by Belgium's Prime Minister about his country's deficit and unemployment problems indicate, many nations are in the same shape, or worse.
right   As the statement by Belgium's Prime Minister about his country's deficit and unemployment problems indicates, many nations are in the same shape, or worse.
        (The subject is the singular noun *statement*, so the verb must be *indicates* rather than *indicate*.)
wrong   Courses offered range from the history of the Greek and Roman world to the 20th century, and covers Britain, Europe, North America, Africa, and the Far East. (History Dept. Prospectus, Birkbeck College, University of London, 1997)
right   Courses offered range from the history of the Greek and Roman world to the 20th century, and cover Britain, Europe, North America, Africa, and the Far East.

Sometimes a long sentence can in itself throw off a writer's sense of subject-verb agreement, even if subject and verb are close together. In the following example the close proximity of the subject *simplifications* to the verb has not prevented error:

wrong   The decline in the quality of leadership is mirrored in the crude simplifications which characterizes the average person's view of the world.
right   The decline in the quality of leadership is mirrored in the crude simplifications which characterize the average person's view of the world.

(b) The error of using *there is* instead of *there are* when the subject is plural has become more and more frequent in writing as well as in speech. When these two expressions are used, remember that the subject comes <u>after</u> the verb; use *is* or *are* depending on whether the subject is singular or plural.

wrong	There's many more opportunities of that sort than there used to be.
right	There are many more opportunities of that sort than there used to be.

3. **habitual action**: The simple present tense is often used to express what is called *habitual* action—the way an action ordinarily, or habitually, occurs. The simple present tense is used to name such action even if the main verb of the sentence is in the past or future tense.

wrong	The professor told us that Jupiter was the largest planet.
right	The professor told us that Jupiter is the largest planet.
	(Jupiter has not stopped being the largest since he spoke.)

THE PRESENT PROGRESSIVE (OR CONTINUOUS) TENSE

	singular	*plural*
1st person	I am saying	we are saying
2nd person	you are saying	you are saying
3rd person	he, she, it is saying	they are saying

4. **verbs not normally used in the continuous tenses**: In English the continuous tenses are not normally used with many verbs which have to do with feelings, emotions, or senses. Some of these verbs are *to see, to hear, to understand, to believe, to hope, to know, to think* (meaning *believe*), *to trust, to comprehend, to mean, to doubt, to suppose, to wish, to want, to love, to desire, to prefer, to dislike, to hate.*

wrong	He is not understanding what I meant.
right	He does not understand what I meant.

THE SIMPLE PAST TENSE

	singular	*plural*
1st person	I finished	we finished
2nd person	you finished	you finished
3rd person	he, she, it finished	they finished

5. **irregular verbs**: The occasional problems that crop up with the simple past tense usually involve irregular verbs—that is to say, verbs that do not follow a regular pattern in the formation of the simple past and other tenses. (See page 32 for a fuller discussion and list.) The use of *may, might* is a good example:

> *wrong*   Bands such as U2 and Simple Minds gained a foothold in North America through campus radio; without it they may not have broken through.
>
> *right*   Bands such as U2 and Simple Minds gained a foothold in North America through campus radio; without it they might not have broken through.

6. **lie/lay**: Two other verbs that often cause problems with the simple past tense are *lie* and *lay*. The difficulty many people have in keeping these straight is often ascribed to other factors, but is in part also attributable simply to the forms of the tenses; the past tense of *lie* is the same as the present tense of *lay*. Also, the past participle of *lie* is *lain*, not *laid*.

> *informal*   Many in our party have just laid down and rolled over; they cannot get over the fact that we have lost control of the House of Representatives.
>
> *right*   Many in our party have just lain down and rolled over; they cannot get over the fact that we have lost control of the House of Representatives.

Given the inherent confusion of the tense forms, the difficulty of getting one's tongue round *lain down* rather than *laid down*, and the fact that almost anyone will know what meaning is intended with these words, many authorities now feel that the distinctions are not worth troubling over except in formal written English.

THE PAST PROGRESSIVE (OR CONTINUOUS) TENSE

	singular	*plural*
1st person	I was leaving	we were leaving
2nd person	you were leaving	you were leaving
3rd person	he, she, it was leaving	they were leaving

The problems that sometimes occur with the past continuous tense are the same as those that occur with the present continuous (see above, number 4). Remember to avoid these tenses when using verbs having to do with feelings, emotions, or senses (e.g. *see, hear, under-*

stand, believe, hope, know, think, trust, comprehend) and when using the verb *to have* to mean *own, possess,* or *suffer from.*

wrong	At that time he was believing that everything on earth was created within one week.
right	At that time he believed that everything on earth was created within one week.

THE SIMPLE FUTURE TENSE

	singular	*plural*
1st person	I will arrive	we will arrive
2nd person	you will arrive	you will arrive
3rd person	he, she, it will arrive	they will arrive

The only significant difficulty in using the simple future tense occurs over the issue of when to use *shall*, which has for the most part given way to *will* in ordinary usage. But it will never disappear; most of us who would never dream of wading through the pages and pages many authorities offer on when to use *will* and when to use *shall* nevertheless sense instinctively moments when *shall* lends the resonance of added conviction to a verb.

milder	We will not fail.
more determined	We shall not fail.

THE FUTURE PROGRESSIVE (OR CONTINUOUS) TENSE

	singular	*plural*
1st person	I will be finding	we will be finding
2nd person	you will be finding	you will be finding
3rd person	he, she, it will be finding	they will be finding

THE PERFECT TENSES

As used to refer to the perfect tenses, the word *perfect* means *completed*; as you might expect, then, the perfect tenses are often (though not always) used to express actions that have been completed. They are formed by combining some form of the verb *to have* with a past participle (e.g., *opened, finished, believed, done*).

THE PRESENT PERFECT TENSE

	singular	*plural*
1st person	I have worked	we have worked
2nd person	you have worked	you have worked
3rd person	he, she, it has worked	they have worked

7. **continuing past actions**: One way in which this tense is used is to speak of past actions which may continue into the present, or be repeated in the present or future. In the sentence, *Margaret Atwood has written a number of books,* for example, the form of the verb shows that she will probably write more; she has neither died nor given up writing.

A simple enough practice in normal usage, but in the long sentences often attempted as part of academic writing, it is easy to become confused:

> *wrong*   Since it called the First World Food Congress in 1963, the Food and Agriculture Organization has said clearly that the world, with the science and technology then known, had enough knowledge to ensure man's freedom from hunger. Successive world congresses and conferences have repeated this contention. (from a paper given by a distinguished professor at an academic conference)

Here the writer has evidently chosen the present perfect, thinking that he is referring to a situation which has continued on into the present. But when he refers to the *science and technology then known* and to *successive world congresses and conferences* he has cut off the 1963 conference from any grammatical connection with the present. This is again the sort of mistake that most writers can only catch during the revision process.

> *right*   When it called the First World Food Congress in 1963, the Food and Agriculture Organization said clearly that the world, with the science and technology then known, had enough knowledge to ensure man's freedom from hunger. Successive world congresses and conferences have repeated this contention.

THE PAST PERFECT TENSE

	singular	*plural*
1st person	I had believed	we had believed
2nd person	you had believed	you had believed
3rd person	he, she, it had believed	they had believed

Since the verb remains unchanged in all these forms, the past perfect is one of the easiest tenses to remember. What is difficult is learning how and when to use it. In English, however, there are quite definite rules about when the past perfect tense should be used. Its chief use is to show that one action in the past was completed before another action in the past began. Here are some examples:

- I told my parents what had happened.
  (The happening occurred before the telling.)
- By the time the group of tourists left Mozambique, they had formed a very favourable impression of the country.
  (The forming occurred before the leaving.)
- When he <u>had gone</u> I thought very seriously about what he <u>had said</u>.
  (Both the going and the saying occurred before the thinking.)

The usefulness of the past perfect tense can be clearly seen in passages in which the writer wishes to flashback, or move backwards in time. If you compare the following passages, you will see that the use of the past perfect tense in the second passage removes any confusion about the order in which the events happened. In the example below, when only the simple past tense is used, it sounds as if the dead snake is able to crawl:

wrong   The tail was still moving, but the snake itself was quite dead. It crawled out from under a rock and slowly moved towards me as I was lowering the canoe at the end of the portage.

right   The tail was still moving, but the snake itself was quite dead. It had crawled out from under a rock and had moved slowly towards me as I had been lowering the canoe at the end of the portage.
(In the second passage it is clear that the snake approached this person <u>before</u> it died, and not afterwards.)

Perhaps the most common occasions in which we use the past perfect tense are when we are using indirect speech:

- She said that she had knocked on my door in the morning, but that there had been no answer.
  (The knocking happened before the saying.)
- The Chair of the Committee repeatedly asked the witness when the President had known of the diversion of funds.
  (The knowing happened before the asking.)

In a few cases it is possible to speak correctly of two actions which happened one after the other in the past by using the simple past tense for both actions. The use of the word *after*, for example, often makes it clear that the first action was completed before the other began.

8. past actions at different times, or over a prolonged period: Writers often neglect to use the past perfect to name the earlier action when they are speaking of two (or more) actions that happened at different times in the past.

wrong   He asked me if I talked to his secretary before coming to him.

right   He asked me if I had talked to his secretary before coming to him.

wrong   By the time the Allies decided to resist Hitler, the Nazis built up a huge military machine.

right   By the time the Allies decided to resist Hitler, the Nazis had built up a huge military machine.

wrong   Johnson's girlfriend, Marsha Dianne Blaylock, said she knew Williams since October 2001, when she and Johnson began their relationship.

right   Johnson's girlfriend, Marsha Dianne Blaylock, said she had known Williams since October 2001, when she and Johnson began their relationship.

    (Note that like the present perfect, the past perfect is very frequently required with *since* or *for*.)

The past perfect is also used to indicate that a past action occurred over a prolonged period:

- In the early 1960s Sonny Bono was a disheveled pop singer and songwriter with hippie tendencies; by the time of his death in 1998 he had become a conservative Republican member of the House of Representatives.

wrong   In 1980, 10 per cent of Chile's families did not have sufficient income to satisfy the minimum food requirements recommended by international organizations; in 2000 the figure grew to 32 per cent.

right   In 1980, 10 per cent of Chile's families did not have sufficient income to satisfy the minimum food requirements recommended by international organizations; by 2000 the figure had grown to 32 per cent.

right   ... in 2000 the figure was 32 per cent.

    (The original suggests that the figure had remained at 10 per cent in every year from 1980 to 2000, and then jumped in the course of one year to 32 per cent.)

THE FUTURE PERFECT TENSE

	singular	*plural*
1st person	I will have gone	we will have gone
2nd person	you will have gone	you will have gone
3rd person	he, she, it will have gone	they will have gone

The Conditional

	singular	*plural*
1st person	I would go	we would go
2nd person	you would go	you would go
3rd person	he, she, it would go	they would go

The conditional tense is used when we are speaking of actions which would happen *if* certain conditions were fulfilled. Here are some examples:

* If I <u>wanted</u> to go to Australia, I <u>would have</u> to fly.
* If I <u>drank</u> a lot of gin, I <u>would be</u> very sick.
* I <u>would lend</u> Joe the money he wants if I <u>trusted</u> him.

Notice that each of these sentences is made up of a main clause, in which the conditional tense *would have, would be*, etc., is used, and a subordinate clause beginning with *if*, with a verb in the simple past tense (*wanted, drank, trusted*, etc.). In all cases the action named in the *if* clause is considered by the speaker to be unlikely to happen, or quite impossible. The speaker does not really want to go to Australia: she is just speculating about what she would have to do if she did. Similarly the second speaker does not expect to drink a lot of gin: if he <u>did</u>, he <u>would be</u> sick, but he does not plan to. In the same way, the speaker of the third sentence does <u>not</u> trust Joe: he is speaking about what the situation would be if he <u>did</u> trust Joe. Situations like these which are not happening and which we do not expect to happen are called *hypothetical situations*: we speculate on what <u>would</u> happen *if* ... but we do not expect the *if* ... to come true.

If we think the *if* ... <u>is</u> likely to come true, then we use the future tense instead of the conditional in the main clause, and the present tense in the subordinate *if* clause, as in these examples:

* If I drink a lot of gin, I will be very sick.
  (Here the speaker thinks that it is very possible or likely that he <u>will</u> drink a lot of gin.)
* If I want to go to Australia, I will have to fly.
  (Here the speaker thinks that she may really want to go.)

Notice the difference between the following two sentences:

* If a socialist government is elected in Brazil, the American administration will not be pleased.
  (Here the writer thinks that it is quite possible or likely that the socialists will be elected.)

- If a socialist government were elected in Brazil, the American administration would not be pleased.
  (Here the writer is assuming that the socialists probably will <u>not</u> be elected.)

9. the subjunctive: Notice in the above example that *were* is used instead of *was*. This is what is known as the subjunctive mood, used in certain cases to denote actions that are wished for or imagined. Years ago there were many more types of sentences in which the subjunctive was used than there are now, but it has by no means disappeared.

- If we can't even get this much done, God help us.
  (not *God helps us*)
- If I were you, I'd do what she says.
  (not *if I was you*)
- Suffice it to say that the subject is a controversial one.
  (not *suffices it* ...)
- Be that as it may, the central assertion of Smith's book is irrefutable.
  (not *is that* ...)
- The doctor advises that he stop smoking immediately.
  (not *that he stops*)

wrong   If a bank was willing to lend new businesses very large amounts without proper guarantees, it would go bankrupt very quickly.

right   If a bank were willing to lend new businesses very large amounts without proper guarantees, it would go bankrupt very quickly.

10. the conditional tense in the main clauses: Some writers mistakenly use the conditional tense or the present tense (instead of the past tense) in the *if* clause when they are using the conditional tense in the main clause.

wrong   If I want to buy a car, I would look carefully at all the models available.

right   If I <u>wanted</u> to buy a car, I would look carefully at all the models available.
          (The speaker does not want to buy a car.)

or   If I <u>want</u> to buy a car, I will look carefully at all the models available.
          (The speaker may really want to buy a car.)

wrong   If television networks would produce fewer series about violent crime, parents would allow their children to watch even more television than they do now.

right   If television networks produced fewer series about violent crime, parents would allow their children to watch even more television than they do now.

Remember that the past tense (or with the verb *to be*, the subjunctive) is used in the *if* clause whenever the conditional tense is being used in the main clause.

THE PAST CONDITIONAL TENSE

	singular	*plural*
1st person	I would have gone	we would have gone
2nd person	you would have gone	you would have gone
3rd person	he, she, it would have gone	they would have gone

This tense is used in conditional sentences in which we are speaking of actions which never happened. It is used in the main clause, with the past perfect tense being used in the *if* clause.

- If I had studied harder, I would have passed.
  (meaning that in fact I did not study very hard, and did not pass)
- If Kitchener had arrived at Khartoum a day earlier, he would have saved Gordon and the rest of the British garrison force.
  (meaning that Kitchener did not come early enough, and was not able to prevent the 1885 massacre at Khartoum)

11. **limiting it to the main clause**: Some people mistakenly use the past conditional tense in both clauses of sentences such as these; remember that the past conditional should be used only in the main clause; use the past perfect in the *if* clause.

wrong   If the Titanic would have carried more lifeboats, hundreds of lives would have been saved.

right   If the Titanic had carried more lifeboats, hundreds of lives would have been saved.

wrong   If the 'Yes' campaign in Quebec would have won 200,000 more votes, the course of Canadian politics in the mid-1990s would have been very different.

right   If the 'Yes' campaign in Quebec had won 200,000 more votes, the course of Canadian politics in the mid-1990s would have been very different.

ACTIVE AND PASSIVE VOICE

12. **reduce wordiness**: As many authorities have pointed out, in most

cases writers can make their sentences less wordy and more effective by using the active voice rather than the passive.

wrong   The election was lost by the premier. (Passive—7 words)
right   The premier lost the election. (Active—5 words)
wrong   Union power was seen by them to have constrained the possibilities for full investment, and for achieving full employment. (from the first draft of a manuscript by a professor)
right   The shareholders thought that union power had constrained the possibilities for full investment, and for achieving full employment.

The vice, one should note, is not the passive voice *per se*, but the wordiness it sometimes gives rise to.

OTHER TENSES

- *The present perfect continuous tense*—I have been running, you have been working, etc.
- *The past perfect continuous tense*—I had been looking, you had been following, etc.
- *The future perfect continuous tense*—I will have been sleeping, they will have been studying, etc.
- *The conditional continuous tense*—I would be bringing, she would be starting, etc.
- *The past conditional continuous tense*—I would have been working, he would have been driving, etc.

DANGLING CONSTRUCTIONS

DANGLING PARTICIPLES AND INFINITIVES

A present participle is an *-ing* word (*going, thinking,* etc.). When combined with a form of the verb *to be*, participles form part of a complete verb. They can also be used in a number of ways on their own, however:

- The President felt that visiting China would be unwise at that time.
  (Here *visiting China* acts as a noun phrase.)
- Having taken into account the various reports, the Committee decided to delay the project for a year.
  (Here *having taken into account the various reports* acts as an adjectival phrase modifying the noun *Committee*.)

13. **dangling present participles or participial phrases**: The danger of dangling occurs with sentences such as the second example above. If the writer does not take care that the participial phrase refers to the subject of the main clause, some absurd sentences can result:

wrong	Waiting for a bus, a brick fell on my head.
	(Bricks do not normally wait for buses.)
right	While I was waiting for a bus, a brick fell on my head.
wrong	Leaving the room, the lights must be turned off.
	(Lights do not normally leave the room.)
right	When you leave the room you must turn off the lights.

In sentences such as these the amusing error is relatively easy to notice; it can be much more difficult with longer and more complex sentences. Experienced writers are especially alert to this pitfall if they begin a sentence with a participle or participial phrase that describes a mental operation; they are wary of beginning by *considering, believing, taking into account, remembering, turning for a moment,* or *regarding.*

wrong	Believing that he had done no wrong, the fact of being accused of dishonesty infuriated the company's CEO.
right	Believing that he had done no wrong, the company's CEO was infuriated at being accused of dishonesty.
or	The company's CEO was infuriated at being accused of dishonesty; he believed he had done no wrong.
wrong	Considering all the above-mentioned studies, the evidence shows conclusively that smoking can cause cancer.

right	Considering all the above-mentioned studies, we conclude that smoking causes cancer.
better	These studies show conclusively that smoking can cause cancer.
wrong	Turning for a moment to the thorny question of Joyce's style, the stream of consciousness technique realistically depicts the workings of the human mind.
right	Turning for a moment to the thorny question of Joyce's style, we may observe that his stream of consciousness technique realistically depicts the workings of the human mind.
better	Joyce's style does not make *Ulysses* easy to read, but his stream of consciousness technique realistically depicts the workings of the human mind.
wrong	Taking into account the uncertainty as to the initial temperature of the beaker, the results are not conclusive.
poor	Taking into account the uncertainty as to the initial temperature of the beaker necessitates that the results be deemed inconclusive.
better	Since the initial temperature of the beaker was not recorded, the results are inconclusive.

Notice that in each case the best way to eliminate the problem is to dispense with the participial phrase entirely. More often than not one's writing is improved by using active verbs rather than participial phrases. Many people seem to feel that writing which is filled with participial phrases somehow sounds more important; in fact, such phrases tend to obscure the writer's meaning under unnecessary padding. This is true even when the participles are not dangling:

wrong	Another significant characteristic having a significant impact on animal populations is the extreme diurnal temperature range on the desert surface.
	(Can a characteristic have an impact? A small point is here buried in a morass of meaningless abstraction.)
better	The extreme diurnal temperature range on the desert surface also affects animal populations.
wrong	Referring generally to the social stratification systems of the city as a whole, we can see clearly that types of accommodation, varying throughout in accordance with income levels and other socio-economic factors, display an extraordinary diversity.
	(Is there anything either clear or extraordinary about this?)
better	In this city rich people and poor people live in different neighborhoods, and rich people live in larger houses than poor people.

By cutting out the padding in this way the writer may occasionally find to his surprise that instead of saying something rather weighty and important as he had thought he was doing, he is in fact saying little or nothing. But he should not be discouraged if this happens; the same is true for all writers. The best response is simply to chuckle and scratch out the sentence!

14. **dangling past participles** (e.g., *considered, developed, regarded*): The same sorts of problems that occur with present participles are frequent with past participles as well:

wrong   Considered from a cost point of view, Combarp Capital Corporation could not really afford to purchase Skinflint Securities.
      (Combarp is not being considered; the purchase is.)

poor   Considered from the point of view of cost, the purchase of Skinflint Securities was not a wise move by Combarp Capital Corporation.

better   Combarp Capital Corporation could not really afford to buy Skinflint Securities.

wrong   Once regarded as daringly modern in its portrayal of fashionable *fin de siècle* decadence, Wilde draws on traditional patterns to create a powerful new Gothic tale. (*The Cambridge Guide to Literature in English*)
      (The novel is an 'it'; Oscar Wilde was a 'he.')

right   *The Picture of Dorian Gray* was once regarded as daringly modern in its portrayal of fashionable *fin de siècle* decadence. In the novel Wilde draws on traditional patterns to create a powerful new Gothic tale.

wrong   Used with frequency, a man will feel refreshed and rejuvenated. (aftershave advertisement)

right   Used with frequency, this product will help a man feel refreshed and rejuvenated.

15. **dangling infinitive phrases**:

wrong   To conclude this essay, the French Revolution was a product of many interacting causes.
      (The French Revolution concluded no essays.)

poor   To conclude this essay, let me say that the French Revolution was a product of many causes.

better   The explanations given for the French Revolution, then, are not mutually exclusive; it was a product of many interacting causes.
      (A good writer does not normally need to tell her readers that she

is concluding an essay; they can see the space at the bottom of the page. A little word such as *then*, set off by commas, is more than enough to signal that this is a summing-up.)

wrong   To receive a complimentary copy, the business reply card should be returned before June 30.
(The card will not receive anything.)

right   To receive a complimentary copy, you should return the business reply card before June 30.

wrong   To appreciate the full significance of the Meech Lake Accord, a range of factors needs to be considered.
(A factor cannot appreciate.)

poor   To appreciate the full significance of the Meech Lake Accord, we need to consider many things.

better   The Meech Lake Accord was important in many ways.

16. dangling gerund or prepositional phrases:

wrong   In reviewing the evidence, one point stands out plainly.
(A point cannot review evidence.)

poor   In reviewing the evidence, we can see one point standing out plainly.

better   One point stands out plainly from this evidence.

wrong   When analyzing the figures, ways to achieve substantial savings can be discerned.
(The ways cannot analyze.)

poor   When we analyze the figures we can see ways to achieve substantial savings.

better   The figures suggest that we can greatly reduce our expenses.

Other sorts of phrases can be caught dangling too. But almost all writers are capable of attaching them properly if they re-read and revise their work carefully.

wrong   On behalf of City Council and the people of Windsor, it gives me great pleasure to welcome you to our city. (from an announcement by the Mayor)
(The Mayor, not a faceless *it*, is acting on behalf of the others.)

right   On behalf of City Council and the people of Windsor, I am pleased to welcome you to our city.

wrong   By adding more component parts to the prototype, this would cause an increase in the price of the product.

right   By adding more component parts to the prototype, we necessitate an increase in the price of the product.

or   Adding more component parts to the prototype makes it necessary to increase the price of the product.

SEQUENCE OF TENSES

If the main verb of a sentence is in the past tense, other verbs must also express a past viewpoint (except when a general truth is being expressed). Some writers have trouble keeping the verb tenses they use in agreement, particularly when indirect speech is involved, or when a quotation is incorporated into a sentence.

17. agreement of tenses in indirect speech—past plus subjunctive:

wrong   He said that he will fix the engine before the end of 2001.
right   He said that he would fix the engine before the end of 2001.
          (*He said that he will fix the engine* implies that the fixing has not yet occurred but may still occur.)

18. agreement of tenses in indirect speech—past plus past perfect:

wrong   He claimed that he smoked drugs many years earlier, but that he never inhaled.
right   He claimed that he had smoked drugs many years earlier, but that he had never inhaled.

19. agreement of tenses—quoted material:

wrong   Prime Minister Blair admitted that "such a policy is not without its drawbacks."
          (The past tense *admitted* and the present tense *is* do not agree.)

There are two ways of dealing with a difficulty such as this:

(a) Change the sentence so as to set off the quotation without using the connecting word *that*. Usually this can be done with a colon. In this case the tense you use does not have to agree with the tense used in the quotation. The words before the colon, though, must be able to act as a complete sentence in themselves.

(b) Use only that part of the quotation that can be used in agreement with the tense of the main verb.

right   Prime Minister Blair did not claim perfection: "such a policy is not without its drawbacks," he admitted.
or   Prime Minister Blair admitted that such a policy was "not without its drawbacks."

Here are some other examples:

wrong   Churchill promised that "we shall fight on the beaches, ...
               we shall fight in the fields and in the streets, we shall fight in
               the hills; we shall never surrender."
               (This suggests that you, the writer, will be among those fight-
               ing.)
right   Churchill made the following promise: "We shall fight on
               the beaches, ... we shall fight in the fields and in the streets,
               we shall fight in the hills; we shall never surrender."
               (Notice that the word *that* is now removed.)
or   Churchill promised that the British people would "fight on
               the beaches, ... in the fields and in the streets, ... in the
               hills," and that they would "never surrender."
wrong   In the 1974 election campaign the Liberals claimed that "the
               Land is strong."
right   In the 1974 election campaign the Liberals slogan was "The
               Land is Strong."
or   In the 1974 election campaign the Liberals asserted that the
               Land was strong.

IRREGULAR OR DIFFICULT VERBS

The majority of verbs in English follow a regular pattern—*I open* in the simple present tense, *I opened* in the simple past tense, *I have opened* in the present perfect tense, and so forth. However, most of the more frequently used verbs are in some way or another irregular. To pick an obvious example, we say *I went* instead of *I goed*, and *I have gone* instead of *I have goed*. What follows is a list of the main irregular or difficult verbs in English. The past participle (column 3) is used in tenses such as the present perfect (e.g., *I have grown, he has found*) and the past perfect (*I had grown, I had found*).

The verbs that most frequently cause problems are given special treatment in the following list:

(Note: In both regular and irregular verbs, the present tense is formed by using the infinitive without the preposition *to*.)

Present & Infinitive	Simple Past	Past Participle
arise	arose	arisen

20.

wrong	A problem had arose even before the discussion began.
right	A problem had arisen even before the discussion began.

Present & Infinitive	Simple Past	Past Participle
awake	awoke/awaked	awoken/awaked/woken
	(passive: *was awakened*)	
be	was/were	been
bear	bore	borne

21.

wrong	It was heartbreaking for her to lose the child after having bore it for so long.
right	It was heartbreaking for her to lose the child after having borne it for so long.

Present & Infinitive	Simple Past	Past Participle
beat	beat	beaten

22.

wrong	The Yankees were badly beat by the Blue Jays.
right	The Yankees were badly beaten by the Blue Jays.

Present & Infinitive	Simple Past	Past Participle
become	became	become

	Present & **infinitive**	**Simple** **past**	**Past** **participle**
23.	begin	began	begun

wrong He had already began treatment when I met him.
right He had already begun treatment when I met him.

	bend	bent	bent
	bite	bit	bitten
	bleed	bled	bled
	blow	blew	blown
	break	broke	broken
	bring	brought	brought
	build	built	built
	burn	burned/burnt	burned/burnt
24.	burst	burst	burst

wrong The pipes bursted while we were on holiday.
right The pipes burst while we were on holiday.

	buy	bought	bought
	can	could	been able
	catch	caught	caught
25.	choose	chose	chosen

wrong In 1949 Newfoundlanders choose to join Confederation.
right In 1949 Newfoundlanders chose to join Confederation.

	cling	clung	clung
	come	came	come
	cost	cost	cost
	dig	dug	dug
	do	did	done
26.	dive	dived	dived

wrong He dove into the shallow water.
right He dived into the shallow water.

27.	drag	dragged	dragged

Present & infinitive	Simple past	Past participle

wrong	The newspapers drug up a lot of scandal about her.	
right	The newspapers dragged up a lot of scandal about her.	

draw	drew	drawn
dream	dreamed/dreamt	dreamed/dreamt

28.

drink	drank	drunk

wrong	He has drank more than is good for him.
right	He has drunk more than is good for him.

HABS SHOULD HAVE DRANK A TOAST TO DISCIPLINE

(Headline, *The Globe and Mail*, Dec. 19, 1990)

SHORT ON EDUCATION

"Re Habs Should Have Drank A Toast To Discipline (Dec.19): Whoever wrote this headline should have went to school longer." *Simon Farrow, North Vancouver*

(Letters to the Editor, *The Globe and Mail*, Dec. 27,1990)

---

drive	drove	driven
eat	ate	eaten
fall	fell	fallen
feel	felt	felt
fight	fought	fought
find	found	found

29.

fit	fitted or fit (US)	fitted

wrong	That dress has fit her since she was married.
right	That dress has fitted her since she was married.

flee	fled	fled

30.

fling	flung	flung

Present & infinitive	Simple past	Past participle

wrong	George flinged his plate across the room.		
right	George flung his plate across the room.		

fly	flew	flown

31.

forbid	forbade	forbidden

wrong	Yesterday he forbid us to climb the fence.
right	Yesterday he forbade us to climb the fence.

32.

forecast	forecast	forecast

wrong	The Weather Office has forecasted more rain.
right	The Weather Office has forecast more rain.

forget	forgot	forgotten
forgive	forgave	forgiven
freeze	froze	frozen
get	got	got
give	gave	given
go	went	gone
grind	ground	ground
	(e.g., I have ground the coffee.)	
grow	grew	grown

33.

hang	hanged/hung	hanged/hung

Note: *Hanged* is used only when referring to a person being killed by hanging. Say *The criminal has been hanged*, but *We have hung the picture on the wall.*

wrong	No one has been hung in Canada since 1962.
right	No one has been hanged in Canada since 1962.

have	had	had
hear	heard	heard
hide	hid	hidden
hit	hit	hit
hold	held	held
hurt	hurt	hurt

Present & infinitive	Simple past	Past participle
keep	kept	kept
kneel	knelt	knelt
know	knew	known

34.   lay   laid   laid

Note: Although many authorities feel that the distinction is not worth troubling over in informal English, formal English still distinguishes between *lay* and *lie*; you *lay* something on a table, and a hen *lays* eggs, but you *lie* down to sleep. In other words, *lie* is an intransitive verb; it should not be followed by a direct object. *Lay*, by contrast, is transitive.

wrong   That old thing has been laying around for years.
right   That old thing has been lying around for years.

lead	led	led
lean	leaned/leant	leaned/leant
leap	leaped/leapt	leaped/leapt
learn	learned/learnt	learned/learnt
leave	left	left
lend	lent	lent
let	let	let

35.   lie   lay   lain

wrong   He asked if I would like to lay down and rest.
right   He asked if I would like to lie down and rest.

See also above, number 34.

light	lighted/lit	lighted/lit
lose	lost	lost
make	made	made
may	might	
mean	meant	meant
meet	met	met
must	had to	
pay	paid	paid

36.   prove   proved   proven

Present & infinitive	Simple past	Past participle

wrong	We have proved the hypothesis to be correct.
right	We have proven the hypothesis to be correct.

Present & infinitive	Simple past	Past participle
put	put	put
read	read	read

37.

Present & infinitive	Simple past	Past participle
ride	rode	ridden

wrong	The actor had never rode a horse before.
right	The actor had never ridden a horse before.

38.

Present & infinitive	Simple past	Past participle
ring	rang	rung

wrong	I rung the bell three times, but no one answered.
right	I rang the bell three times, but no one answered.

Present & infinitive	Simple past	Past participle
rise	rose	risen
run	ran	run
saw	sawed	sawed/sawn
say	said	said
see	saw	seen
seek	sought	sought
sell	sold	sold
sew	sewed	sewed/sewn
shake	shook	shaken
shall	should	

39.

Present & infinitive	Simple past	Past participle
shine	shone	shone

wrong	The moon shined almost as brightly as the sun.
right	The moon shone almost as brightly as the sun.

Present & infinitive	Simple past	Past participle
shoot	shot	shot
show	showed	showed/shown

40.

Present & infinitive	Simple past	Past participle
shrink	shrank	shrunk

wrong	The Government's majority shrunk in the election.
right	The Government's majority shrank in the election.

Present & infinitive	Simple past	Past participle
shut	shut	shut
sing	sang	sung

Present & infinitive	Simple past	Past participle

41. sink   sank   sunk

wrong   The *Edmund Fitzgerald* sunk on Lake Superior.
right   The *Edmund Fitzgerald* sank on Lake Superior.

sit	sat	sat
sleep	slept	slept
slide	slid	slid
smell	smelled/smelt	smelled/smelt
sow	sowed	sowed/sown
speak	spoke	spoken
speed	speeded/sped	speeded/sped
spell	spelled/spelt	spelled/spelt
spend	spent	spent
spill	spilled/spilt	spilled/spilt
spin	spun	spun
spit	spat	spat
split	split	split
spread	spread	spread

42. spring   sprang   sprung

wrong   The soldiers hurriedly sprung to their feet.
right   The soldiers hurriedly sprang to their feet.

stand	stood	stood
steal	stole	stolen
stick	stuck	stuck
sting	stung	stung
strike	struck	struck
swear	swore	sworn
sweep	swept	swept

43. stick   stuck   stuck

44. swim   swam   swum

wrong   Pictures were taken while the royal couple swum in what they thought was a private cove.

Present & infinitive	Simple past	Past participle

right   Pictures were taken while the royal couple swam in what they had thought was a private cove.

swing	swung	swung
take	took	taken
teach	taught	taught
tear	tore	torn
tell	told	told
think	thought	thought
throw	threw	thrown
tread	trod	trodden/trod
understand	understood	understood
wake	waked/woke	waked/woken
wear	wore	worn
weep	wept	wept
win	won	won
wind	wound	wound
wring	wrung	wrung

e.g. She wrings out her clothes if they are wet.

write	wrote	written

INFINITIVES, GERUNDS, OBJECTS: "*TO BE* OR NOT *TO BE?*"

There are no rules in English to explain why some words must be followed by an infinitive *(to go, to do, to be,* etc.), while others must be followed by a gerund *(of going, in doing,* etc.), and still others by a direct object. Here are some of the words with which difficulties of this sort most often arise:

45. **accept** something (<u>not</u> accept to do something): It needs a direct object.

wrong	The Committee accepted to try to improve the quality of the postal service.
right	The Committee accepted the task of trying to improve the postal service.
or	The Committee agreed to try to improve the postal service.

46. **accuse** someone of doing something (<u>not</u> to do)

wrong	Klaus Barbie was accused to have killed thousands of innocent civilians in WW II.
right	Klaus Barbie was accused of having killed thousands of innocent civilians in WW II.

47. **appreciate** something: When used to mean *be grateful*, this verb requires a direct object.

wrong	I would appreciate if you could respond quickly.
right	I would appreciate <u>it</u> if you could respond quickly.
or	I would appreciate a quick response.
	(The verb *appreciate* without an object means *increase in value*.)

48. **assist** in doing something (<u>not</u> to do)

wrong	He assisted me to solve the problem.
right	He assisted me in solving the problem.
or	He helped me to solve the problem.

49. **capable** of doing something (<u>not</u> to do)

wrong	He is capable to run 1500 metres in under four minutes.
right	He is capable of running 1500 metres in under four minutes.
or	He is able to run 1500 metres in under four minutes.

50. **confident** of doing something (<u>not</u> to do)

wrong She is confident to be able to finish the job before dusk.
right She is confident of being able to finish the job before dusk.
or She is confident that she will finish the job before dusk.

51. **consider** something or someone to be something *or* consider it something (<u>not</u> as something)

wrong According to a recent policy paper, the Party now considers a guaranteed annual income as a good idea.
right According to a recent policy paper, the Party now considers a guaranteed annual income to be a good idea.
or According to a recent policy paper, the Party now regards a guaranteed annual income as a good idea.

52. **discourage** someone from doing something (<u>not</u> to do)

wrong The new Immigration Act is intended to discourage anyone who wants to come to Canada to enter the country illegally.
right The new Immigration Act is intended to discourage anyone who wants to come to Canada from entering the country illegally.

53. **forbid** someone to do something (<u>not</u> from doing)

wrong The witnesses were forbidden from leaving the scene of the crime until the police had completed their preliminary investigation.
right The witnesses were forbidden to leave the scene of the crime until the police had completed their preliminary investigation.

54. **insist** on doing something *or* insist that something be done (but <u>not</u> insist to do)

wrong The customer has insisted to wait in the front office until she receives a refund.
right The customer has insisted on waiting in the front office until she receives a refund.

55. **intention**: <u>Have</u> an intention <u>of doing</u> something *but* someone's intention is/was to do something

wrong Hitler had no intention to keep his word.
right Hitler had no intention of keeping his word.

or   Hitler did not intend to keep his word.
or   Hitler's intention was to break the treaty.

56. justified in doing something (<u>not</u> to do something)

wrong   He is not justified to make these allegations.
right   He is not justified in making these allegations.

57. look forward to doing something (<u>not</u> to do something)

wrong   I am looking forward to receive your reply.
right   I am looking forward to receiving your reply.

58. opposed to doing something (<u>not</u> to do something)

wrong   He was opposed to set up a dictatorship.
right   He was opposed to setting up a dictatorship.
or   He was opposed to the idea of setting up a dictatorship.

59. organize something (<u>not</u> to do something)

wrong   We organized to meet at ten the next morning.
right   We organized a meeting for ten the next morning.
or   We arranged to meet at ten the next morning.

60. persist in doing something (<u>not</u> to do something)

wrong   Despite international disapproval and the will of Congress, the Reagan administration persisted to help the rebels in Nicaragua.
right   Despite international disapproval and the will of Congress, the Reagan administration persisted in helping the rebels in Nicaragua.

61. plan to do (<u>not</u> on doing)

wrong   They planned on closing the factory in Windsor.
right   They planned to close the factory in Windsor.

62. prohibit someone from doing something (<u>not</u> to do)

wrong   Members of the public were prohibited to feed the animals.
right   Members of the public were prohibited from feeding the animals.

63. **regarded** as (<u>not</u> regarded to be)

wrong   He is commonly regarded to be one of Canada's best musicians.
right   He is commonly regarded as one of Canada's best musicians.

64. **responsible** for doing (<u>not</u> to do)

wrong   Mr. Dumphy is responsible to market the full line of the company's pharmaceutical products.
right   Mr. Dumphy is responsible for marketing the full line of the company's pharmaceutical products.

65. **sacrifice** something (<u>not</u> to do): The use of *sacrifice* without a direct object may have crept into the language through the use of the verb as a baseball term *(Martinez sacrificed in the ninth to bring home Womack)*.

wrong   He sacrificed to work in an isolated community with no electricity or running water.
right   He sacrificed himself to work in an isolated community with no electricity or running water.
or   He sacrificed a good deal; the isolated community he now works in has no electricity or running water.

66. **seem** to be (<u>not</u> as if)

wrong   The patient seemed as if he was in shock.
right   The patient seemed to be in shock.
          Exception: When the subject is *it*, *seem* can be followed by *as*. (e.g., It seemed as if he was sick, so we called the doctor.)

67. **suspect** someone of doing something (<u>not</u> to do)

wrong   His wife suspected him to have committed adultery.
right   His wife suspected him of committing adultery.
or   His wife suspected that he had committed adultery.

68. **tendency** to do something (<u>not</u> of doing)
wrong   Some Buick engines have a tendency of over-revving.
right   Some Buick engines have a tendency to over-rev.
or   The engine has a habit of over-revving.

PREPOSITION PROBLEMS: "UP WITH WHICH I WILL NOT PUT"

The prepositions used in English often make little or no sense. What good reason is there for saying *inferior to* but *worse than*? None whatsoever, but over the centuries certain prepositions have come to be accepted as going together with certain verbs, nouns, etc. There are no rules to help one learn the combinations; here are some of the ones that most commonly cause difficulty:

69. **agree** <u>with</u> someone, <u>with</u> what someone says; agree <u>to do</u> something, <u>to</u> something; agree <u>on</u> a plan, proposal, etc.

    wrong   The union representatives did not agree with the proposed wage increase.

    right   The union representatives did not agree to the proposed wage increase.

    or   The union representatives did not agree with management about the proposed wage increase.

70. **angry** <u>with</u> someone; angry <u>at</u> or <u>about</u> something

    wrong   He was angry at me for failing to keep our appointment.

    right   He was angry with me for failing to keep our appointment.

71. **annoyed** <u>with</u> someone; annoyed <u>by</u> something

    wrong   The professor is often annoyed with the attitude of the class.

    right   The professor is often annoyed by the attitude of the class.

    or   The professor is often annoyed with the class.

72. **appeal** <u>to</u> someone <u>for</u> something

    wrong   The Premier appealed for the residents to help.

    right   The Premier appealed to the residents for help.

73. **argue** <u>with</u> someone <u>about</u> something

    wrong   They argued against each other for half an hour.

    right   They argued with each other about the merit of exams.

74. **arrive** <u>in</u> a place, <u>at</u> a place (<u>not</u> arrive a place, <u>except</u> arrive home). Airlines are perhaps to blame for the error of using both *arrive* and *depart* without prepositions.

| *wrong* | He won't join the Yankees until tomorrow night when they arrive Milwaukee. |
| *right* | He won't join the Yankees until tomorrow night when they arrive in Milwaukee. |

75. **attach** two or more things (<u>not</u> attach together)

| *wrong* | The Siamese twins were attached together at the hip. |
| *right* | The Siamese twins were attached at the hip. |

76. **borrow** something <u>from</u> someone

| *wrong* | I borrowed him a pair of trousers. |
| *right* | I borrowed a pair of trousers from him. |

77. **cancel** something (<u>not</u> cancel out, except when the verb is used to mean *counterbalance* or *neutralize*)

wrong	She cancelled out all her appointments.
right	She cancelled all her appointments.
or	After playing hockey, he ate a huge snack that cancelled out the calorie loss of the exercise.

78. **care** <u>about</u> something (meaning *to think it worthwhile or important to you*)

wrong	George does not care for what happens to his sister.
right	George does not care what happens to his sister.
or	George does not care about what happens to his sister.

79. **centre**: centred <u>on</u> something (<u>not</u> around something; for one thing to be centred around another is physically impossible)

| *wrong* | The novel is centred around the conflict between British imperialism and Native aspirations. |
| *right* | The novel centres on the conflict between British imperialism and Native aspirations. |

80. **chase** someone or something away for doing something; despite the way the word is misused in baseball slang, the verb *chase* with no preposition means *run after*, not *send away*.

| *wrong* | Starting pitcher Pedro Martinez was chased in the fifth inning. |
| *right* | Starting pitcher Pedro Martinez was pulled from the game in the fifth inning. |

81. **collide** <u>with</u> something (<u>not</u> against something)

    wrong   The bus left the road and collided against a tree.
    right   The bus left the road and collided with a tree.

82. **compare** <u>to</u>, compare <u>with</u>: To compare something <u>to</u> something else is to liken it, especially when speaking metaphorically (e.g., *Can I compare thee to a summer's day?*). To compare something <u>with</u> something else is to judge how the two are similar or different (*If you compare one brand with another you will notice little difference.*). Use *compare with* when noting differences.

    wrong   The First World War was a small conflict compared to the Second World War, but it changed humanity even more profoundly.
    right   The First World War was a small conflict compared with the Second World War, but it changed humanity even more profoundly.

83. **concerned** <u>with</u> something (meaning *having some connection with it, having something to do with it*) and concerned <u>about</u> something (meaning *being interested in it or worried about it*)

    wrong   The Ministry is very concerned with the level of pollution in this river.
    right   The Ministry is very concerned about the level of pollution in this river.

84. **conform** <u>to</u> (<u>not</u> with)

    wrong   The building does not conform with current standards.
    right   The building does not conform to current standards.
    or   The contractors did not comply with current standards.

85. **congratulate** someone <u>on</u> something (<u>not</u> for)

    wrong   The Opposition leaders congratulated the Prime Minister for his success.
    right   The Opposition leaders congratulated the Prime Minister on his success.

86. **connect** two things, connect one thing <u>with</u> another (<u>not</u> connect up with)

    wrong   As soon as he connects up these wires, the system should work.
    right   As soon as he connects these wires, the system should work.

87. **conscious** <u>of</u> something (<u>not</u> that)

    wrong   He was not conscious that he had done anything wrong.
    right   He was not conscious of having done anything wrong.
              (Note: Unlike *conscious*, *aware* can be used with *of* <u>or</u> with a *that* clause.)

88. **consist** <u>in</u> versus consist <u>of</u>: *Consist in* means *to exist in, to have as the essential feature*; *consist of* means *to be made up of.*

    wrong   Success consists of hard work.
              (i.e. The essence of success is hard work.)
    right   Success consists in hard work.
    wrong   The U.S. Congress consists in two houses—the House of Representatives and the Senate.
    right   The U.S. Congress consists of two houses—the House of Representatives and the Senate.

89. **consult** someone (<u>not</u> consult with someone)

    wrong   She will have to consult with the Board of Directors before giving us an answer.
    right   She will have to consult the Board of Directors before giving us an answer.
    or   She will have to talk to the Board of Directors before giving us an answer.

90. **continue** something, <u>with</u> something, <u>to</u> a place (<u>not</u> continue on)

    wrong   We were told to continue on with our work.
    right   We were told to continue with our work.

91. **convenient** <u>for</u> someone, <u>for</u> a purpose; convenient <u>to</u> a place

    wrong   This house is very convenient to me; it is only a short walk to work.
    right   This house is very convenient for me; it is only a short walk to work.

92. **cooperate** <u>with</u> someone (<u>not</u> cooperate together)

    wrong   The Provinces should cooperate together to break down inter-provincial trade barriers.
    right   The Provinces should cooperate with one another to break down inter-provincial trade barriers.

93. **correspond** <u>to</u> (be in agreement with); correspond <u>with</u> (exchange letters with)

wrong	The fingerprints at the scene of the crime corresponded with those of the suspect.
right	The fingerprints at the scene of the crime corresponded to those of the suspect.

94. **couple** <u>of</u> things, times, people, etc.

wrong	The body had been partially hidden under a pier on Lake Union, a couple hundred feet from the Aurora Avenue Bridge.
right	The body had been partially hidden under a pier on Lake Union, a couple of hundred feet from the Aurora Avenue Bridge.
or	The body had been partially hidden under a pier on Lake Union, approximately two hundred feet from the Aurora Avenue Bridge.

(In formal writing it is best to use *two* rather than *a couple of*.)

95. **criticism** <u>of</u> something or somebody (<u>not</u> against)

wrong	His criticisms against her were completely unfounded.
right	His criticisms of her were completely unfounded.

96. **depart** <u>from</u> a place

wrong	One woman was heard saying to a friend as they departed the SkyDome ...
right	One woman was heard saying to a friend as they departed from the SkyDome ...
or	One woman was heard saying to a friend as they left the SkyDome ...

97. **die** <u>of</u> a disease, of old age; die <u>from</u> injuries, wounds

wrong	My grandfather died from cancer when he was only forty-two years old.
right	My grandfather died of cancer when he was only forty-two years old.

98. **different** <u>from, to, than</u>. *Different to* and *different from* are both acceptable British usage; *different from* is the preferred form in Canada; *different than* is a common and entirely acceptable form in the United States.

US	These results are different than those we obtained when we did the same experiment yesterday.
UK	These results are different to those we obtained when we did the same experiment yesterday.
Canada	These results are different from those we obtained when we did the same experiment yesterday.

99. **discuss** something (<u>not</u> discuss about something; no preposition is needed)

wrong	They discussed about what to do to ease tensions in the Middle East.
right	They discussed what to do to ease tensions in the Middle East.

100. **divide** something (no preposition necessary)

wrong	Lear wants to divide up his kingdom among his three daughters.
right	Lear wants to divide his kingdom among his three daughters.

101. **do** something <u>for</u> someone (meaning something that will help); do something <u>to</u> someone (meaning something that will hurt)

wrong	Norman Bethune did a lot to the people of China.
right	Norman Bethune did a lot for the people of China.

102. **end**: at the end <u>of</u> something; in the end (no additional preposition). *In the end* is used when the writer does not say <u>which</u> end he means, but leaves this to be understood by the reader. *At the end of* is used when the writer mentions the end he is referring to.

wrong	In the end of *Things Fall Apart*, we both admire and pity Okonkwo.
right	At the end of *Things Fall Apart*, we both admire and pity Okonkwo.
or	In the end, we both admire and pity Okonkwo.

103. **end** <u>at</u> a place (<u>not</u> end up at)

wrong	We do not want to end up at the same place we started from.
right	We do not want to end at the same place we started from.

104. **fight** someone or <u>with</u> someone (<u>not</u> against; *fight* means *struggle against*, so to add *against* is redundant)

wrong	They fought against each other for almost an hour.
right	They fought with each other for almost an hour.
or	They fought each other for almost an hour.

105. **frightened** <u>by</u> something (when it has just frightened you); frightened <u>of</u> something (when talking about a constant condition)

wrong	He was suddenly frightened of the sound of a door slamming.
right	He was suddenly frightened by the sound of a door slamming.

106. **graduate** <u>from</u> a school

wrong	He graduated McGill in 2002.
right	He graduated from McGill in 2002.

107. **help doing**, as in *be unable to refrain from doing* (<u>not</u> help from doing)

wrong	She could not help from agreeing to his suggestion.
right	She could not help agreeing to his suggestion.

108. **hurry** (<u>not</u> hurry up)

wrong	She told me to hurry up if I didn't want to miss the train.
right	She told me to hurry if I didn't want to miss the train.

109. **identical** <u>with</u> (<u>not</u> to)

wrong	This hotel is identical to the Holiday Inn we stayed in last week.
right	This hotel is identical with the Holiday Inn we stayed in last week.

110. **in**: Do not use *in* where *throughout* is meant; particularly when using such words as *whole* or *entire*, be careful to use *throughout*.

wrong	Political repression is common in the whole world.
right	Political repression is common throughout the world.

111. **independent** <u>of</u> something or someone (<u>not</u> from)

wrong	I would like to live entirely independent from my parents.
right	I would like to live entirely independent of my parents.

112. **inferior** <u>to</u> someone or something (<u>not</u> than)

wrong   Most people think that margarine is inferior than butter.
right   Most people think that margarine is inferior to butter.
            (*Inferior* and *superior* are the only two comparative adjectives which
            are not followed by *than*.)

113. **inside** or **outside** something (<u>not</u> of something)

wrong   Within thirty minutes a green scum had formed inside of
            the beaker.
right   Within thirty minutes a green scum had formed inside the
            beaker.

114. **interested** <u>in</u> something, <u>in</u> doing something (<u>not</u> to)

wrong   She is very interested to find out more about plant genetics.
right   She is very interested in finding out more about plant genetics.

115. **investigate** something (<u>not</u> investigate about or into something)

wrong   The police are investigating into the murder in Brandon last
            week.
right   The police are investigating the murder in Brandon last week.

116. **join** someone (<u>not</u> join up with)

wrong   Conrad Black joined up with his brother Montagu in mak-
            ing the proposal to buy the company.
right   Conrad Black joined his brother Montagu in making the
            proposal to buy the company.

117. **jump** (<u>not</u> jump up)

wrong   Unemployment has jumped up to record levels recently.
right   Unemployment has jumped to record levels recently.

118. **lift** something (<u>not</u> lift up)

wrong   I twisted my back as I was lifting up the box.
right   I twisted my back as I was lifting the box.

119. **lower** something (<u>not</u> lower down something)

wrong   They lowered the coffin down into the grave.
right   They lowered the coffin into the grave.

120. **mercy**: have mercy <u>on</u> someone; show mercy <u>to</u> or <u>towards</u> someone

> *wrong*   We should all have mercy for anyone who is suffering.
> *right*   We should all have mercy on anyone who is suffering.

121. **meet/meet with**: *Meet with* in the sense of *attend a meeting with* is a recent addition to the language. If one is referring to a less formal or less prolonged encounter, however, there is no need for the preposition.

> *wrong*   Stanley finally met with Livingstone near the shores of Lake Victoria.
> *right*   Stanley finally met Livingstone near the shores of Lake Victoria.
>   (The meaning here is *came face to face with for the first time*.)

122. **near** something (<u>not</u> near to something)

> *wrong*   The village of Battle is very near to the place where the Battle of Hastings was fought in 1066.
> *right*   The village of Battle is very near the place where the Battle of Hastings was fought in 1066.

123. **object** <u>to</u> something (<u>not</u> against)

> *wrong*   Some people have objected against being required to wear a seat belt.
> *right*   Some people have objected to being required to wear a seat belt.

124. **off** something (<u>not</u> off of)

> *wrong*   The man stepped off of the platform into the path of the moving train.
> *right*   The man stepped off the platform into the path of the moving train.

125. **opposite**: When used as a noun, *opposite* is followed by *of*; when used as an adjective, it is followed by *to* or *from*, or by no preposition.

> *wrong*   His conclusion was the opposite to mine.
>   (Here, *opposite* is a noun.)
> *right*   His conclusion was the opposite of mine.

or   His conclusion was opposite to mine.
           (Here, *opposite* is an adjective.)

126. **partake** of something or **participate** in something

wrong	They have refused to partake in a new round of talks on the subject of free trade.
right	They have refused to participate in a new round of talks on the subject of free trade.
or	They have refused to partake of a new round of talks on the subject of free trade.

127. **prefer** one thing or person to another (not more than another)

wrong	They both prefer tennis more than squash.
right	They both prefer tennis to squash.

128. **protest** something (not protest against). *To protest* means *to argue against*; the preposition is redundant.

wrong	The demonstrators were protesting against the Government's decision to allow missile testing.
right	The demonstrators were protesting the Government's decision to allow missile testing.

129. **refer** to something (not refer back to something)

wrong	If you are confused, refer back to the diagram on page 24.
right	If you are confused, refer to the diagram on page 24.

130. **regard**: With regard to something

wrong	I am writing in regards to the balance owing on your account.
fair	I am writing with regard to the balance owing on your account.
better	I am writing about the balance owing on your account.

131. **rejoice** at something (not for something)

wrong	He rejoiced for his good fortune when he won the lottery.
right	He rejoiced at his good fortune when he won the lottery.

132. **repeat** something (not repeat again)

wrong	If you miss an answer you must repeat the whole exercise again.
right	If you miss an answer you must repeat the whole exercise.

133. request something *or* request that something be done (but <u>not</u> request for something unless one is using the noun—a request <u>for</u> something)

wrong	He has requested for two more men to help him.
right	He has requested two more men to help him.
or	He has put in a request for two more men to help him.

134. retroactive <u>to</u> a date (<u>not</u> from)

wrong	The tax changes are retroactive from July 1.
right	The tax changes are retroactive to July 1.

135. return <u>to</u> a place (<u>not</u> return back)

wrong	He wanted to return back to Edmonton as soon as possible.
right	He wanted to return to Edmonton as soon as possible.

136. seek something or someone (<u>not</u> seek for something)

wrong	She suggested that we seek for help from the police.
right	She suggested that we seek help from the police.

137. sight: <u>in</u> sight (near enough to be seen); <u>out of</u> sight (too far away to be seen); <u>on</u> sight (immediately after being seen)

wrong	The general ordered that deserters be shot in sight.
right	The general ordered that deserters be shot on sight.

138. speak <u>to</u> someone (when one speaker is giving information to a listener); speak <u>with</u> someone (when the two are having a discussion)

wrong	She spoke harshly with the secretary about his spelling mistakes.
right	She spoke harshly to the secretary about his spelling mistakes.

139. suffer <u>from</u> something (<u>not</u> with)

wrong	He told me that he was suffering with the flu.
right	He told me that he was suffering from the flu.

140. superior <u>to</u> someone or something (<u>not</u> than someone or something)

wrong	The advertisements claim that this detergent is superior than the others.

right	The advertisements claim that this detergent is superior to the others.

141. surprised <u>at</u> or <u>by</u> something: *At* is used to suggest that the person is disappointed or scandalized; unless one wishes to suggest this, *by* is the appropriate preposition.

wrong	I was surprised at the unexpected arrival of my sister.
right	I was surprised by the unexpected arrival of my sister.

142. type <u>of</u> person or thing

wrong	This type carburetor is no longer produced.
right	This type of carburetor is no longer produced.

143. underneath something (<u>not</u> underneath of)

wrong	When we looked underneath of the table, we found what we had been looking for.
right	When we looked underneath the table, we found what we had been looking for.

144. until a time or an event (<u>not</u> up until)

wrong	Up until 1967 the National Hockey League was made up of only six teams.
right	Until 1967 the National Hockey League was made up of only six teams.

145. warn someone <u>of</u> a danger, <u>against</u> doing something (<u>not</u> about something or to do something)

wrong	She warned me about the danger involved in the expedition.
right	She warned me of the danger involved in the expedition.

146. worry <u>about</u> something (<u>not</u> at something or for something)

wrong	He is always worried at what will happen if he loses his job.
right	He is always worried about what will happen if he loses his job.

147. prepositions in pairs or lists: If a sentence includes two or more nouns or verbs that take different prepositions, make sure to include <u>all</u> the necessary words.

wrong	The fire was widely reported in the newspapers and television.

right   The fire was widely reported in the newspapers and on television.

148. **ending a sentence with a preposition**: Some authorities have argued that it is poor English to end a sentence with a preposition. The best answer to them is Winston Churchill's famous remark upon being accused of ending with a preposition: "This is the sort of pedantic nonsense up with which I will not put." Obviously such awkwardness as this can be avoided only by ending with a preposition. It is surely true that in many other cases ending sentences with prepositions is awkward. In practice, however, these are situations that we are already likely to avoid. The following dialogue (a version of which was passed on to me by Prof. A. Levey of the University of Calgary) provides in dramatic form another demonstration of the absurdity of strictures against ending with prepositions:

"Where do you come from?"
"From a place where we don't end sentences with prepositions."
"Let me rephrase. Where do you come from, you stupid pedant?"

SINGULAR & PLURAL DIFFICULTIES

149. unusual plural nouns: A number of nouns are unusual in the way that a plural is formed. Here is a list of some that frequently cause mistakes. The most troublesome—as well as a few pronouns that cause similar difficulties—are also given individual entries below:

appendix	appendices
attorney general	attorneys general
bacterium	bacteria
basis	bases
court martial	courts martial
crisis	crises
criterion	criteria
curriculum	curricula
datum	data
ellipsis	ellipses
emphasis	emphases
erratum	errata
father-in-law	fathers-in-law
focus	foci
governor general	governors general
index	indexes or indices
matrix	matrixes or matrices
medium	media
millennium	millennia
nucleus	nuclei
parenthesis	parentheses
referendum	referenda or referendums
runner-up	runners-up
stratum	strata
symposium	symposia
synthesis	syntheses
thesis	theses

150. accommodation: The plural form is not normally used.

wrong   My family and my friend's family were both unable to find accommodations downtown.

right   My family and my friend's family were both unable to find accommodation downtown.

151. anyone/anybody/no one/none/nobody: All are singular. It is often necessary to spend a few moments puzzling over how to phrase one's ideas before one finds a way to get all the verbs and subjects to agree, and at the same time avoid awkwardness. Ironically, however, the correct solution may in this case not be the best one. (See Bias-Free Language, pp.191.)

not in agreement	Anyone may visit when they like.
in agreement	Anyone may visit when he or she likes.
in agreement	Anyone may visit at any time.
not in agreement	No one likes to leave a place that they have grown fond of.
in agreement	No one likes to leave a place that he or she has grown fond of.
in agreement	No one likes to leave a place that has fond memories attached to it.

152. **bacteria**: A plural word; the singular is *bacterium*.

wrong	There were many bacterias in the mouldy bread.
right	There were a lot of bacteria in the mouldy bread.

153. **behavior**: Although social scientists speak of *a behavior* or of *behaviors* in technical writing, in other disciplines and in conversational English the word is uncountable (i.e. it cannot form a plural or be used with the indefinite article). Say *types of behavior*, <u>not</u> *behaviors*.

wrong	He has a good behavior.
right	His behavior is good.
or	He behaves well.

154. **between/among**: It is often supposed that *between* should always be used for two, *among* for more than two. As the *Oxford English Dictionary* points out, however, "in all senses *between* has been, from its earliest appearance, extended to more than two." Perhaps the most important difference is that *between* suggests a relationship of things or people to each other as individuals, whereas *among* suggests a relationship that is collective and vague. Thus we say *the ball fell among the hollyhocks* where we are expressing the relationship of the ball to many flowers collectively, and where the precise location of the ball is unspecified. But we should <u>not</u> say, as we watch a baseball game, *the ball fell among the three fielders*; here we know the precise location of the ball and are expressing the relationship between it and the three individuals.

wrong   The ball fell among the three fielders.
right   The ball fell between the three fielders.

155. **both/all**: Use *both* to refer to two, and *all* to refer to more than two.

wrong   Harris and Waluchow were the chief speakers in the debate yesterday. They all spoke very well.
right   Harris and Waluchow were the chief speakers in the debate yesterday. They both spoke very well.

156. **brain**: One person can have only <u>one</u> brain. The use of the plural to refer to the brain of one person (e.g., He blew his brains out) is slang, and should not be used in formal written work.

wrong   He used his brains to solve the problem.
right   He used his brain to solve the problem.

157. **children**: Be careful when forming the possessive; the apostrophe should come before the *s*.

wrong   All the childrens' toys had been put away.
right   All the children's toys had been put away.

158. **confusion**: Uncountable—we do not normally speak of *a confusion* or of *confusions*.

wrong   The misunderstanding about his time of arrival caused a confusion.
right   The misunderstanding about his time of arrival caused confusion.

159. **criteria**: Plural; the singular is *criterion*.

wrong   The chief criteria on which an essay should be judged is whether or not it communicates clearly.
right   The chief criterion on which an essay should be judged is whether or not it communicates clearly.

160. **damage**: In its usual meaning, this noun has no plural, since it is uncountable. We speak of *damage*, <u>not</u> *a damage*, and of *a lot of damage*, <u>not</u> *many damages*. The word *damages* means money paid to cover the cost of any damage one has caused.

wrong   The crash caused many damages to his car, but he was unhurt.

right   The crash caused a lot of damage to his car, but he was unhurt.

161. **data**: Like *bacteria, media,* and *phenomena,* the noun *data* is plural. The singular form, which is rarely used, is *datum.*

wrong   This data proves conclusively that the lake is badly polluted.
right   These data prove conclusively that the lake is badly polluted.

162. **each/every/none**: All three are singular. The same problems experienced with *anyone* and *no one* (see above) are common here as well. Even experienced writers often have difficulty phrasing sentences involving these words so as to have the parts agree. (Ironically, however, the 'correct' solution may in this case not always be the best one. See Bias-Free Language.)

not in agreement	Each person applying for the job must fill out this form before they will be granted an interview.
in agreement	Each person applying for the job must fill out this form before he or she will be granted an interview.
in agreement	Each person applying for the job must fill out this form before being granted an interview.

163. **each other/one another**: Use *each other* for two, *one another* for more than two.

wrong	The three brothers always tell stories to each other before going to sleep.
right	The three brothers always tell stories to one another before going to sleep.
wrong	The two men had long since begun to get on one another's nerves. (Alan Moorehead, *The White Nile*)
right	The two men had long since begun to get on each other's nerves.

164. **either/neither**: *Either* and *neither* are both singular. This can create considerable awkwardness in structuring sentences. (See also Bias-Free Language on this point.)

wrong   Somehow, neither Sally nor Great Uncle Magnus were as tidy as they had been when they set out. (Margaret Mahy, *Ultra-Violet Catastrophe*)

Trying to correct the error here by simply changing *were* to *was*, creates a new problem with the *they* in the second half of the sentence; a further change is also necessary.

right	Somehow, neither Sally nor Great Uncle Magnus was as tidy as both had been when they set out.
wrong	So far neither the Liberal rank and file nor the electorate seem satisfied with Jean Chretien's performance.
right	So far neither the Liberal rank and file nor the electorate seems satisfied with Jean Chretien's performance.

165. either/any; neither/none: Use *either* and *neither* for two, *any* and *none* for more than two.

wrong	Shirley has six sisters, but she hasn't seen either of them since Christmas.
right	Shirley has six sisters, but she hasn't seen any of them since Christmas.

166. government: A singular noun.

wrong	The government are intending to build a new terminal at this airport before 2007.
right	The government is intending to build a new terminal at this airport before 2007.

167. graffiti: A plural noun; the singular form is *graffito*.

wrong	Graffiti covers most of the subway cars in the city.
right	Graffiti cover most of the subway cars in the city.

168. media: Plural; the singular is *medium*.

wrong	The media usually assumes that the audience has a very short attention span.
right	The media usually assume that the audience has a very short attention span.

169. money: Some people seem to think that *monies* has a more official ring to it than *money* when they are talking of business affairs, but there is no sound reason for using this plural form in good English.

wrong	The Council has promised to provide some monies for this project.
right	The Council has promised to provide some money for this project.

170. **news**: Despite the *s*, this is a singular collective noun. Make sure to use a singular verb with it.

wrong   Today's news of troubles in the Middle East are very disturbing.

right   Today's news of troubles in the Middle East is very disturbing.

171. **phenomena**: Plural; the singular is *phenomenon*.

wrong   The great popularity of disco music was a short-lived phenomena.

right   The great popularity of disco music was a short-lived phenomenon.

172. **police**: a plural noun. Be sure to use a plural verb with it.

wrong   The police is investigating the case, and hope to make an arrest soon.

right   The police are investigating the case, and hope to make an arrest soon.

173. **someone/somebody**: Both are singular. Be careful with sentences involving one of these pronouns and the pronoun *they*; getting the phrasing right is not always easy.

wrong   Someone has forgotten to turn off the stove; they should be more careful.

fair   Someone has forgotten to turn off the stove; he or she should be more careful.

or   Some careless person has forgotten to turn off the stove.

PRONOUN PROBLEMS: WHO CARES ABOUT WHOM?

Those unfamiliar with the territory may wish to refer to the section on pronouns in the Reference Guide to Basic Grammar at the back of the book. Readers may also wish to refer to the discussion of *y'all* and *youse* in the Preface.

174. **extra pronoun**: It is easy to add an extra pronoun, particularly if the subject of the sentence is separated from the verb by a long adjectival clause.

> *wrong*   The countries which Hitler wanted to conquer in the late 1930s they were too weak to resist him.
>
> *right*   The countries which Hitler wanted to conquer in the late 1930s were too weak to resist him.
>
> *wrong*   The line that is longest in a triangle it is called the hypotenuse.
>
> *right*   The line that is longest in a triangle is called the hypotenuse.

175. **first person**: In formal writing it is customary to use *I* and *me* infrequently or not at all. The object of a formal piece of writing is normally to present an argument, and writers realize that they can best argue their case by presenting evidence rather than by stating that such and such is what they think. Thus many teachers advise their students always to avoid using the first person singular (*I* and *me*) in their writing.

This guideline should not be regarded as a firm and fast rule. George Orwell, often praised as the finest essayist of the last century, uses *I* and *me* frequently. As the following example illustrates, however, he employs the first person to guide the reader through his argument, not to make the points in the argument:

> If one gets rid of these habits one can think more clearly, and to think more clearly is a necessary first step towards political regeneration: so that the fight against bad English is not frivolous and is not the exclusive concern of professional writers. I will come back to this presently, and I hope that by that time the meaning of what I have said will become clearer. ("Politics and the English Language")

Phrases such as *I think* and *I feel,* on the other hand, will not help you convince the reader of the strength of your main points.

wrong   Many authorities assume inflation to be a cause of high interest rates, but I think that high interest rates are a cause of inflation. This essay will prove my argument through numerous examples.

right   Many authorities assume inflation to be a cause of high interest rates; in fact, high interest rates are often a cause of inflation. Let us take the years 1978 to 1983 in the US as an example.

176. I/me: Perhaps as a result of slang use of *me* as a subject pronoun (*Me and him got together for a few beer last night*), the impression seems to have lodged in many minds that the distinction between *I* and *me* is one of degree of politeness or formality rather than one of subject and object.

wrong   There is no disagreement between you and I.
right   There is no disagreement between you and me.
            (Both *you* and *I* are here objects of a preposition—*between*. "Between you and I" is no more correct than is "I threw the ball at he.")

177. than: Does *than* take a subject or an object pronoun? Purists argue that we should say *She's brighter than I* [*am*], and *He's louder than she* [*is*]—that the verb is always understood in such sentences, even when we do not say it or write it, and that the unspoken verb requires a subject. It's hard to argue, however, that the increasingly widespread use of object pronouns after *than* is either ugly or confusing.

less formal   She always sleeps later than him.
more formal   She always sleeps later than he [does].

178. unreferenced or wrongly referenced pronoun: Normally a pronoun must refer to a noun in the previous sentence or clause. In the following sentence, for example, the pronoun *she* clearly refers to the noun *Charity*, which is the subject of the first clause in the sentence:

e.g.   Charity told Alfred that she would start work at nine.

Notice how confusing the sentence becomes, however, if there are two possible *shes* in the first part of the sentence:

e.g.   Charity told Mavis that she would start work at nine.

Does this mean that Charity will start work at nine, or that Mavis will? From the sentence it is impossible to tell. In cases like this, where it is not absolutely clear whom or what a pronoun refers to, use the noun again instead:

clear   Charity told Mavis that she (Charity) would start work at nine.

wrong   My father and my brother visited me early this morning. He told me that something important had happened in Regina.

right   My father and my brother visited me early this morning. Father told me that something important had happened in Regina.

In the following case the writer has gone astray by mentioning two things—one singular, one plural—and then matching only one of the two with a pronoun. In this instance the best remedy is to substitute a noun for the pronoun:

wrong   Shields's characters are so exquisitely crafted and her plot so artfully conceived that it keeps the reader riveted until the final page.

right   Shields's characters are so exquisitely crafted and her plot so artfully conceived that the book keeps the reader riveted until the final page.

Similar mistakes are often made in writing about a general class of people, such as police officers, or doctors, or football players. When writing in this way one can use either the third person singular (e.g., *A doctor helps patients. He* ...) or the third person plural (*Doctors help patients. They* ...). Mixing the two in such situations often leads people to write unreferenced pronouns.

wrong   A herbalist knows a lot about herbs and other plants. They can often cure you by giving you medicine.
        (Here the pronoun *they* is presumably meant to refer to the plural noun *herbalists*, but the writer has referred only to a herbalist.)

right   A herbalist knows a lot about herbs and other plants. He can often cure you by giving you medicine.

or   Herbalists know a lot about herbs and other plants. They can often cure you by giving you medicine.

It may also not be clear what or whom a pronoun refers to if it is placed too far away from the noun:

wrong   The Finance Minister increased corporation taxes by an average of 43 per cent. Other measures in the budget included $100 million in student assistance and a 2 per cent increase in sales taxes. He also introduced a variety of measures to help small businesses.

right   The Finance Minister increased corporation taxes by an average of 43 per cent. Other measures in the budget included $100 million in student assistance and a 2 per cent increase in sales taxes. The Minister also introduced a variety of measures to help small businesses.

Be particularly careful when using *this* as a pronoun; if the preceding sentence is a long one, it may not be at all clear what *this* refers to:

wrong   The deficit was forecast to be $200 million, but turned out to be over $2 billion. This reflected the government's failure to predict the increase in interest rates and the onset of a recession.
            (This <u>what</u>?)

right   The deficit was forecast to be $200 million, but turned out to be over $2 billion. This vast discrepancy reflected the government's failure to predict the increase in interest rates and the onset of a recession.

Sometimes the meaning may be clear, but the omission of a pronoun may create unintended and humorous ambiguity:

wrong   She visited a doctor with a bad case of the flu.
            (Did the doctor have the flu?)

right   She visited a doctor when she had a bad case of the flu.

wrong   The Cougar was a sporty car aimed at the youthful-feeling who wanted luxury in their automobiles. Its buyers were similar to Mustangs, but more affluent.

right   The Cougar was a sporty car aimed at the youthful-feeling who wanted luxury in their automobiles. Its buyers were similar to those who bought Mustangs, but more affluent.

179. **who/whom**: The subject pronoun and the object pronoun, but of course it's not as simple as that. Nor is it—as those who don't feel it worth keeping *whom* around might have us believe—merely a matter of stuffiness or pedantry on the part of linguistic purists. Sound has a great deal to do with it. Even purists must sometimes find themselves saying, *I didn't know who I was talking to*, even though the rules say it should be *whom* (subject—I; object—whom). In similar fashion the

enemies of *whom* must surely be tempted to sacrifice principle rather than attempt such an owlish mouthful as T*o who was he talking?* They would do so not on the grammatical grounds of *whom*, the object pronoun, being correct since it is acting as the object of the preposition *to*, but on the grounds of *whom*, the word with an *m* on the end, being in that sentence a lot easier to say. In such circumstances convenience of pronunciation occasionally overrides arguments either for or against formality.

less formal   Scott Fitzgerald never cared who he irritated.
more formal   Scott Fitzgerald never cared whom he irritated.

PART OF SPEECH CONVERSIONS: A QUESTION OF PRINCIPLE?

A well-known Calvin and Hobbes cartoon strip nicely conveys the amusement that part of speech conversions may engender:

> *Calvin*: "I like to verb words."
> *Hobbes*: "What?"
> *Calvin*: "I take nouns and adjectives and use them as verbs. Remember when "access" was a thing? Now it's something you do. It got verbed....Verbing weirds language."
> *Hobbes*: "Maybe we can eventually make language a complete impediment to understanding."

In fact, however, there is no good reason why a word that has become established as one part of speech should not be used as another; the language has always been changing and growing in this way. As Tom Shippey asks:

> What can be the matter with using nouns as adjectives? Everyone does it; how about "stone wall?" It has been built into the language since before English settlers found Ireland, let alone America.... As for converting nouns to verbs, what about "water?" "Watering the horses" is recorded from before the Conquest. (*Times Literary Supplement*, October 19–25, 1990)

For that matter, what about *chair, table, paper, shelf, bottle, cup, knife, fork, eye, mouth, finger*? The list of nouns that have also become verbs is a very long one, and it includes many of the most basic nouns in the language. The point in being aware of the conversion of one part of speech to another, then, is not that the practice is always a bad one. Rather it is to keep oneself aware of whether or not one is saying something in the best possible way. If the new creation fills a need, saying something more clearly and concisely than it is possible to do otherwise, then it deserves to survive. But if it fulfils no useful purpose—if clearer and more concise ways of saying the same thing already exist—then it's better to avoid it.

180. **access**: Except in the vocabulary of computers, *access* is probably best kept as a noun, not a verb; alternatives such as *enter* and *reach* are usually more precise.

worth checking　　　The cafeteria may be accessed from either the warehouse or the accounts department.

better   The cafeteria may be reached through the warehouse or the accounts department.

181. **adjective for adverb**: If a word is modifying a verb, it should as a general rule be an adverb rather than an adjective. This is normally the case when the descriptive word comes directly after the verb. We say, *The boy laughed quietly*, for example (rather than *The boy laughed quiet*), because the descriptive word *quietly* refers to the verb *laughed*, not the noun *boy*. Similarly, in the sentence *The quiet boy laughed* we use the adjective *quiet* to refer to the noun *boy*. The verb *to be*, however, which of course does not name an action in the way that other verbs do, is normally followed by adjectives rather than adverbs. (Verbs such as *taste*, *smell*, and *feel* resemble *be* in this respect.) Thus we say *The boy is quiet*, not *The boy is quietly*; we use the adjective rather than the adverb because we are again describing the boy, not the action of being. Very few would make the mistake of saying *He laughed quiet*, but almost everyone occasionally chooses an adjective where the adverb should be used.

wrong	I did good on the test yesterday.
right	I did well on the test yesterday.
wrong	She asked us not to talk so loud.
right	She asked us not to talk so loudly.
wrong	The premiers thought it should be worded different.
right	The premiers thought it should be worded differently.
wrong	According to Mr. Adams, "most books will go heavier into evolution, which is a good thing,"
right	According to Mr. Adams, "most books will go more heavily into evolution, which is a good thing."
wrong	He performs bad whenever he is under pressure.
right	He performs badly whenever he is under pressure.

The pragmatists may have a point when it comes to the propriety of using comparative adjectives such as *easier* in place of more long winded adverbs such as *more easily*. Should the *Financial Post* editor have corrected the headline that read "Northern Miners Breathe Easier"? Certainly it's easier to use the adjective here in place of the two-part adverb, *more easily*. Whether or not it's better is less clear; certainly many purists are not pleased by the practice.

less formal	The purpose of desktop publishing is to do the same old thing cheaper, easier, and quicker.
more formal	The purpose of desktop publishing is to do the same old thing more cheaply, more easily, and more quickly.

182. **advice/advise**: *Advice* is the noun, *advise* is the verb.

wrong	They refused to take our advise.
right	They refused to take our advice.

183. **affect/effect**: *Effect* is normally used as a noun meaning *result*. (It can also be used as a verb meaning *put into effect*, as in *The changes were effected by the Committee.*) *Affect* is a verb meaning *cause a result*.

wrong	When the acid is added to the solution, there is no visible affect.
right	When the acid is added to the solution, there is no visible effect.
wrong	"The issues that effect us here on the reserve are the same issues that effect the whole constituency," Mr. Littlechild said. (*The Globe and Mail*)
right	"The issues that affect us here on the reserve are the same issues that affect the whole constituency," Mr. Littlechild said.

184. **author**: A noun, not a verb; there is no need to find a substitute for *write*.

wrong	Smith is a member of the Appeals Court, and has authored two books on the judicial system.
right	Smith is a member of the Appeals Court, and has written two books on the judicial system.

185. **breath/breathe**: *Breath* is the noun, *breathe* the verb.

wrong	When you breath, your lungs take in oxygen.
right	When you breathe, your lungs take in oxygen.

186. **dependent/dependant**: *Dependent* is the adjective, *dependant* the noun. You are dependent on someone or something, and your young children are your dependants; they are dependent on you.

wrong	Emily is still dependant on her parents for financial support.
right	Emily is still dependent on her parents for financial support.

187. **dialogue**: As a verb, *talk* serves perfectly well, even after all these years.

awkward	The two department heads should dialogue with each other more frequently.
better	The two department heads should talk to each other more frequently.

188. enthuse/enthusiastic: *Enthuse* is the verb; *enthused* is its past participle. The adjective is *enthusiastic*.

wrong	In 2002 millions were enthused about South Korea's World Cup performance.
right	In 2002 millions were enthusiastic about South Korea's World Cup performance.
or	In 2002 millions enthused over South Korea's World Cup performance.

189. first/firstly: *Firstly* is now generally thought of as archaic, though it is not incorrect. Be sure to be consistent, though, in the use of *first, second*, etc., in lists.

wrong	There were several reasons for France's reluctance to commit more resources to the New World. First, she was consumed with the battle for supremacy in Europe. Secondly, the returns on previous investments had been minimal.
right	There were several reasons for France's reluctance to commit more resources to the New World. First, she was consumed with the battle for supremacy in Europe. Second, the returns on previous investments had been minimal.

190. good/well: The most common of the adjective-for-adverb mistakes.

wrong	As the manager put it, "He pitched good, but not real good."
fair	He pitched well, but not really well.
better	He did not pitch very well.

191. impact: The use of *impact* as a verb has become widespread even in formal English, but *affect* remains an attractive option.

awkward	The government's decision will impact upon wholesalers in all areas of the country.
better	The government's decision will affect wholesalers in all areas of the country.

192. like/as: *Like* is a preposition, not a conjunction; it introduces a noun or pronoun in a phrase. If introducing a clause, which always includes a verb, use *as* in formal writing.

e.g.	He looks like his father.
	(*Like* introduces the noun *father*.)
	He looks as his father did at his age.
	(*As* introduces the clause *as his father did at his age*.)

He is acting like a drunkard.
(*Like* introduces the noun *drunkard.*)
He is acting as if he were drunk.
(*As* introduces the clause *as if he were drunk.*)

wrong   Like I said before, smoking is forbidden.
right   As I said before, smoking is forbidden.
wrong   He runs like I do—with short, choppy strides.
right   He runs as I do—with short, choppy strides.
or   He runs like me. We both take short, choppy strides.
wrong   Baby Doc ran Haiti like his father had done.
right   Baby Doc ran Haiti the way his father had.

The attempt is also sometimes made to use *like what* in place of *as.*

wrong   Bush wanted to appear tough, like what Reagan did when he ordered the invasion of Grenada.
right   Bush wanted to appear tough, as Reagan did when he ordered the invasion of Grenada.

193. **its/it's**: *Its* is an adjective meaning *belonging to it. It's* is a contraction of *it is*—a pronoun plus a verb. (Similarly, *whose* is an adjective meaning *belonging to whom*, whereas *who's* is a contraction of *who is*.)

wrong   Its important to remember that the population of North America in this period was less than 10 million.
right   It's important to remember that the population of North America in this period was less than 10 million.
wrong   A coniferous tree continually sheds it's leaves.
right   A coniferous tree continually sheds its leaves.

194. **lend/loan**: In formal English *loan* should be used only as a noun; *lend* is the verb.

wrong   He was unwilling to loan his sister any money.
right   He was unwilling to lend his sister any money.

195. **loath/loathe**: *Loath* is the adjective; *loathe* is the verb.

wrong   He told me he is beginning to loath his job.
right   He told me he is beginning to loathe his job.
or   He is loath to return to his old job.

196. **loose/lose**: *Loose* is normally used as an adjective meaning *not tight*; as a verb it means *to make loose* (e.g., *He loosed the reins*). *Lose* is of course always a verb.

wrong	As soon as it became dark she began to loose control of herself.
right	As soon as it became dark she began to lose control of herself.
wrong	If this movie doesn't bring the song back to the hit parade, then you know it's flopped—and that Spielberg is loosing his touch. (*The Toronto Star*)
right	If this movie doesn't bring the song back to the hit parade, then you know it's flopped—and that Spielberg is losing his touch.

197. maybe/may be: *Maybe* is an adverb that should be replaced by *perhaps* in formal writing. *May be* is a compound verb.

wrong	May be he will come, but I doubt it.
right	Maybe he will come, but I doubt it.
or	Perhaps he will come, but I doubt it.
wrong	The prototype maybe ready by 2007.
right	The prototype may be ready by 2007.

198. meantime/meanwhile: *Meantime* is a noun, used most frequently in the phrase *in the meantime. Meanwhile* is an adverb.

wrong	The Germans were preparing for an attack near Calais. Meantime, the Allies were readying themselves for the invasion of Normandy.
right	The Germans were preparing for an attack near Calais. Meanwhile, the Allies were readying themselves for the invasion of Normandy.

199. practice/practise: In Canada and Britain *practise* (verb) and *practice* (noun) should be distinguished; in the U.S. *practice* serves as both noun and verb.

US	The team will practice on Thursday.
UK/CDA	The team will practise on Thursday.

200. predominate/predominant: *Predominate* is the verb, *predominant* the adjective. (Either *predominately* or *predominantly* may be used as adverbs.)

wrong	The Social Credit movement was predominate only in Alberta and British Columbia.
right	The Social Credit movement was predominant only in Alberta and British Columbia.

or   The Social Credit movement predominated only in Alberta and British Columbia.

201. principal/principle: *Principal* can be either a noun or an adjective. As a noun it means *the person in the highest position of authority in an organization* (e.g., a school *principal*) or *an amount of money*, as distinguished from the interest on it. As an adjective it means *first in rank or importance* (*The principal city of northern Nigeria is Kano*). *Principle* is always a noun, and is never used to describe a person; a *principle* is a *basic truth or doctrine*, a *code of conduct*, or a *law describing how something works*.

wrong	We feel this is a matter of principal.
right	We feel this is a matter of principle.
wrong	Up went the shares of the two principle companies in this emerging field.
right	Up went the shares of the two principal companies in this emerging field.

202. prophecy/prophesy: *Prophecy* is the noun, *prophesy* the verb.

wrong	His comment should be regarded as a prediction, not a prophesy.
right	His comment should be regarded as a prediction, not a prophecy.

203. quality: Although in colloquial English *quality* is frequently used as a replacement for *good* or *worthwhile*, in formal writing it should be used as a noun, not an adjective. It should also be remembered that something may as easily be of poor quality as of good quality.

wrong	The salesman claims that this is a quality product.
right	The salesman claims that this is a product of high quality.
or	The salesman claims that this is a good product.
wrong	"It was Mother's Day. I was trying to spend some quality time with my wife." (An NHL vice-president explaining why he had not attended an important playoff game, as quoted in *The Toronto Star*)
right	"It was Mother's Day. I was trying to spend some time with my wife."

204. quote/quotation: In formal English *quote* is the verb, *quotation* the noun.

wrong	The following quote shows just how determined she is to change the Constitution.

right   The following quotation shows just how determined she is
               to change the Constitution.

205. real/really: One of the most commonly made adjective-for-adverb mistakes.

wrong   Some of the fish we caught were real big.
fair   Some of the fish we caught were really big.
better   Some of the fish we caught were very big.

206. verb-noun confusion: Where verbs and nouns have similar forms, be careful not to confuse them. Some of the most common examples are: *advice* (noun) and *advise* (verb); *extent* (noun) and *extend* (verb); *device* (noun) and *devise* (verb); *revenge* (noun) and *avenge* (verb); *loan* (noun) and *lend* (verb).

wrong   Gerald Ford, President from 1974 to 1976, has now to a
               large extend been forgotten.
right   Gerald Ford, President from 1974 to 1976, has now to a
               large extent been forgotten.
wrong   She wanted to revenge the harm he had caused her.
right   She wanted to avenge the harm he had caused her.

207. whose/who's: *Whose* means *belonging to whom*; *who's* is a contraction of *who is*.

wrong   Kennedy is not normally remembered as the President who's
               policies embroiled the US in the Vietnam conflict, but several scholars have suggested that he was as much responsible
               as was Johnson.
right   Kennedy is not normally remembered as the President whose
               policies embroiled the US in the Vietnam conflict, but several scholars have suggested that he was as much responsible
               as was Johnson.

WORD MEANINGS:
ARE CARS EVER STATIONERY?

208. accept/except: These two words are often confused because of their similar sounds. *Accept* is a verb meaning *to receive something favourably (or at least without complaining)*. Examples:

- We accepted the invitation to his party.
- We will have to accept the decision of the judge.

Except, on the other hand, is a conjunction (or sometimes a preposition) which means *not including* or *but*.

wrong	All the permanent members of the Security Council accept China voted to authorize the use of force.
right	All the permanent members of the Security Council except China voted to authorize the use of force.

209. adapt/adopt/adept: To *adapt* something is *to alter or modify it*; to *adopt* something is *to approve it or accept responsibility for it*; *adept* is an adjective meaning *skilful*.

wrong	The Board adapted the resolution unanimously.
right	The Board adopted the resolution unanimously.

210. adverse/averse: *Adverse* means *unfavourable*; *averse* means *reluctant* or *unwilling*.

wrong	The plane was forced to land because of averse weather conditions.
right	The plane was forced to land because of adverse weather conditions.
right	The pilot was averse to the idea of landing in the fog.

211. afflict/inflict: A person *inflicts* pain or hardship on someone else, who is *afflicted* by the pain and hardship.

wrong	The Mugabe government began as early as 1983 to afflict terrible suffering on large numbers of Zimbabweans living in Matorbeleland.
right	The Mugabe government began as early as 1983 to inflict terrible suffering on large numbers of Zimbabweans living in Matorbeleland.

212. **aggravate/annoy/irritate**: *Aggravate* means *make worse.*

e.g. The injury was aggravated by the bumpy ride in the ambulance.

In formal English *aggravate* should not be used to mean *annoy* or *irritate.*

wrong   She found his constant complaints very aggravating.
right   She found his constant complaints very irritating.

213. **alliterate/illiterate**: *Alliterate* is a verb meaning *to use consecutively two or more words that begin with the same sound.*

e.g. The big, burly brute was frighteningly fat.

Illiterate is an adjective meaning either *unable to read* or *unable to read and write well.* Those who confuse the two are sometimes, if unfairly, accused of being illiterate.

wrong   Over forty per cent of the population of Zambia is function-
           ally alliterate.
right   Over forty per cent of the population of Zambia is function-
           ally illiterate.

214. **alternately/alternatively**: *Alternately* means *happening in turn, first one and then the other*; *alternatively* means *instead of.* Be careful as well with the adjectives *alternate* and *alternative.*

wrong   An alternate method of arriving at this theoretical value would
           be to divide the difference between the two prices by the
           number of warrants.
right   An alternative method of arriving at this theoretical value
           would be to divide the difference between the two prices by
           the number of warrants. (*or* "Another method of ... ")
wrong   Professor Beit-Haliahmi seems to have trouble alternatively
           in reading his own book accurately and in reading my re-
           view of it correctly.
right   Professor Beit-Haliahmi seems to have trouble alternately in
           reading his own book accurately and in reading my review
           of it correctly.

215. **ambiguity**: There are many types of ambiguity; for other references see the chapters on Pronoun Problems and Word Order, and the
entries below for such words as *flammable.* Also see the adjacent box.

BRITISH LEFT WAFFLES ON
FALKLAND ISLANDS

The following are all examples of ambiguity in newspaper headlines. In some cases it may take several moments to decipher the intended meaning.

TWO PEDESTRIANS STRUCK BY BRIDGE
MAN HELD OVER GIANT L.A. BRUSH FIRE
ILLEGAL ALIENS CUT IN HALF BY NEW LAW
PASSERBY INJURED BY POST OFFICE
RED TAPE HOLDS UP NEW BRIDGE
VILLAGE WATER HOLDS UP WELL
JERK INJURES NECK, WINS AWARD
BISHOP THANKS GOD FOR CALLING

(The above examples come courtesy of columnist Bob Swift of Knight-Ridder Newspapers, and Prof. A. Levey of the University of Calgary.)

Here are two gems passed on to me by editor Beth Humphries:

THE FOSSILS WERE FOUND BY SCIENTISTS
EMBEDDED IN RED SANDSTONE.

SHE WALKED INTO THE BATHROOM TILED IN
SEA-GREEN MARBLE.

And, from a Global News weather telecast, the following prediction:

"OUT WEST TOMORROW, THEY'RE GOING TO
SEE THE SUN, AS WELL AS ATLANTIC
CANADA."

216. **amiable/amicable**: *Amiable* is used to describe someone's personality; *amicable* describes the state of relations between people.

wrong	Michibata said that the split with his former tennis partner had been an amiable one.
right	Michibata said that the split with his former tennis partner had been an amicable one.

217. **amoral/immoral**: *Amoral* means *not based on moral standards*; *immoral* means *wrong according to moral standards*.

> wrong   The modern reader is unlikely to share Alexander Pope's views as to what constitutes amoral behavior.
>
> right   The modern reader is unlikely to share Alexander Pope's views as to what constitutes immoral behavior.

218. **anti/ante**: If you remember that *anti* means *against* and *ante* means *before* you are less likely to misspell the many words that have one or the other as a prefix.

> wrong   The UN had many anticedents—most notably the League of Nations formed after World War I.
>
> right   The UN had many antecedents—most notably the League of Nations formed after World War I.

219. **anxious/eager**: The adjective *anxious* means *uneasy, nervous, worried*; it should not be used in formal writing to mean *eager*.

> wrong   He was anxious to help in any way he could.
>
> right   He was eager to help in any way he could.

220. **appraise/apprise**: To *appraise* something is *to estimate its value*; to *apprise* someone of something is *to inform him or her of it*.

> wrong   The house has been apprised at $160,000.
>
> right   The house has been appraised at $160,000.
>
> or   He apprised her of the house's jump in value.

221. **assure/ensure/insure**: To *assure* someone of something is *to tell them with confidence or certainty*; to *insure* (or *ensure*) that something will happen is *to make sure* that it does; to *insure* something is *to purchase insurance* on it so as to protect yourself in case of loss.

> wrong   Our inventory is ensured for $10,000,000.
>
> right   Our inventory is insured for $10,000,000.
>
> right   I assure you that it will never happen again.
>
> right   I will ensure that it never happens again.

222. **attitude**: In colloquial English in recent years *attitude* has undergone a considerable transformation, becoming first a synonym for *bad attitude* and then a word more broadly denoting strength of character. In conversational English *She's got attitude* is more likely to be in-

tended as a compliment than a criticism. But in formal written English such colloquial usages should be used sparingly, if at all.

223. be/become: The difference between the two is that *to be* simply indicates existence, while *to become* indicates a process of change. Whenever you are talking about a change, use *become* instead of *be.*

wrong	I had been quite contented, but as time went by I was unhappy.
right	I had been quite contented, but as time went by I became unhappy.
wrong	After years of struggle, East Timor finally was independent in 2002.
right	After years of struggle, East Timor finally became independent in 2002.

224. beg the question: The original meaning of *beg the question* is *take for granted the very thing to be argued about*—<u>not</u> *invite the question.* In the words of Thomas Hurka, the former *Globe and Mail* 'Principles' columnist, "'begging the question' is *not* what Alex Trebek does on *Jeopardy.*" The extension of the phrase to mean *invite the question* has become so widespread in recent years that it may be vain to think of the tide being reversed, but the original concept of question begging is a useful one, and we should be reluctant to allow it to disappear.

wrong	This sort of sexual abuse case begs the question as to how such behavior could be hidden for so many years.
right	This sort of sexual abuse case makes us wonder how such behavior could be hidden for so many years.

225. bored/boring: *Bored* is the opposite of *interested* and *boring* is the opposite of *interesting.* In other words, one is quite likely to be bored when someone reads out what one has already read in the newspaper, or when one is watching a football game when the score is 38–0, or when one is doing an uninteresting job. To be bored, however, is <u>not</u> the same as being sad, or depressed, or irritated, or angry.

wrong	She was so bored with her husband that she tried to kill him.
right	She was so angry with her husband that she tried to kill him.

226. breach/breech: To *breach* a wall or a contract is to break or break through it, and the breach is the breaking. *Breech* refers to a part of a cannon or rifle—or to the buttocks (hence a "breech birth" in which the buttocks or feet emerge before the head).

wrong	The lawyers claimed that her actions constituted a breech of contract.
right	The lawyers claimed that her actions constituted a breach of contract.

227. **brusque/brisk**: To be *brusque* is *to be abrupt or slightly rude in speech or manner*; *brisk* means *quick or lively*.

wrong	He didn't say anything rude to me, but his manner was rather brisk.
right	He didn't say anything rude to me, but his manner was rather brusque.

Beating Around the Bush?

Anyone who speaks a good deal in public on an impromptu basis will utter the odd absurdity, but George W. Bush has had more problems with meaning than most. A few examples:

- "The future will be better tomorrow."
- "I believe we are on an irreversible trend toward more freedom and democracy—but that could change."
- "It isn't pollution that's harming our environment. It's the impurities in our air and water that are doing it."
- "A low voter turnout is an indication of fewer people going to the polls."
- "Republicans understand the importance of bondage between a mother and child."
- "I am not part of the problem. I am a Republican."
- "I stand by all the misstatements that I've made."

---

228. **can/may**: In formal writing *can* should be used to refer to ability, *may* to refer to permission.

wrong	Can I leave the room?
	(This makes literal sense only if you are an injured person conversing with your doctor.)
right	May I leave the room?

229. capital/capitol: As a noun, *capital* can refer to *wealth*, to *the city from which the government operates*, to *an upper case letter*, or to *the top of a pillar*. It can also be used as an adjective to mean *most important* or *principal*. *Capitol* is much more restricted in its meaning—*a specific American legislative building* or *Roman temple*.

wrong	The prosecution alleged that he had committed a capitol offence.
right	The prosecution alleged that he had committed a capital offence.

230. career/careen: As a verb, *career* means *to swerve wildly*. *Careen* originally meant *to tilt or lean*, but now in North America especially is often treated as a synonym for *career*. Since *careen* has other specifically nautical meanings, some authorities resist the conflation of the two verbs.

231. careless/uncaring: *Careless* means *negligent* or *thoughtless*; you can be careless about your work, for example, or careless about your appearance. Do not use *careless*, however, when you want to talk about not caring enough about other people.

wrong	He acted in a very careless way towards his mother when she was sick.
right	He acted in an uncaring way towards his mother when she was sick.

232. censor/censure: To *censor* something is *to prevent it, or those parts of it that are considered objectionable, from being available to the public*. To *censure* someone is *to express strong criticism or condemnation*.

wrong	The Senate censored the Attorney General for his part in the scandal.
right	The Senate censured the Attorney General for his part in the scandal.

233. classic/classical: As an adjective *classic* means *of such a high quality that it has lasted or is likely to last for a very long time*. *Classical* is used to refer to *ancient Greece and Rome*, or, particularly when speaking of music, to refer to *a traditional style*.

wrong	Sophocles was one of the greatest classic authors; his plays are classical.

right   Sophocles was one of the greatest classical authors; his plays are acknowledged classics.

234. childish/childlike: The first is a term of abuse, the second a term of praise.

wrong   Her writing expresses an attractive childish innocence.
right   Her writing expresses an attractive childlike innocence.

235. climatic/climactic: Weather is not necessarily the most exciting part of life.

wrong   Difficulties in predicting long-term trends are inherent in any climactic projections.
right   Difficulties in predicting long-term trends are inherent in any climatic projections.

236. collaborate/corroborate: To *collaborate* is *to work together*, whereas to *corroborate* is *to give supporting evidence*.

wrong   He collaborated her claim that the Americans had corroborated with the Nazi colonel Klaus Barbie.
right   He corroborated her claim that the Americans had collaborated with the Nazi colonel Klaus Barbie.

237. compliment/complement: To *compliment* someone is *to praise* him, and a *compliment* is *the praise*; to *complement* something is *to add to it to make it better or complete*, and a *complement* is *the number or amount needed to make it complete*.

wrong   None of the divisions had its full compliment of troops.
right   None of the divisions had its full complement of troops.
wrong   Gretzky's mission in New York will be to compliment Mark Messier, the team's captain and franchise player. (Associated Press story, Oct. 1, 1996)
            (Literally, this would mean that the hockey player's job was to keep saying "Nice work, Mark," and so on.)
right   Gretzky's mission in New York will be to complement Mark Messier, the team's captain and franchise player.

238. comprise/compose: The whole *comprises* or includes the various parts; the parts *compose* the whole.

wrong   The British government is comprised of far fewer ministries than is the Canadian government.

right	The British government comprises far fewer ministries than does the Canadian government.
or	The British government is composed of far fewer ministries than is the Canadian government.

239. conscience/conscious/consciousness: To be *conscious* is to be *awake and aware of what is happening*, whereas *conscience* is *the part of our mind that tells us it is right to do some things and wrong to do other things* (such as steal or murder). *Conscience* and *consciousness* are both nouns; the adjectives are *conscientious* (aware of what is right and wrong) and *conscious* (aware).

wrong	She was tempted to steal the chocolate bar, but her conscious told her not to.
right	She was tempted to steal the chocolate bar, but her conscience told her not to.

240. contemptuous/contemptible: We are *contemptuous* of anyone or anything we find *contemptible*.

wrong	The judge called the delinquent's behavior utterly contemptuous.
right	The judge called the delinquent's behavior utterly contemptible.

241. continual/continuous: If something is *continuous* it *never stops*; something *continual* is *frequently repeated but not unceasing*. The same distinction holds for the adverbs *continually* and *continuously*.

wrong	He has been phoning me continuously for the past two weeks. (Surely he stopped for a bite to eat or a short nap.)
right	He has been phoning me continually for the past two weeks.

242. copyright: *Copyright* is *the right to make copies of something*. The fact that these are often of written material has encouraged a confusion of spelling.

wrong	The software company plans to copywrite some of the advances it will introduce this year.
right	The software company plans to copyright some of the advances it will introduce this year.

243. council/counsel; councillor/counsellor: A *council* is *an assembled group of officials*, and a *councillor is a member of that group*. *Counsel* is *advice*, or in the special case of a lawyer, *the person offering advice*. In other situations the person offering *counsel* is a *counsellor*.

wrong	The city counsel met to discuss the proposed bylaw.
right	The city council met to discuss the proposed bylaw.
wrong	The lawyer offered sound council as to the advisability of launching a suit.
right	The lawyer offered sound counsel as to the advisability of launching a suit.
wrong	Overall, she enjoyed summer camp, but she did not like her councillor.
right	Overall, she enjoyed summer camp, but she did not like her counsellor.

244. credible/credulous: Someone *credulous* (believing) is likely to believe anything, even if it is not *credible* (believable).

wrong	"Maybe I'm too credible," she said. "I believe everything my husband tells me."
right	"Maybe I'm too credulous," she said. "I believe everything my husband tells me."

245. decimate: Most etymologists agree that originally this word meant *kill one of every ten*. It has come to be used more loosely to mean *destroy a considerable number of*, and sometimes *kill nine of every ten*, but it is best not to use it in a way that some authorities feel, as H.W. Fowler puts it, "expressly contradicts the proper sense."

wrong	The regiment was decimated; fewer than 40 per cent of the troops survived.
right	The regiment suffered extreme losses; fewer than 40 per cent of the troops survived.

246. deduce/deduct: *Deduction* is the noun stemming from both these verbs, which is perhaps why they are sometimes confused. To *deduce* is *to draw a conclusion*, whereas to *deduct* is *to subtract*.

wrong	Sherlock Holmes deducted that Moriarty had committed the crime.
right	Sherlock Holmes deduced that Moriarty had committed the crime.

247. definite/definitive: If something is *definite* then *there is no uncertainty* about it; a *definitive* version of something fixes it in its *final* *or permanent form*—just as a dictionary definition attempts to fix the meaning of a word. Often a sentence is better with neither of these words.

wrong   Glenn Gould's recording of Bach's Brandenburg Concertos is often thought of as the definite modern version.

right   Glenn Gould's recording of Bach's Brandenburg Concertos is often thought of as the definitive modern version.

wrong   Once we have completed our caucus discussion I will be making a very definitive statement.

right   Once we have completed our caucus discussion I will be making a statement.

or   Once we have completed our caucus discussion I will have something definite to say.

248. degradation/decline: *Degradation* carries the connotation of shame and disgrace. To *degrade* something is not to reduce it, or downgrade it, or destroy it.

wrong   Among those units in which women played a combat role there was no degradation in operational effectiveness.

right   Among those units in which women played a combat role there was no decline in operational effectiveness.

or   ... there was no reduction in operational effectiveness.

wrong   According to some authorities, the Iraqi threat has now been significantly degraded.

right   According to some authorities, the Iraqi threat has now been significantly reduced.

249. deny/refute: To *deny* something is *to assert that it is not true*; to *refute* it is *to prove conclusively that it is not true*.

wrong   During yesterday's press conference the President angrily refuted the allegations: "There has been no improper relationship," he said.

right   During yesterday's press conference, the President angrily denied the allegations: "There has been no improper relationship," he said.

250. deprecate/depreciate: To *deprecate* something is *to suggest that it is not valuable or worthy of praise*; something that *depreciates* loses its value.

wrong   Robert Stanfield is a very self-depreciating man.

right   Robert Stanfield is a very self-deprecating man.

251. **discrete/discreet**: *Discrete* means *separate* or *distinct*, whereas *discreet* means *prudent and tactful; unwilling to give away secrets.*

wrong	David Letterman is not renowned for being discrete.
right	David Letterman is not renowned for being discreet.

252. **disinterested/uninterested**: A *disinterested* person is *unbiased; uninfluenced by self-interest, especially of a monetary sort.* It is thus quite possible for a person who is entirely *disinterested* in a particular matter to be completely fascinated by it. If one is *uninterested* in something, on the other hand, one is *bored* by it.

wrong	He was so disinterested in the game that he left after the fifth inning with the score at 2–2.
right	He was so uninterested in the game that he left after the fifth inning with the score at 2–2.
wrong	The controlling shareholders had grown tired of the CEO's futuristic strategies and disinterest in day-to-day operations.
right	The controlling shareholders had grown tired of the CEO's futuristic strategies and lack of interest in day-to-day operations.

253. **disorient/disorientate**: Both are considered correct by many authorities, but the extra syllable of the second grates on the ear.

poor	I was entirely disorientated in the darkness.
better	I was entirely disoriented in the darkness.

254. **dissemble/disassemble**: To *dissemble* is *to disguise your feelings*—a mild form of lying. To *disassemble* is *to take apart.*

wrong	For the test we are required to first assemble and then dissemble a six-cylinder engine.
right	For the test we are required to first assemble and then disassemble a six-cylinder engine.

255. **dissociate/disassociate**: There is no need for the extra syllable.

poor	T.S. Eliot speaks of the disassociation of sensibility that began in the seventeenth century.
better	T.S. Eliot speaks of the dissociation of sensibility that began in the seventeenth century.

256. **distinct/distinctive**: *Distinct* means *able to be seen or perceived clearly; easily distinguishable from those around it.* *Distinctive* means

unusual; not commonly found. There is a similar contrast between the adverbs *distinctly* and *distinctively*, and the nouns *distinction* and *distinctiveness*.

wrong	I distinctively heard the sound of a car engine.
right	I distinctly heard the sound of a car engine.

257. economic/economical: *Economic* means *pertaining to economics*, or *sufficient to allow a reasonable return for the amount of money or effort put in. Economical* is a word applied to people, which means *thrifty.* The difference applies as well to *uneconomic* and *uneconomical.*

wrong	Controversy over whether it would be economical to develop the vast Hibernia oilfield continued for many years.
right	Controversy over whether it would be economic to develop the vast Hibernia oilfield continued for many years.

258. effective/efficacious/effectual/efficient: *Effective, efficacious,* and *effectual* all mean *sufficient to produce the desired effect. Efficacious,* however, applies only to things: a person cannot be efficacious. *Effectual* was once applied only to actions, but is now sometimes applied to people as well. *Effective* can apply to actions or people. *Efficient* has an added connotation: *producing results with little waste of money or effort.* Thus a promotional campaign to persuade people to buy a product by giving away free samples to every man, woman, and child in the country might be *effective,* but it would certainly not be *efficient;* a good deal of waste would be involved. The same difference applies to the nouns *effectiveness* and *efficiency.* (*Efficacy* is a rather pretentious noun that is usually best avoided.)

wrong	The Board wants to increase the efficacy of the machinery we use.
right	The Board wants to increase the efficiency of the machinery we use.
poor	It would not be efficacious to launch a direct mail campaign with a product of this sort.
better	It would not be effective to launch a direct mail campaign with a product of this sort.

259. e.g./i.e.: The abbreviation *e.g.* is short for *exempli gratia* ("examples given"). It is sometimes confused with the abbreviation *i.e.,* which is short for *id est* ("that is to say").

wrong	Those citizens of India who speak Hindi (e.g., the vast majority of the population) are being encouraged by the government to learn a second language.
right	Those citizens of India who speak Hindi (i.e. the vast majority of the population) are being encouraged by the government to learn a second language.

260. elemental/elementary: A thing is *elemental* if it forms *an important or essential element of the whole*; it is *elementary* if it is *easy to understand*, or *at a relatively simple level.*

wrong	He lacked even the most elemental understanding of the problem.
right	He lacked even the most elementary understanding of the problem.

261. elicit/illicit: *Elicit* is a verb; one *elicits* information about something. *Illicit* is an adjective meaning *illegal* or *not approved.*

wrong	She has been dealing in elicit drugs for some time.
right	She has been dealing in illicit drugs for some time.
or	The police elicited details about her drug use.

262. eligible/illegible: One is *eligible* for a job or for membership in an organization *if one meets the standard set for applicants*. One of the requirements might be that one's handwriting not be *illegible*.

wrong	He regretted that I was not illegible to join his club.
right	He regretted that I was not eligible to join his club.

263. emigrant/immigrant: To *migrate* is to move from one place to another. The prefix *ex*, shortened to *e*, means *out of*, so an *emigrant* from a country is *someone who is moving out of it*. The prefix *in* or *im* means *in* or *into*, so an *immigrant* to a country is *someone moving into it*. Similarly, *emigration* is *the movement of people out of a country*, while *immigration* is *the movement of people into a country*. Notice the spelling in both cases; e-migrant (one *m*), im-migrant (two *m*s).

wrong	More than 100,000 emigrants entered America last year.
right	More than 100,000 immigrants entered America last year.

264. eminent/imminent/immanent: A person is *eminent* if she is *well-known and well-respected*; an event is *imminent* if it is *about to happen*; a quality (or a god) is *immanent* if it *pervades everything.*

wrong	Even those working for the party in the campaign did not believe that a majority victory was immanent.
right	Even those working for the party in the campaign did not believe that a majority victory was imminent.

265. enervate/invigorate:

Because of the similarity in sound between *enervate* and *energy*, it is often thought to mean *make more energetic*. In fact it means just the opposite—*to lessen the strength of*. If something makes you more energetic it *invigorates* you.

wrong	She found the fresh air quite enervating; I haven't seen her so lively in months.
right	She found the fresh air quite invigorating; I haven't seen her so lively in months.

266. enormity/enormousness:

Originally the adjective *enormous* simply meant *deviating from the norm*, but by the early nineteenth century it had also come to mean *abnormal, monstrous*, or *extraordinarily wicked*. Today the only meaning is of course *vast* in size or quantity, but the connotation of wickedness is preserved in the noun *enormity*. We may speak of the *enormity* of a person's crime, but if we want a noun to express vast size we should use *enormousness* or *vastness*.

wrong	What most impresses visitors to the Grand Canyon is usually its sheer enormity.
right	What most impresses visitors to the Grand Canyon is its sheer enormousness.
better	What most impresses visitors to the Grand Canyon is its vastness.

267. epithet/epigraph/epitaph/epigram:

four words often confused. Here are their meanings:

- *Epithet*—an adjective or short phrase describing someone ("The Golden Brett, the epithet often used to describe Brett Hull, involves an allusion to the nickname of his famous father.").
- *Epigraph*—an inscription, especially one placed upon a building, tomb, or statue to indicate its name or purpose.
- *Epitaph*—words describing a dead person, often the words inscribed on the tomb.
- *Epigram*—a short, witty, or pointed saying.

wrong	His epigram will read, "A good man lies here."
right	His epitaph will read, "A good man lies here."

268. equal/equitable/equable: Things that are *equal* have the *same value*. Arrangements that are *equitable* are *fair and just*. An *equable* person is one who is *moderate and even-tempered*.

> *wrong*   The distribution of Commons and Senate seats is an equable one; in almost every case the percentage of combined seats allocated to a province closely approximates the percentage of the Canadian population made up by its inhabitants.
>
> *right*   The distribution of Commons and Senate seats is an equitable one; in almost every case the percentage of combined seats allocated to a province closely approximates the percentage of the Canadian population made up by its inhabitants.

269. explicit/implicit: If something is *explicit* it is *unfolded*—stated in precise terms, not merely suggested or implied. Something that is *implicit* is *folded in*—not stated overtly. By extension *implicit* has also come to mean *complete* or *absolute* in expressions such as *implicit trust* (i.e., trust so complete that it does not have to be put into words).

> *wrong*   I told you implicitly to have the report on my desk first thing this morning.
>
> *right*   I told you explicitly to have the report on my desk first thing in the morning.

270. financial/fiscal/monetary/economic: The terms used in personal, business, and government finance are not always the same. Here are four that are often not clearly understood:

- *Financial*—having to do with finance or the handling of money.
- *Fiscal*—having to do with public revenue.
- *Monetary*—having to do with the currency of a country. (Only in very limited circumstances, such as the expression *monetary value*, can monetary have the more general meaning of *having to do with money*.)
- *Economic*—having to do with the economy. Thus a government's *economic* program embraces both *fiscal* and *monetary* policies.

> *wrong*   My brother is a nice person, but he has no monetary ability.
>
> *right*   My brother is a nice person, but he has no financial ability.

271. finish/be finished/have finished: In slang usage *to be finished* means *to be at the end of one's life or career* (*If that player's knee is* *seriously injured again, he is finished*). This special use should not be extended to the verb *finish* in its normal meaning.

wrong	Are you finished your work?
right	Have you finished your work?

272. flammable/inflammable: The two words share the same meaning; *flammable* may have originated because of the possibility for confusion over the word *inflammable*, which looks like a negative but isn't. *Non-flammable* should be used to mean *difficult or impossible to burn*.

wrong	Asbestos is an inflammable material.
right	Asbestos is a non-flammable material.

273. flout/flaunt: To *flout* is *to disobey or show disrespect for*; to *flaunt* is *to display very openly*.

wrong	Aggressive policing seems to have increased the number of people flaunting the law.
right	Aggressive policing seems to have increased the number of people flouting the law.

274. formerly/formally: The similarity of sound often leads to confusion.

wrong	In August Mr. Laurel formerly broke with Mrs. Aquino.
right	In August Mr. Laurel formally broke with Mrs. Aquino.

275. fortunate/fortuitous: *Fortunate* means *lucky*; *fortuitous* means *happening by chance*.

wrong	This combination of circumstances is not a fortuitous one for our company; we shall have to expect reduced sales in the coming year.
right	This combination of circumstances is not a fortunate one for our company; we shall have to expect reduced sales in the coming year.

276. forward/foreword: You find a *foreword* before the other words in a book.

wrong	The author admits in the forward to her book that the research was not comprehensive.
right	The author admits in the foreword to her book that the research was not comprehensive.

277. founder/flounder: As a verb, *founder* means *to get into difficulty, to stumble or fall, to sink* (when speaking of a ship), or *to fail* (when speaking of a plan). To *flounder* is *to move clumsily or with difficulty*, or *to become confused* in an effort to do something.

wrong	He foundered about in a hopeless attempt to solve the problem.
right	He floundered about in a hopeless attempt to solve the problem.

278. further/farther: *Farther* refers only to physical distance.

wrong	Eisenhower argued that the plan should receive farther study.
right	Eisenhower argued that the plan should receive further study.

279. historic/historical: *Historic* means *of sufficient importance that it is likely to become famous in history*; *historical* means *having to do with history* (historical research, historical scholarship, etc.).

wrong	We are gathered here for a historical occasion—the opening of the city's first sewage treatment plant.
right	We are gathered here for a historic occasion—the opening of the city's first sewage treatment plant.

280. hopefully: one of the greatest causes of disagreement among grammarians. Traditionalists argue that the correct meaning of the adverb *hopefully* is *filled with hope*, and that the use of the word to mean *it is to be hoped that* is therefore incorrect. On the other side it is plausibly argued that many adverbs can function as independent comments at the beginning of a sentence. (*Finally, let me point out that* ...; *Clearly, we have much to do if we are to* ... ; *Obviously, it will not be possible to* ...). Why should *hopefully* be treated differently? Why indeed? Using *hopefully* for this purpose may not make for beautiful English, but it should not be regarded as a grievous error.

poor	Hopefully, it will be possible to finish before tomorrow. (As usually happens, "hopefully" is here used with the passive, making for a wordy sentence.)
better	We hope we can finish before tomorrow.
poor	Hopefully, we will arrive before dusk. (This sentence should be rewritten in order to ensure that the sentence does not suggest the meaning, "we will arrive filled with hope before dusk.")
better	I hope we will arrive before dusk.

281. human/humane: Until the eighteenth century there was no distinction made between the two in either meaning or pronunciation; they were simply alternative ways of spelling the same word. In recent centuries *humane* has come to be used to refer exclusively to the more attractive human qualities—kindness, compassion, and so forth.

> *wrong*   Their group is campaigning for the human treatment of animals.
>
> *right*   Their group is campaigning for the humane treatment of animals.

282. idioms: Similarity in sound and meaning between words often leads to the mixing-up of idioms.

> *wrong*   Authorities termed it a democratic transition, but for all intensive purposes it was a *coup d'état*.
>
> *right*   Authorities termed it a democratic transition, but for all intents and purposes it was a *coup d'état*.
>
> *wrong*   The new recruits were reminded that they would have to tow the line.
>
> *right*   The new recruits were reminded that they would have to toe the line.

283. illusion/allusion: An *allusion* is *an indirect reference to something*; an *illusion* is *something falsely supposed to exist.*

> *wrong*   Joyce is making an illusion in this passage to a Shakespearean sonnet.
>
> *right*   Joyce is making an allusion in this passage to a Shakespearean sonnet.

284. imply/infer: To *imply* something is *to suggest it without stating it directly*; the other person will have to *infer* your meaning. It may be a comfort to the many who have confused the two to know that the mistake goes back at least as far as Milton:

> *wrong*   Great or Bright infers not Excellence. (*Paradise Lost* viii, 91)
> *right*   Great or Bright implies not Excellence.
>   (The fact that a thing is great or bright does not imply that it is also excellent.)
>
> *wrong*   I implied from his tone that he disliked our plan.
> *right*   I inferred from his tone that he disliked our plan.

285. in to/into: The difference is that *into* is used to indicate movement from outside to inside.

wrong	Writers in Britain generally expressed sympathy for Rushdie's decision, although some said he was caving into pressure.
right	Writers in Britain generally expressed sympathy for Rushdie's decision, although some said he was caving in to pressure.

286. incidents/incidence: *Incidents* is the plural of *incident* (happening), whereas *incidence* is a singular noun meaning *the rate at which something occurs.*

wrong	The incidents of lung cancer is much lower in Zambia than it is in North America.
right	The incidence of lung cancer is much lower in Zambia than it is in North America.

287. ingenious/ingenuous: *Ingenious* means *clever*; *ingenuous* means *pleasantly open and unsophisticated.*

wrong	Her manner was completely ingenious; I cannot imagine she was trying to deceive us.
right	Her manner was completely ingenuous; I cannot imagine she was trying to deceive us.

288. innumerable: so numerous that it is impossible to count; do not use as a synonym for *many.*

wrong	Scholars have advanced innumerable explanations for the dinosaurs' disappearance.
right	Scholars have advanced many explanations for the dinosaurs' disappearance.

289. insist/persist: To *insist* (that something be done, or on doing something) is *to express yourself very forcefully*. To *persist* in doing something is *to keep on doing it*, usually despite some difficulty or opposition.

wrong	Even after he had been convicted of the crime, he persisted that he was innocent.
right	Even after he had been convicted of the crime, he insisted that he was innocent.

290. instinctive/instinctual: There is no difference in meaning; it is thus better to stay with the older (and more pleasant sounding) *instinctive.*

poor	Biologists disagree as to what constitutes instinctual behavior.
better	Biologists disagree as to what constitutes instinctive behavior.

291. **judicial/judicious**: *Judicial* means *having to do with law courts and the administration of justice. Judicious* means *having good judgement.*

wrong	He made one or two judicial comments about the quality of the production.
right	He made one or two judicious comments about the quality of the production.

292. **know**: When one *knows* something, that piece of knowledge has been in one's mind for some time. The process of gathering or acquiring knowledge is called *discovering*.

wrong	Although I noticed the new employee on Monday, I did not know her name until today.
right	Although I noticed the new employee on Monday, I did not discover her name until today.

293. **later/latter**: *Later* means *afterwards in time*, whereas the *latter* is *the last mentioned* (of two things).

wrong	I looked up the battle of Stalingrad in both the *World Book* and the *Encyclopaedia Britannica*. The later provided much more information.
right	I looked up the battle of Stalingrad in both the *World Book* and the *Encyclopaedia Britannica*. The latter provided much more information.

294. **laudable/laudatory**: *Laudable* means *worthy of praise*; *laudatory* means *expressing praise.*

wrong	His efforts to combat poverty are very laudatory.
right	His efforts to combat poverty are very laudable.

295. **liable/likely**: *Liable* means *obliged by law* (*You will be liable for any damage caused when you are driving the vehicle*), or *in danger of doing or suffering from something undesirable* (*That chimney is liable to fall*). Since in the latter meaning *likely* can often be used in place of *liable*, it is often assumed that there is really no distinction between the two. Careful writers, however, do not use *liable* unless they are referring to possible consequences of an undesirable nature.

poor	Last Sunday Woods won the Colonial Open. He's liable to win again before the Canadian Open.
better	Last Sunday Woods won the Colonial Open. He's likely to win again before the Canadian Open.

296. libel/slander: *Libel is written* (and published); *slander is oral.*

wrong	He was careful in his speech to avoid making any libellous remarks.
right	He was careful in his speech to avoid making any slanderous remarks.

297. lightning/lightening: One is not likely to see the sky *lightening* until after the thunder and *lightning* are over.

wrong	Three of the men were severely injured by the lightening.
right	Three of the men were severely injured by the lightning.

298. literally: *Literal* means *by the letter*—in exact agreement with what is said or written. A literal meaning is thus the opposite of a figurative or metaphorical meaning. Do not use the adverb *literally* simply to emphasize something.

wrong	As silviculturalists we are—literally—babes in the woods. (Ken Drushka, *Stumped: The Forest Industry in Transition*) (Silviculturalists may be literally in the woods, but they are not literally babes.)
right	As silviculturalists we are babes in the woods.

299. make/allow/make possible: To *make* someone do something is *to force them to do it* (often against their wishes); to *allow* someone to do something is *to permit them* or *make it possible* for them to do something that they want to do.

wrong	A new hospital wing is being built; this will make many more people come for treatment.
right	A new hospital wing is being built; this will allow many more people to come for treatment.
or	A new hospital wing is being built; this will make it possible for many more people to come for treatment.

300. masterful/masterly: *Masterful* means *domineering*; *masterly* means *exhibiting mastery* or *great skill.*

wrong	Once again last night, Liona Boyd gave the audience a masterful performance.
right	Once again last night, Liona Boyd gave the audience a masterly performance.

301. **mitigate/militate**: To *mitigate* something is *to make it less harsh or severe*; thus *mitigating* circumstances are those that make a criminal offence less serious. To *militate* against something is *to act as a strong influence against it.*

wrong	The natural history orientation of early anthropology also mitigated against studies of change. (Bruce G. Trigger in *Natives and Newcomers*)
right	The natural history orientation of early anthropology also militated against studies of change.

302. **momentarily**: *Momentarily* means *lasting only a moment* (*He was momentarily confused*). Common usage also allows the word to mean *in a moment* or *soon*; in formal writing it is best to avoid this use.

poor	Ms. Billings has informed me that she will join us momentarily.
better	Ms. Billings told me that she will join us soon.

303. **need/want**: The verb *need* conveys the idea that it would be difficult or impossible for you to do without the needed thing. If you are talking about acquiring something that is not necessary or essential, use *want* instead; everyone *needs* water and food, but no one really *needs* a television. Be careful too not to commit to paper the slang use of *need to* for *should.*

wrong	I need to marry someone who is very beautiful, very intelligent, very kind, and very rich.
right	I want to marry someone who is very beautiful, very intelligent, very kind, and very rich.
wrong	The government needs to improve the roads in this area.
right	The government should improve the roads in this area.

304. **non sequitur**: A *non sequitur* is a *statement that has no clear relationship with what has preceded it.* There may be some connection within the mind of the speaker or writer, but it has not been expressed in words.

wrong	It's time our government did something to help southern Africa. Besides, consumers appreciate inexpensive clothes.
right	It's time our government did something to help southern Africa. Lowering the current barriers against importing cheap food and textiles would be an important step in that direction. Such a move would benefit our own citizens too; consumers appreciate inexpensive food and clothing.

305. **obligate/oblige**: These two words share the same Latin root but have different shades of meaning and are used rather differently. One feels a sense of obligation, but feels obliged to do something.

wrong	She felt obligated to finish the book her friend had lent her.
right	She felt obliged to finish the book her friend had lent her.

306. **of/have**: The difference in meaning is obvious, but the similarity in sound consistently leads people to write sentences involving such meaningless expressions as *should of, would of, could of, may of, might of,* and *must of.*

wrong	The experiment would of succeeded if the solution had been prepared correctly.
right	The experiment would have succeeded if the solution had been prepared correctly.
wrong	Hitler believed that Rommel should of been able to defeat Montgomery at El Alamein.
right	Hitler believed that Rommel should have been able to defeat Montgomery at El Alamein.

307. **other**: if one uses the words <u>the</u> *other* it suggests that the thing or person one is about to mention is the <u>only</u> other one is going to write about. If there are several *others* to be mentioned, *another* is the word to choose.

wrong	One reason Germany lost the Second World War was that she underestimated the importance of keeping the United States out of the conflict. The other reason was that her intelligence network was inferior to that of the Allies. Moreover, Hitler's decision to invade Russia was a disastrous mistake.
	(Here the use of *the other* in the second sentence leads the reader to believe this is the <u>only</u> other reason. When a third reason is mentioned in the next sentence, the reader is taken by surprise.)
right	One reason Germany lost the Second World War was that she underestimated the importance of keeping the United

States out of the conflict. Another reason was that her intelligence network was inferior to that of the Allies. Moreover, Hitler's decision to invade Russia was a disastrous mistake.

308. **our/are**: Like the substitution of *of* for *have*, the confusion of *our* and *are* should never survive the rough draft stage.

wrong	Almost all are time is spent together.
right	Almost all our time is spent together.

309. **palate/palette/pallet**: Your *palate* is in your mouth. An artist uses a *palette* to mix paint on. (By extension people often refer to the range of colors typically used by a painter as her palette.) Finally, a *pallet* (or skid) is a wooden frame designed for transporting goods.

wrong	In his later work Matisse's pallet was more limited; much of his work was in unmodulated, primary colors.
right	In his later work Matisse's palette was more limited; much of his work was in unmodulated, primary colors.

310. **partake/participate**: *Partake* refers to things (especially food and drink), *participate* to activities.

wrong	The Governor General made a brief appearance, but did not partake in the festivities.
right	The Governor General made a brief appearance, but did not participate in the festivities.

311. **persecute/prosecute**: To *persecute* someone is *to treat them in a harsh and unfair manner*, especially because of their political or religious beliefs. To *prosecute* someone is *to take legal action against them* in the belief that they have committed a crime.

wrong	Catholics began to be prosecuted in England in the sixteenth century.
right	Catholics began to be persecuted in England in the sixteenth century.

312. **persuade**: To *persuade* someone <u>of</u> something is *to make that person believe that it is true*. To persuade someone <u>to do</u> something is *to lead that person, through what one says, to do the desired thing*. If one does not succeed in making people believe or do what one wants, then one has not persuaded or convinced them, but only <u>tried</u> to persuade

them. (The confusion of *refute* with *deny* [above, number 249] is a parallel mistake.)

wrong	After all Portia's persuasion Shylock still refuses to change his mind.
right	After all Portia's attempts to persuade him, Shylock still refuses to change his mind.

313. **pore/pour**: As *The Globe and Mail Style Book* puts it, one should "not write of someone pouring over a book unless the tome in question is getting wet."

wrong	After pouring over the evidence, the committee could find no evidence of wrongdoing.
right	After poring over the evidence, the committee could find no evidence of wrongdoing.

314. **practical/practicable**: *Practical* means *suitable for use*, or *involving activity rather than theory*. *Practicable* means *able to be done*. Changing the railway system back to steam locomotives would be *practicable* but extremely *impractical*. In most cases *practical* is the word the writer wants; excessive use of *practicable* will make writing sound pretentious rather than important.

wrong	We do not feel that the construction of a new facility would be practicable at this time.
right	It would not be practical to construct a new facility now.

315. **prescribe/proscribe**: To *prescribe* something is *to recommend or order its use*; to *proscribe* something is *to forbid its use*.

wrong	One local physician has already proscribed this new drug for a dozen of her patients, and in every case their condition has improved after taking it.
right	One local physician has already prescribed this new drug for a dozen of her patients, and in every case their condition has improved after taking it.

316. **presently**: The subject of much disagreement among grammarians; should *presently* be restricted to its original meaning of *soon*, or should common usage of the word to mean *now* be allowed to spread unopposed? Traditionalists argue that the acceptance of both meanings encourages ambiguity, but in fact the verb tense usually makes clear whether the speaker means *soon* or *now* (*I will be there presently,*

I am presently working on a large project, etc.). Perhaps the best solution is to avoid the rather pompous *presently* altogether, and stick to those fine Anglo-Saxon words *soon* and *now.*

poor	I am seeing Mr. Jones presently.
better	I am seeing Mr. Jones now.
or	I will be seeing Mr. Jones soon.

317. **proposition/proposal:** The only formally correct meaning of *proposition* is *a statement that expresses an idea,* as in *This country is dedicated to the proposition that all humans are created equal.* It is better not to use it to mean *proposal.*

poor	The department has put forward a proposition for increasing sales.
better	The department has put forward a proposal for increasing sales.

318. **prove:** To *prove* something is *to eliminate any doubt whatsoever as to its truth.* Outside of mathematics, science, or philosophical logic *proof* is rarely possible; what one is doing when writing about history or political science or English is presenting an argument, not a *proof.* Be cautious in the claims you make in formal writing.

poor	The following passage proves that T.S. Eliot was anti-Semitic.
better	The following passage strongly suggests that T.S. Eliot was anti-Semitic.

319. **raise/rise:** Raise means *to lift;* rise means *to come up.*

wrong	They rose the curtain at 8 o'clock.
right	They raised the curtain at 8 o'clock.
or	The curtain rose at 8 o'clock.

320. **rational/rationale:** *Rational* is an adjective meaning *logical* or *sensible.* A *rationale* is *an explanation* for something.

wrong	The underlying rational for the proliferation of soaps and detergents is not to make our skin or clothes any cleaner, but to increase the profits of the manufacturers.
right	The underlying rationale for the proliferation of soaps and detergents is not to make our skin or clothes any cleaner, but to increase the profits of the manufacturers.

321. **ravish/ravage**: *Ravish* has two quite unrelated meanings—*to rape*, or *to fill with delight*. To *ravage* is *to damage or destroy*.

wrong   The tree had been ravished by insects.

right   The tree had been ravaged by insects.

322. **real/genuine**: The basic meaning of *real* is *existing*; the opposite of *fake* or *forged* is *genuine*.

poor   The buyer had thought the painting was a Cezanne, but he soon discovered it was not real.

better   The buyer had thought the painting was a Cezanne, but he soon discovered it was not genuine.

323. **reign/rein**: A monarch *reigns* over a territory; to control a horse you *rein* it in (using the reins).

wrong   Megawati has so far shown no signs of reigning in the armed forces. (*The Economist*, April 21, 2001)

right   Megawati has so far shown no signs of reining in the armed forces.

324. **respectively/respectfully**: *Respectively* means *in the order mentioned*; *respectfully* means *done with respect*.

wrong   Green Bay, Denver, and San Francisco were, respectfully, the three best teams in the NFL last season.

right   Green Bay, Denver, and San Francisco were, respectively, the three best teams in the NFL last season.

325. **reticent/reluctant**: *Reticent* means *reluctant to speak; reserved about speaking*. A country may be *reluctant* to go to war; it cannot be *reticent* to go to war. And to say *reticent to speak* is to repeat oneself.

wrong   She was reticent to speak up, even when her family's reputation had been attacked.

right   She was reluctant to speak up, even when her family's reputation had been attacked.

or   She remained reticent, even when her family's reputation had been attacked.

326. **sensory/sensuous/sensual**: Advertising and pornography have dulled the distinction among these three adjectives. The meanings of *sensory* and *sensuous* are similar—*sensual* is the sexy one:

- *Sensory*—having to do with the senses.
- *Sensuous*—having to do with the senses, or appealing to the senses.
- *Sensual*—offering physical pleasure, especially of a sexual sort.

wrong	Boswell suggested they go to a house of ill repute, but Johnson had no desire for sensuous pleasures.
right	Boswell suggested they go to a house of ill repute, but Johnson had no desire for sensual pleasures.

327. **set/sit**: *Set* means *to place something somewhere.*

wrong	I could remember everything, but I had difficulty sitting it down on paper.
right	I could remember everything, but I had difficulty setting it down on paper.
wrong	He asked me to set down on the couch.
right	He asked me to sit down on the couch.

328. **simple/simplistic**: *Simplistic* is a derogatory word meaning *too simple* or *excessively simplified.*

wrong	The questions were so simplistic that I was able to answer all but one correctly.
right	The questions were so simple that I was able to answer all but one correctly.

329. **somehow**: *Somehow* means *by some method* (*Somehow I must repair my car so that I can arrive in time for my appointment*). It does not mean *in some ways, to some extent,* or *somewhat.*

wrong	His brother is somehow mentally disturbed.
right	His brother is mentally disturbed in some way.
or	His brother is somewhat disturbed mentally.

330. **specially/especially**: *Specially* means *for a particular purpose* (*These utensils are specially designed for left-handed people*). *Especially* means *particularly* or *more than in other cases.*

wrong	The entire system pleased her, but she was was specially happy to see that the computer program had been especially created for small business users.
right	The entire system pleased her, but she was especially happy to see that the computer program had been specially created for small business users.

331. stationary/stationery: *Stationary* means *not moving*; *stationery* is *what you write on*.

wrong	As Mr. Blakeney remembered it, Lord Taylor "would always park his car in the no-parking zone outside the Bessborough Hotel, leaving House of Lords stationary on the windshield."
right	As Mr. Blakeney remembered it, Lord Taylor "would always park his car in the no-parking zone outside the Bessborough Hotel, leaving House of Lords stationery on the windshield."

332. stimulant/stimulus: *Stimulus* (plural stimuli) is the more general word for *anything that produces a reaction*; *stimulant* normally refers to *a drink or drug* that has a *stimulating* effect.

wrong	The shocks were intended to act as stimulants to the rats that we used as subjects for the experiment.
right	The shocks were intended to act as stimuli to the rats that we used as subjects for the experiment.

333. tack/tact: *Tack* is a sailing term; a different tack means *a different direction relative to the wind*. *Tact* is *skill in saying or doing the right or polite thing*.

wrong	We will have to exercise all our tack in the coming negotiations.
right	We will have to exercise all our tact in the coming negotiations.

334. than/that: The difference in meaning is obvious, but slips of the pen or typewriter too often allow this error to make it to the final draft.

wrong	It turns out that the company needs more money that we had expected.
right	It turns out that the company needs more money than we had expected.

335. they/their/there/they're: Four words that are confused perhaps more frequently than any others. *They* is a pronoun used to replace any plural noun (e.g., books, people, numbers). *There* can be used to mean *in* (or at) *that place*, or can be used as an introductory word before various forms of the verb *to be* (*there is, there had been*, etc.). *Their* is a possessive adjective meaning *belonging to them*. Beware in particular of substituting *they* for *there*:

wrong	They were many people in the crowd.
right	There were many people in the crowd.

The easiest way to check whether one is making this mistake is to ask if it would make sense to replace *they* with a noun. In the above sentence, for example, it would obviously be absurd to say, *The people were many people in the crowd.*

The confusion of *they, there,* and *their* is the sort of mistake that all writers are able to catch if they check their work carefully before writing the final draft.

wrong	Soviet defenceman Mikhail Tatarinov is considered to be there enforcer. (*Peterborough Examiner*)
right	Soviet defenceman Mikhail Tatarinov is considered to be their enforcer.
wrong	There all going to the dance this Saturday.
right	They're all going to the dance this Saturday.
or	They are all going to the dance this Saturday.

336. **tiring/tiresome**: Something that is *tiring* makes you feel *tired*, though you may have enjoyed it very much. Something that is *tiresome* is *tedious* and *unpleasant*.

wrong	Although it is tiresome for him, my father likes to play tennis at least twice a week.
right	Although it is tiring for him, my father likes to play tennis at least twice a week.

337. **to/too/two**: *Too* can mean *also* or be used to indicate *excess* (*too many, too heavy*); *two* is of course the number.

wrong	She seemed to feel that there was to much to do.
right	She seemed to feel that there was too much to do.

338. **to/towards**: *Towards* indicates motion.

wrong	The deer moved slowly to me through the tall grass.
right	The deer moved slowly towards me through the tall grass.

339. **unexceptional/unexceptionable**: *Unexceptional* means *ordinary, not an exception*; *unexceptionable* means *you do not object* (or *take exception*) to the thing or person in question.

| *wrong* | One way the President pays for this is in the confusion and controversy that surround the unexceptional White House |

plan to reflag 11 Kuwaiti tankers with the Stars and Stripes. It is a modest proposal that in itself should not cause the handwringing now being observed on Capitol Hill.

(The plan to reflag the tankers clearly <u>was</u> an exception; the U.S. had not done anything similar for years. What the writer means to say is that the plan is unexceptionable—that no one should have any objection to it.)

right   One way the President pays for this is in the confusion and controversy that surround the unexceptionable White House plan to reflag 11 Kuwaiti tankers with the Stars and Stripes. It is a modest proposal that in itself should not cause the handwringing now being observed on Capitol Hill.

340. unique/universal/perfect/complete/correct: None of these can be a matter of degree. Something is either unique or not unique, perfect or imperfect, and so on.

wrong   Frida Kahlo made a rather unique contribution to twentieth century art.

right   Frida Kahlo made a unique contribution to twentieth century art.

or   It is arguable that Frida Kahlo made a unique contribution to twentieth-century art.

341. valid/true/accurate: An *accurate* statement is one that is *factually correct*. A combination of *accurate* facts may not always give a *true* picture, however. For example, the statement *Former Canadian Prime Minister Mackenzie King often visited prostitutes* is entirely *accurate*, but gives a false impression; in fact King visited prostitutes to try to convince them of the error of their ways, not to use their services. *Valid* is often used carelessly and as a consequence may seem fuzzy in its meaning. Properly used it can mean *legally acceptable*, or *sound in reasoning*; do not use it to mean *accurate, reasonable, true*, or *well-founded*.

poor   Churchill's fear that the Nazis would become a threat to the rest of Europe turned out to be valid.

better   Churchill's fear that the Nazis would become a threat to the rest of Europe turned out to be well-founded.

poor   Bergson (2002) makes a valid point about the motives of the French government being suspect in its dealings with African nations.

better   Bergson (2002) has shown conclusively that the motives of the French government in its dealings with African nations were deeply suspect.

342. vein/vain: *Veins* run through your body; to be *vain* is to be *conceited*; an effort that fails to brings any of the desired results has been in vain.

wrong	Shakespeare portrays Sir John Oldcastle—or Falstaff, as he is usually known—as vein and irresponsible but immensely amusing and likeable.
right	Shakespeare portrays Sir John Oldcastle—or Falstaff, as he is usually known—as vain and irresponsible but immensely amusing and likeable.

343. verbal/oral: *Oral* means *spoken rather than written*, whereas *verbal* means *having to do with words*. A person who is unable to speak may have a high level of *verbal* skill.

wrong	I can write well enough, but I have difficulty in expressing ideas verbally.
right	I can write well enough, but I have difficulty in expressing ideas orally.

344. were/where: *Were* is of course a past tense form of the verb *to be*, while *where* refers to a place. Spell-check will not tell you if you have used the wrong word.

wrong	This is the place were Dante met Beatrice.
right	This is the place where Dante met Beatrice.

WORD ORDER PROBLEMS

Word order problems are of many sorts. See also, for example, the discussions elsewhere in this book of syntax; of ambiguity; of split infinitives; of indefinite pronouns such as *each, every,* and *anyone*; and of *not only ... but also.*

345. ambiguity/confusion: Inappropriate word order is one of the most common sources of ambiguity and confusion. Often a change in punctuation may also be required to correct the problem.

wrong	The liner tilted dramatically after fire broke out in the engine room, 50 miles south of Cyprus.
right	The liner tilted dramatically after fire broke out in the engine room. At the time the ship was 50 miles south of Cyprus.
wrong	He has not come under any pressure to make way for a new leader, despite the failure of any tangible benefits from his government's economic policies.
right	He has not come under any pressure to make way for a new leader, despite the failure of his government's economic policies to bring any tangible benefits.
wrong	Proportion of overweight people between 18 and 64 years trying to lose weight by sex in Alberta 1990. (Heading on chart, Alberta Heart Health Survey, reprinted in *The Calgary Herald*, June 3, 1994)
right	Proportion in Alberta of overweight people between 18 and 64 years, by sex, who were trying to lose weight, 1990.

346. amounts: For no good reason, adjectives having to do with amounts or quantities (e.g., *much, few, many*) normally precede the noun or pronoun to which they refer, even when the verb *to be* is used. In this way such adjectives differ from other adjectives. For example, we can talk about *a happy man*, putting the adjective *happy* before the noun *man*, or we can use the present tense of the verb *to be* and say, *The man is happy*, in which case the adjective *happy* comes after the noun *man*. In contrast, it is not correct to say, *We were many at the meeting*, or *The people here are few*. Instead the sentence must be changed around, and the adjectives put before the nouns. The easiest way to do this is by using *there* and the verb *to be*. The revised versions of the above sentences are:

right	There were many of us at the meeting.
right	There are few people here.

A further example:

wrong	The students at the football game were many.
right	There were many students at the football game.

347. balance: Often paired connectives (*if... then, either ... or* [given a separate entry below], *not only ... but also, both ... and*) can help in achieving balance. But here, as always, the writer must be careful that the words are in the right places; otherwise the fragile element of balance is lost:

wrong   Hardy was not only a prolific novelist but wrote poetry too, and also several plays.

right   Hardy was not only a prolific novelist but also a distinguished poet and a dramatist.
> (The noun *novelist* is balanced by the later nouns *poet* and *dramatist*.)

wrong   To subdue Iraq through sanctions, the United Nations felt, was better than using military force.

right   To subdue Iraq through sanctions, the United Nations felt, was better than to use military force.
> (The infinitive *to subdue* is balanced by the infinitive *to use*.)

wrong   In 1972 there was a stop-McGovern movement and a stop-Carter movement in 1976.

right   In 1972 there was a stop-McGovern movement and in 1976 a stop-Carter movement.

or   In 1972 there was a stop-McGovern movement and in 1976 there was a stop-Carter movement.

wrong   As a critic she is both fully aware of the tricks used by popular novelists to score easy successes with readers through stylized depictions of sex and violence, as well as realizing that "serious" novelists are sometimes not above resorting to the very same tricks.

right   As a critic she is fully aware both of the tricks used by popular novelists to score easy successes with readers through stylized depictions of sex and violence, and of the fact that "serious" novelists are sometimes not above resorting to the very same tricks.

348. direct object position: The normal position for direct objects is after the verb. When the direct object is put at the beginning of a sentence it sounds awkward, and the word order may lead writers to include an extra, unwanted pronoun later in the sentence. It is therefore always best to keep the direct object after the verb.

wrong   Some of the money I put it in the bank.
> (Notice the extra pronoun *it*.)

right   I put some of the money in the bank.
            (*I* is the subject; *some of the money* is the direct object of *put*.)

349. either ... or: These words should directly precede the pair of things to which they refer. The same applies to *neither ... nor*.

wrong   I will either pick an apple or a banana.
right   I will pick either an apple or a banana.
            (*Either* and *or* refer to *apple* and *banana*. Therefore they must come immediately before those words.)
wrong   He will go either to New York for the holiday or remain here.
right   He will either go to New York for the holiday or remain here.
            (The choice is between going and remaining.)
wrong   The experiment can either be performed with hydrogen or with oxygen.
right   The experiment can be performed with either hydrogen or oxygen.
            (The choice is between the two gases, not between performing and doing some other thing.)

350. except: A phrase beginning with *except* should appear directly after the noun or pronoun to which *except* refers.

wrong   We all had to wait except for those who had bought tickets in advance.
right   All except those who had bought tickets in advance had to wait.

351. first person last: When speaking about both yourself and another person (or other people), always mention the other person first. The first person pronoun (*I*, *me*) should come last.

wrong   I and my brother decided to go shopping yesterday.
right   My brother and I decided to go shopping yesterday.

352. only: The adverb *only* should come directly before the word or words it refers to. *She could only see him* implies that she could not hear, smell, or touch him; *She could see only him* implies that she had eyes for no one else.

wrong   She only asked six people to the party.
right   She asked only six people to the party.

353. questions in indirect speech: In a question we normally reverse the order of the subject and the verb. For example, to change the statement *She was sad* to a question, we reverse the order of *she* and *was* and ask, *Was she sad?* The same rule does not apply, however, to questions in indirect speech. These are considered to be part of a statement and, as in any other statement, the entire verb should come after the subject. For example, to turn the above sentence into indirect speech we would say, *I asked her whether she was sad* (<u>not</u> *I asked her was she sad*).

wrong	I asked him how was he.
right	I asked him how he was.
wrong	She asked her brother where was he going.
right	She asked her brother where he was going.

Notice as well that these sentences are statements, not questions. They therefore do not end with a question mark.

354. relative pronouns: Relative pronouns (*who, which, whom, whose,* etc.) normally refer to the word that has come immediately before them. This may sometimes turn out to be difficult, in which case the word order may have to be changed.

wrong	He purchased his friend's shop, whom he had known for many years.
	(The relative pronoun *whom* refers to *friend,* not *shop.* Change the word order to put *whom* directly after *friend.*)
right	He purchased the shop from his friend, whom he had known for many years.
wrong	On Saturday I went to my brother's wedding, whose new wife is a senior government official.
right	On Saturday I went to the wedding of my brother, whose new wife is a senior government official.

TOO MANY WORDS,
TOO FEW WORDS

Wordiness is perhaps the most persistent disease afflicting modern writing; references to it permeate this book. The mistake of including too few words in a sentence is much less common; most of the following entries, therefore, are instances of too many words rather than too few.

355. **actual/actually**: Usually redundant.

> *wrong*   Many people assume that Switzerland is made up entirely of bankers and watchmakers. In actual fact, the Swiss economy is very diversified.
>
> *right*   Many people assume that Switzerland is made up entirely of bankers and watchmakers. In fact, the Swiss economy is very diversified.

356. **as regards**: Use *about,* or rephrase.

> *wrong*   As regards your request for additional funding, we have taken the matter under advisement.
>
> *right*   We are considering your request for more money.

357. **as stated earlier**: If so, why state it again?

> *wrong*   The Venus flytrap, which as stated earlier is an insectivorous plant, grows only in a restricted area of New Jersey.
>
> *right*   The Venus flytrap grows only in a restricted area of New Jersey.

358. **as you know, as we all know**: Usually better omitted.

> *wrong*   As we all know, George W. Bush was elected President in 2000, even though more votes were cast for Al Gore.
>
> *right*   George W. Bush was elected President in 2000, even though more votes were cast for Al Gore.

359. **aspect**: Often a pointer to an entire phrase or clause that can be cut.

> *wrong*   The logging industry is a troubled one at the present time. One of the aspects of this industry that is a cause for concern is the increased production of cheaper timber in South America.

right   The logging industry is now a troubled one. Increased production of cheaper timber in South America has reduced the market for North American wood.

360. at a later date: *Later.*

wrong   We can decide this at a later date.
right   We can decide this later.

361. at the present time: *Now,* or nothing.

wrong   At the present time the company has ten employees.
right   The company has ten employees.

362. attention: *It has come to my attention that* is almost always unnecessarily wordy.

wrong   It has come to my attention that shipments last month were 15 per cent below targeted levels.
right   Shipments last month were 15 per cent below targeted levels.

363. basis/basically: Both are often pointers to wordiness.

wrong   On the basis of the information we now possess it is possible to see that William Bligh was not the ogre he was once thought to be. Basically, he was no harsher than most captains of the time.
right   Recent research suggests that William Bligh was not the ogre he was once thought to be. He was no harsher than most captains of the time.

364. cause: Sentences using *cause* as a verb can often be rephrased more concisely; try to think of other verbs.

wrong   The increased sales tax caused the people to react with fury.
right   The increase in sales tax infuriated the people.
wrong   The change in temperature caused the liquid to freeze within seventeen minutes.
right   The liquid froze within seventeen minutes of the temperature change.

365. close proximity to: *Near.*

wrong   The office is situated in close proximity to shops and transportation facilities.
right   The office is near a shopping centre and a bus stop.

366 e.g ... etc.: If you begin by saying *for example*, it is redundant to add *and others* at the end of your list. See also immediately below, and under *such as* in the chapter on joining ideas together.

wrong	In several African nations (e.g., Rwanda, Malawi, Zaire, etc.) tyrannical or murderous regimes were overthrown in the 1990s.
right	In several African nations (e.g., Rwanda, Malawi, Zaire) tyrannical or murderous regimes were overthrown in the 1990s.

367. etc.: The Latin *et cetera,* or *etc.* for short, means *and the rest* or *and others.* To say *and etc.* is really to say *and and others.* Beware as well of combining *etc.* with expressions such as *such as.*

wrong	During recent years several countries (Mexico, Argentina, and etc.) have amassed huge debts, which they are now unable to pay.
right	During recent years several countries (Mexico, Argentina, etc.) have amassed huge debts, which they are now unable to pay.
wrong	Plants such as Venus flytraps, pitcher plants, etc. feed on insects.
right	Plants such as Venus flytraps and pitcher plants feed on insects.
or	Some plants (Venus flytraps, pitcher plants, etc.) feed on insects.

368. exists: Often a pointer to wordiness.

wrong	A situation now exists in which voters suspect the government's motives, regardless of whether or not they approve of its actions.
right	Voters now suspect the government's motives even if they approve of its actions.

369. fact: Be wary of *the fact that.*

wrong	Due to the fact that we have discontinued this product, we are unable to provide spare parts.
right	Because we have discontinued this product we are unable to provide spare parts.
wrong	The fact that every member nation has one vote in the General Assembly does not give each one equal influence.
right	Each member nation has one vote in the General Assembly, but some have more influence than others.

wrong   Despite the fact that virtually no one in those days could foresee the end of American surpluses, Jones could.

right   Jones was one of the few to foresee the end of American surpluses.

370. **factor**: Heavily overused, and a frequent cause of wordiness.

wrong   An important factor contributing to the French Revolution was the poverty of the peasantry.

right   The poverty of the peasantry was a major cause of the French Revolution.

371. **from my point of view, according to my point of view, in my opinion**: All three expressions are usually redundant.

wrong   From my point of view, basic health care is more important than esoteric and expensive machines or procedures that benefit few.

fair   I think that basic health care is more important than esoteric and expensive machines or procedures that benefit few.

better   Basic health care is more important than esoteric and expensive machines or procedures that benefit few.

372. **I myself**: In almost all cases the addition of *myself* is needlessly repetitive.

wrong   I myself believe in freedom of speech.

right   I believe in freedom of speech.

373. **in all probability**: *Probably.*

wrong   In all probability we will be finished tomorrow.

right   We will probably be finished tomorrow.

374. **include**: Often a needed word or two is omitted after this verb. The best solution may be to rephrase or find another verb.

wrong   The report includes both secondary and post-secondary education.

right   The report includes material on both secondary and post-secondary education.

or   The report deals with both secondary and post-secondary education.

wrong   The Thirty Years War included most countries in Europe.

right   The list of countries that fought in the Thirty Years War includes almost every European nation.

right   Almost every European country fought in the Thirty Years War.

375. interesting: In most cases the writer should not have to tell the reader that what he is saying is interesting.

wrong   It is interesting to observe that illiteracy affects almost as high a proportion of native-born Americans as it does immigrants.

right   Illiteracy affects almost as high a proportion of native-born Americans as it does immigrants.

376. mean for: The preposition is unnecessary.

wrong   I did not mean for him to do it all himself.
right   I did not mean that he should do it all himself.

377. nature: Often contributes to wordiness.

wrong   The nature of the brain is to process information incredibly swiftly.
right   The brain processes information extremely swiftly.

378. personally: It is safe to let your reader take it for granted that you are speaking for yourself rather than on behalf of others.

wrong   Personally, I feel that the Supreme Court has usually exercised its constitutional authority wisely in recent years.

right   I feel the Supreme Court has usually exercised its constitutional authority wisely in recent years.

379. point in time: *Now* or *then*.

wrong   At that point in time central Africa was very sparsely populated.
right   Central Africa was then very sparsely populated.

380. really: If an intensifier must be used, *very* is preferable.

wrong   It is really important that this be done today.
right   It is very important that this be done today.
or   This must be done today.

Often, however, your point may be made more effectively without using intensifiers—and even without using adjectives:

needs checking	Like any other animal raised in a modern factory farm, a factory-farmed pig leads a terribly appalling life. It spends its entire life in really hideous pens that do not permit it to turn around, let alone to walk or run. Such incredibly barbaric cruelty is justified on the grounds that without it, humans would be forced to pay somewhat more for bacon and ham.
revised	Like any other animal raised in a modern factory farm, a factory-farmed pig leads an appalling life. It spends its entire life in pens that do not permit it to turn around, let alone to walk or run. Such cruelty is justified on the grounds that without it, humans would be forced to pay somewhat more for bacon and ham.

381. regard, with regard to, as regards: Try *about* or *over*, or rephrase.

wrong	I am writing with regard to your proposal to centralize production.
right	I am writing about your proposal to centralize production.
wrong	As regards the trend in interest rates, it is likely to continue to be upward.
right	Interest rates are likely to continue to increase.
wrong	This Act gave the government powers with regard to the readjustment of industry.
right	This Act gave the government powers over the readjustment of industry.

382. redundancy: Redundancies are words or expressions that repeat in different words a meaning already expressed. Commonly used expressions that involve redundancy include *end result, plans for the future, general public, nod your head, optimistic about the future, a personal friend of mine, mutual cooperation*. Sometimes a case may be made for using a phrase of this sort in order to emphasize a point. What is to be avoided is thoughtless and purposeless wordiness.

wordy	This property will appreciate greatly in value.
better	This property will appreciate greatly.
wordy	The house is very large in size.

better	The house is very large.
wordy	It was decided it would be mutually beneficial to both of us if he left.
better	It was decided it would be mutually beneficial if he left.
or	We agreed it would be better for both of us if he left.

383. **situation**: By avoiding this word you will usually make your sentence shorter and better.

wrong	This treaty created a situation in which European countries gave up a degree of autonomy in return for greater security.
right	Through this treaty European countries gave up a degree of autonomy in return for greater security.

384. **there is/are/was/were**: These constructions often produce sentences that are needlessly long.

wrong	There were many factors which undermined the government's popularity in this period.
right	Many things undermined the government's popularity in this period.
wrong	There are many historians who accept this thesis.
right	Many historians accept this thesis.

385. **too few words**: This mistake can happen anywhere in a sentence. One of the best tests of whether or not a writer has checked her work is whether or not there are missing words. In almost all cases, such omissions will be noticed through careful proofreading.

wrong	She rushed home to tell my family and about the accident.
right	She rushed home to tell my family and me about the accident.
wrong	Mrs. Gandhi reminded the Conference that just one intercontinental ballistic missile could plant 200 million trees, irrigate one million hectares of land, or build 6,500 health care centers. (United Nations official)
right	Mrs. Gandhi reminded the Conference that the money spent on just one intercontinental ballistic missile could be used to plant 200 million trees, irrigate one million hectares of land, or build 6,500 health care centers.

386. **too many words**: Many of the causes of this problem have been given separate entries.

wrong	So far as the purpose of this essay is concerned, it will concentrate on the expansion of Soviet power.
right	This essay will concentrate on the expansion of Soviet power.
wrong	Although the author does not claim to be writing a social study, the question arises whether the social implications of his analysis can be ignored.
right	Although the author does not claim to be writing a social study, his analysis does have social implications.

387. tragic/tragically: Unnecessary use of either the adjective or the adverb constitutes overkill.

redundant	Her husband, her child, and more than a hundred others died in a tragic plane crash in 1997.
better	Her husband, her child, and more than a hundred others died in a plane crash in 1997.

388. would like to take this opportunity to: *Would like.*

wrong	I would like to take this opportunity to thank my cousin in Peoria.
right	I am very grateful to my cousin in Peoria.
or	I would like to thank my cousin in Peoria.

ONE WORD OR TWO?

A number of very commonly used English words have over many years become accepted as one word because they are combined so often. Other similar combinations, however, should still be written as two words. In a few cases one can see English usage changing on this point right now. A generation ago, for example, *alright* as one word could not have been found in any dictionary. Now a few authorities are beginning to regard *alright* as acceptable, and perhaps in another generation or two it will have completely replaced *all right*. For the moment, though, it is best to stick with *all right* rather than the more colloquial *alright*.

389. **one word preferred**: What has been written as two words should be one. Here are some common examples:

> **already**: one word when used as an adverb ("He has finished already.")
> **altogether**: one word when used as an adverb to mean *completely* or *entirely* ("He is not altogether happy with the result.")
> **awhile**: one word when used as an adverb
> **another**
> **anybody**
> **anyone**: one word unless it is followed by *of*
> **bathroom**
> **bloodshed**
> **businessman** (but see Bias-free Language page 191)
> **cannot**: *can not* is less common, but still acceptable
> **everybody**
> **everyday**: one word when used as an adjective (e.g., "Brushing your teeth should be part of your everyday routine"—here *everyday* is an adjective modifying the noun *routine*.)
> **everyone**: one word unless it is followed by *of*
> **everything**
> **forever**
> **furthermore**
> **indeed**
> **intact**
> **into**: one word except in the relatively few cases where the senses of *in* and *to* are clearly separate (Fowler uses the example, "the Prime Minister took her in to dinner.")
> **maybe**: when used as an adverb meaning *perhaps* (e.g., *Maybe I will join you later*—here the verb is *will join* and *maybe* is an adverb.)
> **nearby**

nobody
onto: see *into*
ourselves
somebody
someone
straightforward
themselves
wartime
whatever
whenever

390. **two words preferred**: What has been written as one word should be two words. Here are some common examples:

a lot
all ready: two words when not used as an adverb (*We are all ready to go.*)
all right
all together: two words when not used as an adverb (e.g., *They were all together when I left them.*)
every day: two words when not used as an adjective (e.g., *We see each other every day.*)
every time
in fact
in front
in order
in spite of
may be: two words when used as a verb (e.g., *He may be here later tonight—may be* is the verb in the sentence.)
no one

USAGE: WORD CONVENTIONS

391. according to: This expression normally is used only when one is referring to a <u>person</u> or to a group of people (e.g., *ccording to his lawyer, the accused was nowhere near the scene when the crime was committed, According to Shakespeare, Richard III was an evil king*).

wrong	According to geography, Congo is larger than all of Western Europe.
right	As we learn in geography, Congo is larger than all of Western Europe.
wrong	According to the story of *Cry the Beloved Country*, Stephen Kumalo has a quick temper.
right	The events of the story show that Stephen Kumalo has a quick temper.

392. age/aged: Do not use the noun *age* as a participle.

wrong	A woman age 35 was struck and killed by the car.
right	A woman aged 35 was struck and killed by the car.

393. all of: Many authorities advise that the expression *all of* should be avoided in the interests of economy. Perhaps so, but there is certainly no error involved, and in many cases the addition of the word *of* improves the rhythm of the sentence; Lincoln's famous maxim "You can not fool all the people all of the time" would not be improved by dropping the *of.*

394. amount: This word should be used only with things that are uncountable (sugar, goodwill, etc.).

wrong	A large amount of books were stolen from the library last night.
right	A large number of books were stolen from the library last night.

395. and: In most cases *or* rather than *and* should be used as a connective if the statement is negative.

wrong	Moose are not found in South America, Africa, and Australia.
right	Moose are not found in South America, Africa, or Australia.

396. anyways/anywheres: There is never a need for the *s*.

wrong	We were unable to find him anywheres.
right	We were unable to find him anywhere.

397. as: When this word is used to relate the times at which two actions happened, the actions must have happened at the same time (e.g., *As I got out of bed, I heard the sound of gunfire,* where the hearing happens <u>during</u> the action of getting out; *As he was walking to work, he remembered that he had left the stove on,* where the remembering happens <u>during</u> the walking). *As* should <u>not</u> be used in this way if the two actions happened at different times; if one action is completed before the other begins, always use *when*.

wrong	As I had finished my geography assignment, I started my history essay.
right	When I had finished my geography assignment, I started my history essay.
	(The finishing happens before the starting.)
wrong	As she discovered that the engine was overheating, she stopped the car immediately.
right	When she discovered that the engine was overheating, she stopped the car immediately.
	(The discovering happens before the stopping.)

Note: Since *when* can be used both when actions happen simultaneously and when they happen at different times, anyone who is at all uncertain about this point is wise to avoid using *as* to refer to time, and always stick to *when*. This has the added advantage of avoiding the possible ambiguity as to whether *as* is being used to mean *because* or to mean *when*.

398. as/that/whether: Do not use *as* to mean *that* or *whether*.

wrong	I don't know as how I can do the job in time.
right	I don't know whether I can do the job in time.

399. back formations: A back formation is the formation of a word from what one would expect to be its derivative. The verb *laze,* for example, is a back formation from the adjective *lazy;* a more recent (and similar-sounding) back formation is the verb *liaise* from the noun *liaison.* Many back formations may be created from negatives that lack a positive form *(kempt, gruntled, couth, gainly, continent, wieldy, solent,* etc.). These should of course be avoided in formal written English.

wrong	Toronto is a pretty ruly place to watch a game. (Baseball Manager Lou Piniella, as quoted by Robertson Cochrane in *The Globe and Mail,* Oct. 29, 1994)
right	Toronto is a pretty civilized place to watch a game.

400. because of the following reasons/some reasons/many reasons:
The word *because* makes it clear that a cause or reason is being introduced. The addition of a phrase such as *of the following reasons* is redundant. Either use *because* on its own, or use <u>*for* the following reasons/many reasons</u>, etc.

wrong	During her first few years in Canada, Susanna Moodie was unhappy because of several reasons.
right	During her first few years in Canada, Susanna Moodie was unhappy for several reasons.

401. both: The expressions *both alike, both equal,* and *both together* involve repetition.

poor	Macdonald and Cartier both arrived together at about eight o'clock.
better	Macdonald and Cartier arrived together at about eight o'clock.

402. can be able: *I can do it* and *I am able to do it* mean the same thing. Using both verbs together is redundant.

wrong	He thinks Minnesota can be able to win the Cup.
right	He thinks Minnesota can win the Cup.
or	He thinks Minnesota will be able to win the Cup.

403. cannot help but: One too many negatives; use *can but* or *cannot help*.

wrong	He couldn't help but think he had made a mistake.
right	He couldn't help thinking he had made a mistake.
or	He could but think he had made a mistake.

404. change: You *make* a change (<u>not</u> do a change).

wrong	The manager did several changes to the roster before the match with Russia.
right	The manager made several changes to the roster before the match with Russia.

405. comment: We *make* comments (<u>not</u> say or do them).

wrong	Anyone who wishes to say any comments will have a chance to speak after the lecture.
right	Anyone who wishes to make any comments will have a chance to speak after the lecture.

406. compared to/than: The use of *compared to* as a participial phrase often leads to ambiguity and error. Unless one is speaking of one person *comparing* something to something else, it is usually better to use *than*.

wrong	There were far fewer frogs in the area in 2002 compared to previous years.
right	There were far fewer frogs in the area in 2002 than there had been in previous years.

407. convince: You *convince* people *that* they should do something, or *persuade* them *to* do it.

wrong	Reagan's advisers convinced him to approve the arms for hostages deal with Iran.
right	Reagan's advisers persuaded him to approve the arms for hostages deal with Iran.

408. elder/older: *Elder* can act as an adjective (*my elder son*) or a noun (*the elder of the two*). *Older* can act only as an adjective. If using than, use *older*.

wrong	She is four years elder than her sister.
right	She is four years older than her sister.

409. for: One use of this preposition is to show purpose. Normally, however, *for* can be used in this way only when the purpose can be expressed in one word (e.g., *for safety, for security*). It is <u>not</u> usually correct to try to express purpose by combining *for* with a pronoun and an infinitive: expressions such as *for him to be happy, for us to arrive safely* are awkward and should be avoided. Instead, one can express purpose either by beginning with an infinitive (e.g., *in order to make life easier, in order to increase yield per hectare*), or by using *so that* (e.g., *so that life will be made easier, so that yield per hectare will be increased*).

wrong	Please speak slowly for me to understand what you say.
right	Please speak slowly so that I can understand what you say.
wrong	The team must work hard for it to have a chance at the Grey Cup.
right	The team must work hard if it is to have a chance at the Grey Cup.

410. forget: To *forget* something is to fail to remember it, <u>not</u> to leave it somewhere.

wrong	I forgot my textbook at home.
right	I left my textbook at home.
or	I forgot to bring my textbook from home.

411. **had ought/hadn't ought**: Use *ought* or *ought not* instead.

wrong	He hadn't ought to have risked everything at once.
right	He ought not to have risked everything at once.
or	He should not have risked everything at once.

412. **hardly**: *Hardly* acts as a negative; there is thus no need to add a second negative.

wrong	The advertisers claim that you can't hardly tell the difference.
right	The advertisers claim that you can hardly tell the difference.

413. **how/what**: One may talk about *how* something (or someone) *is*, or *what* something (or someone) is *like*, but <u>not</u> *how* they are *like*.

wrong	Tell me how it looks like from where you are.
right	Tell me how it looks from where you are.
or	Tell me what it looks like from where you are.
wrong	I do not know how the roads are like between St. John's and Cornerbrook.
right	I do not know what the roads are like between St. John's and Cornerbrook.
or	I do not know how the roads are between St. John's and Cornerbrook.

414. **increase**: Numbers can be *increased* or *decreased*, as can such things as *production* and *population* (nouns which refer to certain types of numbers or quantities). Things such as *houses*, however, or *books* (nouns which do not refer to numbers or quantities) cannot be *increased*; only the <u>number</u> of houses, books, etc. can be *increased* or *decreased, raised* or *lowered*.

wrong	The government has greatly increased low-rent houses in the suburbs of Seattle.
right	The government has greatly increased the number of low-rent houses in the suburbs of Seattle.

415. **information**: One *gives* information (<u>not</u> tells it).

wrong	He told me all the information I wanted about how to apply.
right	He gave me all the information I wanted about how to apply.

416. investigation: We *make, carry out,* or *hold* an investigation (<u>not</u> do one).

wrong	The manager did a thorough investigation into the disappearance of funds from his department.
right	The manager made a thorough investigation into the disappearance of funds from his department.

417. irregardless: The result of confusion between *regardless* and *irrespective*. Use *regardless*.

wrong	She told us to come for a picnic, irregardless of whether it is rainy or sunny.
right	She told us to come for a picnic, regardless of whether it is rainy or sunny.

418. is when/is where: Many people use these phrases when attempting to define something. There is always a better way.

wrong	Osmosis is when a fluid moves through a porous partition into another fluid.
right	Osmosis occurs when a fluid moves through a porous partition into another fluid.
or	Osmosis is the movement of a fluid through a porous partition into another fluid.

419. journey: You *make* a journey (<u>not</u> do one).

wrong	If we do not stop along the way, we can do the journey in an hour.
right	If we do not stop along the way, we can make the journey in an hour.

420. law: A law is *passed, made,* or *put into effect* by the government, and *enforced* by the police. Laws are <u>not</u> *put* or *done*.

wrong	I think the government should put a law increasing the penalty for drunken driving.
right	I think the government should pass a law increasing the penalty for drunken driving.

421. less/fewer: When something can be counted (e.g., people, books, trees), use *fewer*. Use *less* only with uncountable nouns (e.g., sugar, meat, equipment).

wrong	As the modern economy spreads through the countryside, less people will die of tropical diseases or infected wounds. (*The New York Times*, May 12, 1997)
right	As the modern economy spreads through the countryside, fewer people will die of tropical diseases or infected wounds.
wrong	There are less steps, and that means there is more room for error.
right	There are fewer steps, and that means there is more room for error.

422. lie (meaning *speak falsely*): You lie *about* something, <u>not</u> *that* something.

wrong	He lied that he was eighteen years old.
right	He lied about his age, stating that he was eighteen.
or	He lied when he said he was eighteen years old.

423. mistake: Mistakes are *made* (<u>not</u> done).

wrong	He did seven mistakes in that short spelling exercise.
right	He made seven mistakes in that short spelling exercise.

424. more/most: Most adjectives and adverbs have comparative and superlative forms; the comparative is used when comparing two things, the superlative when comparing three or more.

needs checking	Smith was the most accomplished of the two.
revised	Smith was the more accomplished of the two.

To use *more* with a comparative adjective, or *most* with a superlative adjective is to repeat oneself.

wrong	The bride looked like the most happiest person in the world.
right	The bride looked like the happiest person in the world.
or	The bride looked like the most happy person in the world.
wrong	Gandalf is much more wiser than Frodo.
right	Gandalf is much wiser than Frodo.

425. nor: This word is usually used with *neither*. Do <u>not</u> use it with *not*; when using *not*, use *or* instead of *nor*.

wrong	She does not drink nor smoke.

right	She does not drink or smoke.
or	She neither drinks nor smokes.
wrong	Graham does not have the money nor the organization to work with that Atkins enjoys.
right	Graham does not have the money or the organization to work with that Atkins enjoys.
or	Graham has neither the money nor the organization to work with that Atkins enjoys.

426. nothing/nobody/nowhere: These words should not be used with another negative word such as *not*. If one uses *not*, then one should use *anything* instead of *nothing*, *anybody* instead of *nobody*, *anywhere* instead of *nowhere*.

wrong	He could not do nothing while he was in prison.
right	He could not do anything while he was in prison.

427. opposed: You are opposed *to* something or someone (<u>not</u> with or against)

wrong	Charles Darwin was opposed against the literal interpretation of the story of Creation, as found in Genesis.
right	Charles Darwin was opposed to the literal interpretation of the story of Creation, as found in Genesis.

428. per cent/percentage: If you use *per cent*, you must give the number. Otherwise, use *percentage*.

wrong	The per cent of people surveyed who reported any change of opinion was very small.
right	The percentage of people surveyed who reported any change of opinion was very small.
or	Only six per cent of the people surveyed reported any change of opinion.

Note: *Percentage* is always one word; authorities differ as to whether *per cent* should always be written as two words, or whether it also may be written as one word.

429. preclude: To *preclude* something is to exclude any possibility of it happening; people cannot be *precluded*.

wrong	Our cash flow problems preclude us from entering into any new commitments before 2003.
right	Our cash flow problems preclude any new commitments before 2003.

> *or*   We do not have enough money to make a commitment to you now.

430. position/theory: Positions and theories are held or argued; they do not hold or argue themselves.

> *wrong*   Devlin's position holds that a shared public morality is essential to the existence of society.
>
> *right*   Devlin's position is that a shared public morality is essential to the existence of society.
>
> *or*   Devlin holds that a shared public morality is essential to the existence of society.

431. reason: The phrase *the reason is because* involves repetition; use *that* instead of *because*, or eliminate the phrase completely.

> *wrong*   The reason ice floats is because it is lighter than water.
>
> *right*   The reason ice floats is that it is lighter than water.
>
> *or*   Ice floats because it is lighter than water.
>
> *wrong*   The reason I have come is because I want to apply for a job.
>
> *right*   I have come to apply for a job.

432. short/scarce: If a person is *short* of something, that thing is *scarce*.

> *wrong*   Food is now desperately short throughout the country.
>
> *right*   Food is now extremely scarce throughout the country.
>
> *or*   The country is now desperately short of food.

433. since/for: Both these words can be used to indicate length (or duration) of time, but they are used in slightly different ways. *Since* is used to mention the point at which a period of time began (*since 6 o'clock, since the beginning of 2002, since last Christmas,* etc.). *For* is used to mention the amount of time that has passed (*for two years, for six months, for centuries,* etc.).

> *wrong*   She has been staying with us since three weeks.
>
> *right*   She has been staying with us for three weeks.
>
> *or*   She has been staying with us since three weeks ago.

434. so: When used to show degree or extent, *so* is normally used with *that*: *so big that ...* , *so hungry that ...* , etc. *So* should not be used as an intensifier in the way that *very* is used.

wrong	When she stepped out of the church she looked so beautiful.
right	When she stepped out of the church she looked very beautiful.
or	When she stepped out of the church she looked so beautiful that it was hard to believe she had once been thought of as plain.

435. some/any/someone/anyone: With negatives (*not, never,* etc.) *any* is used in place of *some.*

wrong	He never gives me some help with my work.
right	He never gives me any help with my work.

436. speech: You *make* a speech or *give* a speech (<u>not</u> do a speech).

wrong	The Dean was asked to do a speech at the Convocation.
right	The Dean was asked to give a speech at the Convocation.

437. start: If <u>both</u> the time at which an event begins <u>and</u> the time that it finishes are mentioned, it is not enough to use only the verb *start.*

wrong	The dance started from 9 p.m. till midnight.
right	The dance started at 9 p.m. and finished at midnight.
or	The dance continued from 9 p.m. until midnight.
or	The dance lasted from 9 p.m. until midnight.

438. suppose/supposed: Be sure to add the *d* in the expression *supposed to.*

wrong	We are suppose to be there by eight.
right	We are supposed to be there by eight.

439. supposed to/should: These two are very similar in meaning, and may often be used interchangeably; if a person is *supposed to* do something, then that is what she *should* do. In the past tense, however, the question of when and when not to use *supposed to* is quite tricky. You <u>may</u> use it when you are clearly talking about a fixed plan that has not been carried out (e.g., *He was supposed to arrive before two o'clock, but he is still not here*). You should not use it to apply to any action that you think was wrong, or you feel should not have been carried out. The safe solution to this problem is always to use *should* instead of *supposed to.*

wrong	What she said was impolite, but he was not supposed to hit her for saying it.

right	What she said was impolite, but he should not have hit her for saying it.
wrong	The National Party government was not supposed to keep Nelson Mandela in jail for so many years.
right	The National Party government should not have kept Nelson Mandela in jail for so many years.

440. thankful/grateful: We are *thankful* that something has happened, and *grateful* for something we have received.

wrong	I am very thankful for the kind thoughts expressed in your letter.
right	I am very grateful for the kind thoughts expressed in your letter.

441. too: The word *too* suggests that something is more than necessary, or more than desired. Do not use it indiscriminately to lend emphasis.

wrong	She looked too beautiful in her new dress.
right	She looked very beautiful in her new dress.

442. try/sure: Perhaps the most common error of all, in published books and articles as well as in less formal writing, is the use of *and* rather than *to* after *try* and *sure*.

wrong	No Montrealers stepped in to try and save the franchise.
right	No Montrealers stepped in to try to save the franchise.
wrong	Burton had agreed with the Sultan not to try and convert the Africans to Christianity. (Alan Moorehead, *The White Nile*)
right	Burton had agreed with the Sultan not to try to convert the Africans to Christianity.
wrong	Be sure and take out the garbage before you go to bed.
right	Be sure to take out the garbage before you go to bed.

443. use/used: Be sure to add the *d* in the expression *used to*.

wrong	He use to be much more reckless than he is now.
right	He used to be much more reckless than he is now.

444. where: Do not use *where* for *that*.

wrong	I read in the paper where the parties are now tied in popularity.
right	I read in the paper that the parties are now tied in popularity.

PUTTING IDEAS TOGETHER

There are many ways of putting ideas together. Most of this chapter is concerned with the particulars of joining-words and how to use them; it may be useful, however, to begin with a brief look at some of the processes involved in putting ideas together.

NARRATION

The mode of thought involved in narratives is a very simple one: one thing happens, and then another thing happens, and then another thing happens. Narration is particularly useful in an academic context when the writer is describing the steps in a procedure, such as a scientific experiment. (Normally, the body of a lab report is largely taken up by narration, though the most important sections—outlining the hypothesis, drawing conclusions, etc.—are not written in a narrative mode.)

Narrative is the most straightforward mode of thinking and of writing, and perhaps for that reason many of us tend to overuse it. Business people, for example, are sometimes tempted to rely too much on narrative rather than analysis in writing reports. And among students there is a special temptation to employ the narrative mode in writing history or literature essays. In a few cases this may be appropriate. If the writer is discussing the Whitewater affair during the administration of Bill Clinton, for example, the narrative mode may well be the best one to adopt; the sequence is a complex one, and getting it straight is crucial to establishing the degrees of guilt (who knew what when) of those involved. But the narrative should be introduced in support of the writer's argument. It must not overwhelm the ideas.

CAUSE AND EFFECT

A great deal of writing involves discerning and analyzing causes and effects. Whereas the natural connectives in narrative writing are *and* and *then*, the natural connectives in writing about causes and effects are words such as *because, since,* and *therefore*. These particular connectives—and how they relate to causes and effects—are treated fully below. But before turning to them it may be useful to understand something of the difference between sequence and cause—between *and ... then* and *since ... therefore*.

sequences and causes: It is all too easy to confuse the fact that one thing happens after another thing with the notion that the first thing caused the second. Below, for example, are two arguments that were advanced against a provision in a piece of labour legislation introduced by a government in the year 2000 (I'll call it the government of Alpaca). This provision restricted the conditions under which employers would be permitted to hire outside workers during a strike. Both arguments drew comparisons with similar legislation that had been passed by another government (called here the government of Llama) some years earlier. Here is the first argument:

- This provision would lead to the closing of newspapers here in Alpaca, just as happened in Llama; the *Llama Star* suffered a long strike and was forced to close down after the introduction of similar legislation.

The facts in this argument are right. The legislation went into effect, and then the *Star* suffered from a strike, and subsequently closed down. But do they tell the whole story? Can we conclude from these facts that the first of these events was primarily or even partially responsible for causing the third? The era was a time of contraction in the newspaper business in Llama; at least one other newspaper in the area had closed down <u>before</u> this legislation went into effect. At the time, the population of newspaper-reading age was shrinking.

Let us look at the second argument:

- The provision will inevitably lead to an increase in the frequency and the duration of strikes. By 1998 in Llama, two years after similar legislation was introduced there, the number of days lost to strikes had increased over fifty per cent.

The facts are right here too; days lost to strikes *were* much higher in 1998 than in 1996. But again, can we assume that the first event caused the second? Hardly. First, we should look at other possible causes. For example, how was the overall economy performing in 1998 versus 1996? We should also look at other years as a basis for comparison; why should the year 1998 be singled out as a later point of comparison? Was it an unusually good or bad year for strikes? As it turns out, 1998 was indeed exceptional; there were far more strikes in that year than in most. On average, in the years since the controversial legislation had been passed, the number and duration of strikes in Llama had actually decreased. Another lesson in the care that deserves to be taken in making—and in responding to—arguments about cause and effect.

multiple causes: Events often have more than one cause, and claims must often be justified by more than one reason. This sounds straight-forward enough, but it is easy to forget, as the following examples show.

Many of the arguments against military intervention in the Persian Gulf (before the 1991 Gulf War, in 1998, and again in 2002–3) took this form:

- The Americans are willing to fight Saddam Hussein because they believe the oil reserves of the Gulf region are of strategic and economic importance to them. This is not a good moral justification for going to war. Therefore we should not fight.

To begin with, this sort of argument confuses explanation with justification. To inquire into American motives is to ask why the Americans were willing to go to war—a very different thing from asking if they should have been willing at those points to go to war. It is always possible to do "the right deed for the wrong reason."

Beyond this, however, the argument assumes that if one explanation can safely be advanced for an action, it is also safe to conclude that it is the only explanation. In fact, of course, it is entirely possible for the US and its allies to have been willing to go to war both out of a self-interested desire to protect oil reserves and out of unselfish desires to resist aggression, to prevent the development of chemical and biological weapons, and so on.

Reasoning used by many on the opposite side of such debates may be equally flawed. The gist of the argument of the American, British, and Canadian political leaders in 1991 was this:

- In an act of brutal aggression, Iraq invaded and annexed Kuwait, killing many of its citizens in the process. Aggression must be resisted. Therefore we should be willing to go to war.

And in 1998, as well as in 2002–3:

- In a flagrant flouting of UN resolutions, Iraq has refused to allow monitoring of strategic sites on which it has probably been developing chemical and biological weapons. Contempt for international law must be resisted. Therefore we should be willing to go to war.

As with the anti-war arguments above, the pro-war arguments here suffer from incomplete reasoning—reasoning that fails to allow for any multiplicity of causes, reasons, and effects. Did Iraq in 1991 have a legitimate historical claim on the territory of Kuwait (which, like Iraq, was carved out of what had been a part of the Ottoman Empire by the British)? What are the casualties likely to be in the event of war? Should aggression be resisted in all circumstances, and at any cost? These are some of the questions left unanswered.

And similarly in 1998 and 2002–3: Should defiance of UN resolutions be resisted at any cost? Who is likely to suffer, and how much? Does military intervention carry with it the risk of sparking a larger conflict? Have other means short of military action been exhausted? Depending on the answers one provides to such questions, the appropriate course of action may become far less clear.

necessary and sufficient conditions: A useful distinction to use in sorting out the relative importance of multiple causes, effects, and reasons is the one between necessary and sufficient conditions. The presence of oxygen is a <u>necessary</u> condition for there to be fire; there can be no fire without oxygen. But it is not a <u>sufficient</u> condition; everything in the presence of oxygen does not automatically catch fire.

Similarly (in the argument discussed above), the 1991 political leaders were in effect arguing that the fact of Iraq having invaded and annexed another sovereign country was in itself a sufficient condition to justify going to war. Someone arguing against going to war in the same circumstances might claim that the invasion of one country by another was a necessary condition for going to war, but not a sufficient one—that other, additional justification was required. And a third person might say that the invasion constituted neither a necessary nor a sufficient condition; that we should stay out of such affairs in any circumstances.

cause and correlation: Another useful distinction—particularly in the sciences and social sciences—is that between cause and correlation. Again, this may be made clear by example. A recent study has shown that the rate of breast cancer in women has increased markedly over the past twenty years. Over the same period, the average childbearing age has also risen dramatically. Now it is possible that the connection between those two occurrences may be causal in nature—that, for example, waiting until later in life to have children increases one's risk of breast cancer. But researchers caution that we should not assume this to be the case; more research needs to be done. As it stands, the connection is merely a correlation: an interrelationship of variable qualities. In this case, over the same period and under the same conditions, both variables changed.

When a correlation between two things exists, there may be a common cause or common causes for both; one may cause the other (or help to cause the other; again, more than one cause may be involved); the two may happen coincidentally as a result of quite separate causes.

Arguing in English

It is widely accepted that problems with writing are often closely intertwined with a lack of training in thinking critically; for that reason coverage of some basic concepts in critical thinking is included here. Of course thousands of books have been written on critical thinking and logical argument—and on the subtleties of logical argument in English. In a book of this sort it is not possible to do more than touch on a few key distinctions.

deductive/inductive: The conclusion of a deductive argument is based on its premises, and the conclusion must follow logically from the premises if the argument is sound. The classic examples of deductive arguments are syllogisms such as the following:

- A successful baseball team must have good starting pitchers to succeed. This year's White Sox team does not have good starting pitching. Therefore, this year's White Sox team will not be successful.

Note that the reasoning of a deductive argument may be sound even if one of its premises are false. For example, the above syllogism makes a valid argument in terms of its reasoning regardless of whether or not it is in fact true that to be successful a team must have good starting pitching.

Inductive arguments, on the other hand, rest on factual evidence; typically they generalize from a particular number or percentage to a general conclusion. Here is an example:

- Since the creation of the National League, every World Series winner has had at least three outstanding starting pitchers on its roster. It seems reasonable to conclude from this that the chances of a team with fewer than three outstanding starting pitchers winning the World Series are extremely slight.

From this observation it seems safe to generalize that a team needs outstanding starting pitchers if it is to succeed. Notice that inductive arguments are based on numbers, percentages, and estimates of probabilities.

In practice arguments very frequently combine inductive and deductive elements. Here is another example:

- Nobody ever dies from this sort of operation. If Frank dies during the operation, then it must be as a result of malpractice on the part of the surgeons. We should sue!

The initial claim here involves an inductive claim. It can be settled only by reference to the facts:

- What percentage of people have in fact died during this sort of operation?

The follow-up claim represents a deductive argument, and can be addressed by reasoning, without reference to the facts of the case:

- If it is indeed true that others have not died during this sort of operation, then what are the possible explanations? Is it in fact true that the only possible explanation is medical malpractice?

some/all: It is particularly important in sorting out both inductive and deductive arguments to be sensitive to the difference between *some* and *all*. This may seem an obvious point, but it is one that it is easy to lose in the twists and turns of an argument—or indeed in making off-hand observations about things that seem self-evident:

- I don't know about that candidate. We've hired people from that school before and, to be honest, they really haven't worked out. Let's look again at the other candidates.

The implicit assumption here is of course that since *some* graduates of a particular school have not worked out, it follows that *all* graduates of the same school will not work out at this particular sort of job.

The distinction between *some* and *all* should also be kept in mind when it comes to arguments with several interconnected strands. Does what one is saying apply to all the facts of the argument, or only to some of them? Here is an example:

- What on earth is wrong with *spinster, chairman, mankind*, or, for that matter, adjectives such as *blind* and *deaf*, to name just a few? These are perfectly legitimate and serviceable terms, yet an arbitrary, malevolent connotation has been assigned them. In their place we are asked to draw from a silly artificial glossary of convoluted euphemisms to describe people and events, a glossary replete with all manner of adverbs with the word *challenged* suffixed leech-like to them.

The writer here is arguing against bias-free language. The core of the argument is that the new terms we are asked to use are silly, artificial, and convoluted. And that may well be true of a term such as *mentally challenged*. But notice how difficult it is to make such claims stick with all or even most of the examples here. The non-sexist alternatives for *chairman* and *mankind*—*chair*, *humanity*, and the like—are hardly silly, artificial, or convoluted. And are we in fact asked to replace the word *deaf* with *aurally-challenged*? Not at all. Those working in the field do indeed use *aurally-challenged* as a blanket term to refer to all those who have any hearing impairment, ranging from mild loss of hearing to complete deafness, but they do not shy away from using terms such as *deaf* and *partially deaf*. In short, the objection raised by this writer to "politically correct" language in general turns out to apply only to a very few instances.

if/then: The *if ...then* syntactical structure is a basic form of both deductive and inductive arguments. It may be helpful here to look out for necessary and sufficient conditions; these are discussed above under the section on Cause and Effect.

trends: In matters of any complexity involving numbers and trends, it is easy to lose sight of the big picture—and many verbal arguments are constructed in a way that encourages those listening to the arguments to lose sight of the big picture. Here is an example:

- Even many of those who support the Kyoto protocol say that it will cost jobs—perhaps hundreds of thousands of jobs. We cannot afford to let our economy shrink; it is essential that we oppose ratification of the Kyoto accord.

The unstated premise in this argument is that if jobs are lost, the economy shrinks. That <u>might</u> be the case if what were being spoken of was an <u>absolute</u> reduction in the number of jobs. In fact, however, no discussion of the issue has suggested that this would happen. Some have suggested that the total number of jobs and the economy in general would grow somewhat more slowly if the Kyoto protocol were adopted, whereas others have suggested that the economy would grow almost as fast or just as fast if the accord were adopted. Here, as in many other cases, it is important to be aware of distinctions between a decline, and a decline in the rate of increase, and so on.

relevance: It is often much more difficult than one would think to judge what is relevant or irrelevant to a given argument. Here is an example:

- I don't agree with the arguments of the animal rights activists. Before we worry about any troubles the animals might have, we should take care of the problems that people have.

The argument here may seem at first glance quite powerful, but in fact the claims being made are entirely irrelevant to all but one of the arguments put forward by animal rights activists. The argument here says nothing as to the inductive claims made by these activists about the prevalence of cruelty to animals in factory farming, for example, and nor does it address the argument that it is wrong to cause unnecessary pain to other creatures. The only argument that it does address is the suggestion that we should pay some attention to the plight of animals even while we are also attempting to address human problems. There are no doubt legitimate arguments of a variety of sorts to be made concerning the priority we should give to the plight of animals as against that of humans who are suffering. But that is a separate question from the one that this argument purports to be addressing.

fallacies: A fallacious argument is one that suffers from faulty reasoning. Many forms of faulty reasoning have been identified; following is a list of some of the most common forms of fallacy:

ad hominem: This is the fallacy of attacking the person making the argument rather than the argument itself. Here is an example:

- What George Bush says about energy policy makes no sense at all. Remember, he made a fortune in the oil industry.

straw man argument: A common practice in argument is to ascribe to one's opponent an extreme view that in fact one's opponent has never put forward, and then suggest that in knocking down the extreme "straw man" argument you have won. Here are two examples:

- I fully support capital punishment. How can anyone claim that the life of a convicted murderer is as valuable as the life of the innocent person he has killed?

- I oppose capital punishment. How can anyone claim that there is no chance of a criminal reforming, and no intrinsic value in human life itself?

Of course, neither the opponents nor the supporters of capital punishment make the suggested claims—but often people are able to get away with this sort of sleight of hand in the midst of an argument.

begging the question: To beg the question is to avoid the question by taking for granted the very thing to be argued about. Here is an example:

- The situation in Afghanistan remains turbulent, and in this context it is vital that we support good government in surrounding countries. How, then, should we best support the current government in Pakistan?

By moving straight to asking how best to support the current government of Pakistan, the arguer here avoids (or "begs") the question of whether or not the current government of Pakistan is indeed providing good government that is deserving of support. (For common misunderstanding of *beg the question* to mean *raise the question*, see above, page 80.)

formally invalid arguments: If the formal structure of one's argument is not sound, then the argument is fallacious.

Two common forms of formally invalid arguments are those which *deny the antecedent*, and those which *affirm the consequent*. Here is an example of the former:

- If water starts dripping from this ceiling during a rainstorm, then you can be sure there is a problem with your roof. No water drips from the ceiling during a rainstorm. Therefore, there is no problem with the roof.

In this case it is certainly true that water dripping from the ceiling is a reliable sign of there being some problem with the roof. But of course there can be a problem with the roof even without there being such a visible sign; very frequently roof leaks result in water saturating rafters and seeping down inside walls without there being any drips from the ceiling. (Like so many elements of reasoning, the ability to recognize this fallacy connects to the ability to be sensitive to the distinction between *some* and *all*; some roof leaks result in dripping ceilings, but others don't.) The *if ...* part of an argument such as this is known as the *antecedent*. And, as the example above shows, denying the antecedent has no argumentative force.

- If a lake is very seriously affected by acid rain, no fish can survive in it. This lake has no fish living in it whatsoever. This lake must be seriously affected by acid rain.

It is entirely true that lakes seriously affected by acid rain cannot support any aquatic life. But that is not the only possible cause for the disappearance of aquatic life from a lake. If, for example, a company had been using the lake as a toxic waste dump, that would also have the effect of killing all the fish. (Again, the distinction between *some* and *all* is crucial; some lifeless lakes got that way because of acid rain, but not all.) The *then ...* part of an argument is called the *consequent*. As this example shows, affirming the consequent does nothing to prove the argument.

slippery slope arguments: The fallacy of the slippery slope argument is the suggestion that one development in a certain direction will inevitably lead to further developments in the same direction or "down the same slope." Here is an example:

- The idea of people being required to carry identity cards may seem innocuous enough, but in fact it should be resolutely opposed. If we allow the government to force us to carry identity cards, pretty soon they'll be keeping track of all our movements with video cameras, and placing all sorts of restrictions on our privacy. We have to stop these government intrusions into our lives!

This argument says nothing about the issue of identity cards *per se*. It is entirely based on the premise of one move by the government being followed by other, more drastic moves. Sometimes, of course, developments are part of long-term trends, but sometimes they are not part of any trend—or may represent the furthest extent of a particular trend. Certainly there is no inevitability about any particular move in one direction being followed by subsequent moves in the same direction.

false dichotomy: A dichotomy occurs when things or ideas are split into two distinct alternatives. An argument that tries to insist on two and only two alternatives when in fact three or more possibilities exist (or gradations among possibilities exist) is one that poses a *false dichotomy*. Here is an example:

"There should be laws prohibiting people from inciting hate against those of other races or religions."

"So you're against freedom of speech? Without freedom of speech we wouldn't have a democracy!"

"No, I support freedom of speech—but with certain limits to prevent the most harmful extreme views from being promulgated. It sounds to me as if you are not willing to do anything to combat bigotry and racism."

"Not at all. But I believe that people speaking out freely against freely expressed bigoted or racist opinions will combat them more effectively than government attempts to prohibit them."

In this case both arguers pose false dichotomies in their characterizations of the other's viewpoint—whereas in fact both hold nuanced views.

missing or unacknowledged premises: Many real-life arguments take short cuts and do not spell out all the underlying premises. In many cases this does not in fact damage the argument, but sometimes a missing or unacknowledged premise is the key to a fatal weakness in an argument. Here is an example:

- Many have suggested that the presence of extreme poverty and oppression in the world makes it more likely that terrorism will take root. But that just doesn't square with the facts; the vast majority of the September 11th terrorists and the Al Qaeda leadership did not come from backgrounds of extreme hardship. Some, including Osama bin Laden, were among the most privileged members of Saudi Arabian society.

The missing or unacknowledged premise in this argument is that people will always struggle only on behalf of those from their own nationality or social class. In fact, however, history is filled with examples of individuals from one nation or social class who became so involved with the plight of another that they devote all their energies to fighting for change.

An example like this illustrates just how readily our perceptions of argument are influenced by emotion and ideology. In this case, the entirely appropriate sense of anger and revulsion that we feel at the terrorist acts makes it difficult for us to imagine that the terrorists might consider themselves to be acting altruistically on behalf of the poor and the oppressed. And maybe most of them do not in fact think of themselves in this way. The only point here is that the fact of someone coming from a privileged background does not in itself preclude the possibility that such a person will act in a way he or she perceives as benefiting the less privileged.

post hoc, propter hoc: The fallacy here is to imagine that if one thing happens <u>after</u> the other, then it will have happened <u>because of</u> the other. (The Latin *post hoc, propter hoc* translates as *after this, because of this*.) Here is an example:

- The decline of frog populations throughout the world started to happen just after the thinning of the ozone layer; there *has* to be a connection!

But there doesn't have to be a connection—as becomes plain if we substitute a different event in the same logical structure:

- The decline of frog populations throughout the world started to happen just after the Montreal Canadiens stopped winning the Stanley Cup with any degree of frequency; there *has* to be a connection!

In this case damage from ultraviolet radiation is indeed one possible cause for the decline of frog populations—but scientists are still weighing the evidence, and are far from certain if it is one of several contributing causes, the primary cause, or simply an unrelated event. (For more on this sort of problem in reasoning, see under Cause and Effect.)

JOINING WORDS

The art of combining correct clauses and sentences logically and coherently is as much dependent on taking the time to think through what we are writing—and how the reader will respond to what we write—as it is on knowledge of correct usage. It is all too easy for most of us to assume that the flow of our thoughts will be as clear to the reader as it is to us. In practical terms this leads to the omission of links in the argument or of joining words that help the reader to see those links. Almost as common is the tendency to give too many or contradictory cues to the reader—a tendency that is often an indication that ideas have not yet been thoroughly thought out. That in itself is nothing to be ashamed of; the key is to be willing to take the time to re-read and revise the work. Every good writer makes at least two and sometimes as many as five or six drafts of any piece of writing before considering it finished. Here are two examples, both taken from early drafts of books published by Broadview Press:

- At the end of World War II there was substantial optimism that the application of Keynesian analysis would lead to economic stability and security. Over the post-war period optimistic rationalism weakened in the face of reality.
- A short report in which you request an increase in your department's budget should be written in the persuasive mode. Most reports, however, do not have persuasion as their main objective. Persuasion, though, will often be one of their secondary objectives. In reports like these, some parts will be written in the persuasive mode.

445. **too few cues** (see also *non sequitur*): The first of these passages gives the reader too few cues. What is the connection between the idea of the first sentence and that of the second? One can figure it out without too much difficulty, but the flow of the argument is briefly interrupted while one does so. The problem is easily solved by the addition of one word to the second sentence:

right   At the end of World War II there was substantial optimism that the application of Keynesian analysis would lead to economic stability and security. Over the post-war period, however, optimistic rationalism weakened in the face of reality.

446. **too many or contradictory cues**: The second passage suffers from the opposite problem; the use of *however* and *though* in consecutive sentences gives the reader the sense of twisting back on himself without any clear sense of direction. This sort of difficulty can be removed by rewording or rearranging the ideas:

right   A short report in which you request an increase in your department's budget should be written in the persuasive mode. Most reports, however, do not have persuasion as their main objective. Persuasion will thus be at most a secondary objective. In reports like these, some parts will be written in the persuasive mode.

The following pages list the chief words and expressions used in English to join ideas together, and discuss problems that are often experienced with them.

WORDS TO CONNECT IDEAS THAT ARE OPPOSED TO EACH OTHER

All these words are used to indicate that the writer is saying two things which seem to go against each other, or are different from each other.

For example, in the sentence, *He is very rich, but he is not very happy,* the fact that he is not happy is the reverse of what we might expect of a rich man. The word *but* indicates this opposition of ideas to the reader.

although	nevertheless
but	though
despite	whereas
even if	while
however	yet
in spite of	

Although

This word indicates that in the same sentence two things that seem to go against each other are being said. *Although* is usually used to introduce subordinate clauses, <u>not</u> phrases.

- Although he has short legs, he can run very quickly.
- Hume and Dr. Johnson, indeed, have a good deal in common, although Hume's attitude towards religion earned him Johnson's scorn.

447. **although/but**: Be careful not to use <u>both</u> *although* and *but* in the same sentence; one is enough:

wrong	Although in many African countries the government is not elected by the people, but in Botswana the government is democratically elected.
right	Although in many African countries the government is not elected by the people, in Botswana the government is democratically elected.
or	In most African countries the government is not elected by the people, but in Zimbabwe the government is democratically elected.

But

This word is usually used in the middle of a sentence to show that the two ideas in the sentence oppose or seem to oppose each other. It is also quite correct, however, to use *but* at the beginning of a sentence, if what one is saying in the sentence forms a complete clause and if the idea of the sentence seems to oppose the idea of the previous sentence.

e.g.	The civilization of ancient Greece produced some of the world's greatest works of art and gave birth to the idea of democracy, but the Greeks also believed in slavery.

or   The civilization of Greece produced some of the world's great-
              est works of art and gave birth to the idea of democracy. But
              the Greeks also believed in slavery.

448. opposing or supporting ideas: When one is dealing with complex combinations of ideas it is sometimes easy to forget which ideas
are in fact in opposition and which in support.

wrong   Brandy and bourbon, with the most "congenors," have the
              highest hangover ratings. Red wine is a close second, fol-
              lowed by dark rum, sherry, scotch, rye, beer, white wine,
              gin, and vodka. Vintage red wines have 15 times as much
              histamine (it triggers allergic reactions) as white wine, but
              vintage whites have fewer congenors.
                   (The use of *but* is inappropriate here; that whites have both less
                   histamine and fewer congenors is as one would expect; the two
                   facts are both instances of white wines having fewer side effects
                   than reds.)
right   Brandy and bourbon, with the most "congenors," have the
              highest hangover ratings. Red wine is a close second, fol-
              lowed by dark rum, sherry, scotch, rye, beer, white wine,
              gin, and vodka. Vintage red wines also have 15 times as much
              histamine (it triggers allergic reactions) as white wine does.

449. but: Experienced writers are careful not to use *but* more than
once in a single sentence, or in consecutive sentences; they realize that
doing so tends to confuse the reader. (It is also unwise to use any
combination of *but* and *however* in this way.)

wrong   Chief Constable Smith said that Ryan had been legally in
              possession of three handguns and two rifles, but he thought
              it "incredible" that someone should be allowed to keep am-
              munition at his home. But he said any change in the firearms
              law was something which would not be discussed by him.
right   Chief Constable Smith said that Ryan had been legally in
              possession of three handguns and two rifles. Smith said he
              thought it "incredible" that someone should be allowed to
              keep ammunition at his home, but he would not comment
              directly on whether there should be a change in the firearms
              law.

Despite

This word means the same as *although*, but it is used to introduce
phrases, not clauses.

- Despite his old age, his mind is active and alert.
  (*Despite his old age* is a phrase; it has no verb.)
- Although he is very old, his mind is active and alert.
  (*Although he is very old* is a clause, with *he* as a subject and *is* as a verb.)
- Despite the rain, she wanted to go out to the park.
- Although it was raining hard, she wanted to go to the park.

450. **despite**: Remember not to introduce clauses with *despite*.

wrong	Despite that the drink tasted very strong, there was very little alcohol in it.
right	Despite its strong taste, there was very little alcohol in the drink.
or	Although the drink tasted very strong, there was very little alcohol in it.

Even if

This expression is used when one is introducing a clause giving a condition. The word *even* emphasizes that the condition is surprising or unusual. Examples:

- Even if I have to stay up all night, I am determined to finish the job.
  (Staying up all night would be very unusual.)
- Even if Bangladesh doubled its food production, some of its people would still be hungry.
  (Doubling its food production would be very surprising.)

However

This word shows that what one is saying seems to go against what one has said in the previous sentence. It should normally be placed between commas in the middle of the sentence:

- The country suffered greatly during the three-year drought. This year, however, the rains have been heavy.

451. **however**: *However* should not be used to combine ideas within one sentence, unless a semi-colon is used.

wrong	Hitler attempted to conquer the Soviet Union however he was defeated.
right	Hitler attempted to conquer the Soviet Union; however, he was defeated.
or	Hitler attempted to conquer the Soviet Union. However, he was defeated.

or   Hitler attempted to conquer the Soviet Union but he was defeated.

wrong   There will not be regular mail pick-up from boxes this Friday, however regular mail pick-up will resume Saturday.

right   There will not be regular mail pick-up from boxes this Friday, but regular mail pick-up will resume Saturday.

or   There will not be regular mail pick-up from boxes this Friday. However, regular mail pick-up will resume Saturday.

(Note that *however* in the sense of *to whatever extent* may be used to introduce a clause: *However tired we are, we must finish the job tonight.*)

Nevertheless

Like *however, nevertheless* is normally used to show that the idea of one sentence seems to go against the idea of the previous sentence. It should not be used to join two clauses into one sentence. Example:

- According to the known laws of physics it is not possible to walk on water. Nevertheless, this is what the Bible claims Jesus did.

Whereas

This word is commonly used when one is comparing two things and showing how they differ. Like *although*, it must begin a subordinate clause, and may be used either at the beginning or in the middle of a sentence.

e.g.   Whereas Americans are usually thought of as being loud and confident, Canadians tend to be more quiet and less sure of themselves.

or   Americans are usually thought of as being loud and confident, whereas Canadians tend to be more quiet and less sure of themselves.

452. **whereas**: Any sentence that uses *whereas* must have at least two clauses—a subordinate clause beginning with *whereas* <u>and</u> a main clause.

wrong   In "The Rain Horse" a young person feels unhappy when he returns to his old home. Whereas in "The Ice Palace" a young person feels unhappy when she leaves home for the first time.

right   In "The Rain Horse" a young person feels unhappy when he returns to his old home, whereas in "The Ice Palace" a young person feels unhappy when she leaves home for the first time.

While

453. while: *While* can be used in the same way as *although*. If there is any chance of confusion with the other meanings of *while*, however, it is better to use *although* in such circumstances.

wrong	While I support free trade in principle, I think it hurts this industry.
right	Although I support free trade in principle, I think it hurts this industry.

Yet

This word can be used either to refer to time (e.g., *He is not yet here*), or to connect ideas in opposition to each other. When used in this second way, it may introduce another word or a phrase, or a completely new sentence.

- His spear was firm, yet flexible.
- Barthes decries the language of "realism"—the pretense that one can represent on the page life as it really is. Yet it is difficult to see how following his prescriptions for an art of signs that "draw attention to their own arbitrariness" can entirely escape a tendency towards art that calls too much attention to its own surface, even art that is self-indulgent.

454. yet: *Yet,* like the other words in this group, should not be paired with another conjunction in such a way as to create too many twists and turns in the argument.

wrong	Varying the pace, altering the tone, director Joseph Rubens keeps us off balance. Ultimately, though, that pedestrian script catches up with him, yet not before *Sleeping with the Enemy* has made its point.
	(The combination of *yet* and *though* is confusing for the reader.)
right	Varying the pace, altering the tone, director Joseph Rubens keeps us off balance. Ultimately, that pedestrian script catches up with him, yet not before *Sleeping with the Enemy* has made its point.

WORDS TO JOIN LINKED OR SUPPORTING IDEAS

also	indeed
and	in fact
as well	moreover

further	similarly
furthermore	: [colon]
in addition	; [semi-colon]
not only ... but also	

Also, as well

These two are very similar both in meaning and in the way that they are used. It is best not to use *also* to start sentences or paragraphs. Examples:

- He put forward his simplistic credo with enormous conviction. "To do well at school," he assured us, "you must be willing to study. It is also important to eat the right foods, exercise regularly, and get plenty of sleep." While the one thing we all wanted, and none of us had managed to get, was plenty of sex.
- He put forward his simplistic credo with enormous conviction. "To do well at school," he assured us, "you must be willing to study. It is important as well to eat the right foods, exercise regularly, and get plenty of sleep." While the one thing we all wanted, and none of us had managed to get, was plenty of sex.

455. **also:** *Also* should not be used in the way that we often use *and*— to join two clauses together into one sentence.

wrong	We performed the experiment with the beaker half full also we repeated it with the beaker empty.
right	We performed the experiment with the beaker half full and we repeated it with the beaker empty.
or	We performed the experiment with the beaker half full. We also repeated it with the beaker empty.

And

456. **and:** If this word appears more than once in the same sentence, it's worth stopping to ask if it would not be better to start a new sentence. Usually the answer will be yes.

wrong	All my family attended the celebration and most of my friends were there and we enjoyed ourselves thoroughly.
right	All my family attended the celebration and most of my friends were there too. We enjoyed ourselves thoroughly.

457. **as ... as:** When making comparisons one may use the *as ... as* combination or use a comparative adjective with *than*. But the two should not be combined.

wrong	Recent studies indicate that the average smoker is three times as likely to develop cancer than his non-smoking counterpart.
right	Recent studies indicate that the average smoker is three times more likely to develop cancer than his non-smoking counterpart.

458. **as well**: To avoid repetition, do not use *as well* in combination with *both*.

wrong	This method should be rejected, both because it is very expensive as well as because it is inefficient.
right	This method should be rejected, both because it is very expensive and because it is inefficient.

In addition, further, furthermore, moreover

All of these are commonly used to show that what the writer is saying gives additional support to an earlier statement she has made. An example:

- It is easy to see why many countries still trade with South Africa, despite their intense dislike of apartheid. For one thing, it is the richest country in Africa. Many of its resources, moreover, are of strategic importance.

Notice that all four expressions are often used after sentences that begin with words such as *for one thing* or *first*.

Indeed, in fact

Both of these are used to indicate that what the writer is saying is a restatement or elaboration of the idea he has expressed in the previous sentence. Notice that a colon or semi-colon may also be used to show this. Examples:

- Asia is the world's most populous continent. In fact, more people live there than in all the other continents combined.
- Asia is the world's most populous continent: more people live there than in all the other continents combined.

Not only ... but also

459. **not only ... but also**: This combination is used to join two pieces of supporting evidence in an argument. The combination can

help to create balanced, rhythmic writing, but if it is to do so it must be used carefully. Notice that it is not necessary to use *but also* in all cases, but that if the phrase is omitted a semi-colon is normally required in order to avoid a run-on sentence.

wrong	Not only was Nirvana a commercial success, it was also among the first grunge bands to achieve musical respectability.
right	Not only was Nirvana a commercial success; it was also among the first grunge bands to achieve musical respectability.
or	Nirvana was not only a commercial success, but also a critical one; it was among the first grunge bands to achieve musical respectability.

Plus

460. **plus**: Do not use this word in the same way as *and* or *as well*.

wrong	For one thing, the Council did not much like the design for the proposed new City Hall. Plus, there was not enough money available to build it that year.
right	For one thing, the Council did not much like the design for the proposed new City Hall. As well, there was not enough money available to build it that year.

Words Used to Introduce Causes or Reasons

The core of most arguments involves reasons why the writer's statements can be claimed to be true, and relationships of cause and effect. It is common to experience some difficulty at first in understanding such relationships clearly. The discussion below of the word *because* may be helpful in this respect. To begin with, though, here is a list of words that are used to introduce causes or reasons:

as
for
as a result of
on account of
because
since
due to

As

This word can be used either to show the relationship between two events in time, or to indicate that one event is the cause of another.

This sometimes leaves room for confusion about meaning (ambiguity). The following sentence is a good example:

* As he was riding on the wrong side of the road, he was hit by a car.

This can mean either *When he was riding on the wrong side of the road* ... or *Because he was riding on the wrong side of the road* .... Unless the writer is absolutely certain that the meaning is clear, it may be better to use *while* or *when* instead of *as* to indicate relationships in time, and *because* instead of *as* to indicate relationships of cause and effect.

Because

This word creates many problems for writers. The first thing to remember is that any group of words introduced with *because* must state a cause or reason. It must not state a result or an example.

461. **because**: In the following sentences, *because* has been wrongly used:

wrong	The wind was blowing because the leaves were moving to and fro.
wrong	He had been struck by a car because he lay bleeding in the road.

A moment's reflection leads to the realization that both of these sentences are the wrong way round. The movement of the leaves is the <u>result</u> of the blowing of the wind, and the man's bleeding is the <u>result</u> of his having been hit. When the sentences are turned around, they become correct:

right	The leaves were moving to and fro because the wind was blowing.
right	He lay bleeding on the road because he had been struck by a car.

What leads many people to make mistakes like these is the sort of question that begins, *How do you know that* ... or *Prove that* ... or *Show that* .... The person who is asked, "How do you know that the wind is blowing?" is likely to answer wrongly, "The wind is blowing because the leaves are moving to and fro." What he really means is, "I know the wind is blowing because I see the leaves moving to and fro." That answer is quite correct, since here the <u>seeing</u> is the cause of the

<u>knowing</u>. Similarly, someone who is asked to show that the man in a newspaper story has been hit by a car might answer wrongly, "He had been struck by a car because he lay bleeding in the road." What he really means is, "I <u>know</u> that he had been struck by a car because I <u>read</u> that he lay bleeding in the road." It is of course awkward to use a lot of phrases such as *I know that* and *I see that*. Here are some easier and better ways of answering such questions:

- The movement of the trees shows that the wind is blowing.
- The fact that the leaves are moving proves that the wind is blowing.
- Since the man lay bleeding in the road, it seems likely that he had been hit by a car.

462. **because**: *Because* is also often used incorrectly to introduce examples.

Look carefully at the following sentences:

wrong	The Suharto regime detained people in jail for long periods without ever bringing them to trial because it had little respect for the law.
wrong	In the story, "The Hero," Dora feels sorry for Julius because she sheds tears when he is expelled from school.

In these sentences the source of confusion may not be immediately clear. If we ask ourselves whether the regime's actions <u>caused</u> it to have little respect for the law, however, we realize that the answer is no. Are Dora's tears a <u>cause</u> of her feeling sorry for Julius? Again, no. It may be a result of her feeling sorry, or an example chosen to show that she felt sorry, but it is certainly not a cause. Again, it is possible to correct these sentences as we did the ones above—by reversing the order of the ideas. But this may not always be an appropriate solution to the problem, particularly if what the writer is trying to show is an example or an illustration rather than a relationship of cause and effect. If, for example, one had been asked, "How do you know that Dora feels sorry for Julius?" or told to "Show that the Suharto regime had little respect for the law," one would not normally want to answer using *because*. Here are various ways of dealing with such difficulties:

- Dora feels sorry for Julius when he is expelled, as we can see when she sheds tears for him.
- It is clear that Dora feels sorry for Julius, since she sheds tears for him.

- We can see from the fact that Dora sheds tears for Julius that she feels sorry for him.
- The fact that the Suharto regime in Indonesia detained people for long periods without ever bringing them to trial shows that it had little respect for the law.
- The Suharto regime in Indonesia showed little respect for the law. It detained people for long periods, for example, without ever bringing them to trial.
- The Suharto regime in Indonesia had little respect for the law; it detained people for long periods without ever bringing them to trial.

Of all these examples the last is perhaps the best, since it is the most succinct.

463. **because**: It is best not to use *because* when listing several reasons for something; otherwise the writer gives the reader the impression that the first reason given is to be the <u>only</u> reason. The reader will then be surprised when others are mentioned.

wrong	He was happy because it was Friday. He was also happy because his team had won the game that morning and he had scored the winning goal. Finally, he was happy because he had done well on his exams.
right	He was happy for several reasons: it was Friday, he had scored the winning goal for his team that morning. and he had done well on his exams.
wrong	Frederick was able to enjoy such success because he was enormously adroit at waiting for the right opportunity, and seizing it when it was handed him. He was also successful because he created a military machine that had no equal.
right	One reason Frederick was able to enjoy such success was that he was enormously adroit at waiting for the right opportunity, and seizing it when it was handed him. But none of this would have been possible had he not also created a military machine that had no equal.

464. **because**: Some people like to answer *How ...?* questions by using *because*. Instead, the word *by* should be used.

wrong	How did she help him? She helped him because she lent him some money.
right	How did she help him? She helped him by lending him some money.

Due to

465. **due to**: *Due* is an adjective and therefore should always modify a noun (as in the common phrase *with all due respect*). When followed

by *to* it can suggest a causal relationship, but remember that the word *due* must in that case refer to the <u>previous</u> noun:

> *e.g.*   The team's success is due to hard work.
> (*Due* refers to the noun *success*.)

It is not a good idea to begin a sentence with a phrase such as *Due to unexpected circumstances ...* or *Due to the fact that ....* To avoid such difficulties it is best to use *because*.

> *wrong*   Due to the departure of our Sales Manager, the Marketing Director will take on additional responsibility for a short time.
> *right*   Because our Sales Manager has resigned suddenly, the Marketing Director will take on additional responsibility for a short time.

Since

When used to introduce causes or reasons (rather than as a time word) *since* is used in essentially the same way as *because*.

WORDS USED TO INTRODUCE RESULTS OR CONCLUSIONS

as a result	therefore
consequently	thus
hence	to sum up
in conclusion	in consequence
it follows that ...	so, and so

As a result, hence

Both of these are used to show that the idea being talked about in one sentence follows from, or is the result of, what was spoken of in the previous sentence.

> *e.g.*   His car ran out of gas. As a result, he was late for his appointment.
> *or*   His car ran out of gas. Hence, he was late for his appointment.

Notice the difference between these two and words such as *because* and *since*; we would say *Because (or since) his car ran out of gas, he was late for the appointment.*

466. **hence**: *Hence* should not be used to join two clauses into one sentence, or to join words or phrases.

wrong	Her phone is out of order hence it will be impossible to contact her.
right	Her phone is out of order. Hence, it will be impossible to contact her.
wrong	It is not the film but the advertising that is exploitative, hence pornographic.
right	It is not the film but the advertising that is exploitative, and hence pornographic.

So

This word may be used to introduce results when one wants to mention both cause and result in the same sentence (e.g., *Her phone is out of order, so it will be impossible to contact her*). It is usually best not to use *so* to begin a sentence, in order to avoid writing sentence fragments.

467. **so**. If *so* is used, *because* is not needed, and vice versa. One of the two is enough.

wrong	Because he was tired, so he went to bed early.
right	Because he was tired, he went to bed early.
or	He was tired, so he went to bed early.

Therefore

468. **therefore**: *Therefore* should not be used to join two clauses into one sentence.

wrong	Training is perceived as good, therefore the payment of a $30 million subsidy to McDonalds can be made to look like a benign act.
right	Training is perceived as good; therefore the payment of a $30 million subsidy to McDonalds can be made to look like a benign act.

WORDS USED TO EXPRESS PURPOSE

in order to	so that
in such a way as to	so as to

So that

469. **so that**: When used beside each other (see also *so ... that* below) these two words show purpose; they indicate that we will be told <u>why</u> an action was taken. Examples:

- He sent the parcel early so that it would arrive before Christmas.
- She wants to see you so that she can ask you a question.

The words *such that* should never be used in this way to indicate purpose.

wrong	The doctor will give you some medicine such that you will be cured.
right	The doctor will give you some medicine so that you will be cured.
wrong	Fold the paper such that it forms a triangle.
right	Fold the paper so that it forms a triangle.
or	Fold the paper in such a way that it forms a triangle.

WORDS USED TO INTRODUCE EXAMPLES

for example	such as
for instance	: [colon]
in that	

For example, for instance, such as

The three expressions are used differently, even though they all introduce examples. *Such as* is used to introduce a single word or short phrase. It always relates to a plural noun that has appeared just before it.

- Crops such as tea and rice require a great deal of water.
     (Here *such as* relates to the noun *crops*.)
- Several African peoples, such as the Yoruba of Nigeria and the Makonde of Tanzania, attach a special ceremonial importance to masks.
     (*Such as* relates to *peoples*.)

For example and *for instance*, on the other hand, are complete phrases in themselves, and are normally set off by commas. Each is used to show that the entire sentence in which it appears gives an example of a statement made in the previous sentence. Examples:

- Some crops require a great deal of water. Tea, for example, requires an annual rainfall of at least 1500 mm.
- Several African peoples attach a special ceremonial importance to masks. The Yoruba and the Makonde, for example, both believe that spirits enter the bodies of those who wear certain masks.

- Tornadoes are not only a Deep South phenomenon. In 1987, for instance, over 20 people were killed by a tornado in Edmonton, Alberta.

470. for example, for instance: *For example* and *for instance* should not be used to introduce phrases that give examples. In such situations use *such as* instead.

wrong	In certain months of the year, for example July and August, Penticton receives very little rainfall.
right	In certain months of the year, such as July and August, Penticton receives very little rainfall.
or	In certain months of the year Penticton receives very little rainfall. July and August, for example, are almost always extremely dry.

In that

471. in that: Do not confuse with *in the way that*.

wrong	He is cruel in the way that he treats his wife harshly.
right	He is cruel in that he treats his wife harshly.
or	He is cruel in the way that he treats his wife.

Such as

472. such as: The addition of *and others* at the end of a phrase beginning with *such as* is redundant.

wrong	In contrast to this perspective, sociological studies of ethnicity written from the "class" perspective (such as Bollaria and Li's 2001 paper, Chan's 1999 monograph, and others) have argued that ethnic inequality is only a special class of inequality in general.
right	In contrast to this perspective, sociological studies of ethnicity written from the "class" perspective (such as Bollaria and Li's 2001 paper, and Chan's 1999 monograph) have argued that ethnic inequality is only a special class of inequality in general.

WORDS USED TO INDICATE ALTERNATIVES

either ... or	otherwise
if only	rather than
instead, instead of	unless
in that case	whether ... or
neither ... nor	or

If only

This expression is normally used when we wish that something would happen, or were true, but it clearly will not happen, or is not true.

- If only he were here, he would know what to do.
  (This indicates that he is not here.)
- "If only there were thirty hours in a day ..." she kept saying.

In that case

This expression is used when we wish to explain what will happen if the thing spoken of in the previous sentence happens, or turns out to be true. Examples:

- He may arrive before six o'clock. In that case we can all go out to dinner.
- It is quite possible that many people will dislike the new law. In that case the government may decide to change it.

Do not confuse *in that case* with *otherwise*, which is used in the reverse situation (i.e., when one wishes to explain what will happen if the thing spoken of in the previous sentence does <u>not</u> happen, or turns out to be false).

Otherwise

This word has two meanings. The first is *in other ways* (e.g., *I have a slight toothache. Otherwise I am healthy*). The second meaning can sometimes cause confusion: *otherwise* used to mean *if not*. Here the word is used when we want to talk about what will or may happen if the thing spoken of in the previous sentence does not happen. Examples:

- I will have to start immediately. Otherwise, I will not finish in time.
  (This is the same as saying, *If I do not start now, I will not finish in time.*)
- The general decided to retreat. Otherwise, he believed, all his troops would be killed.
  (This is the same as saying. *The general believed that if he decided not to retreat, all his troops would be killed.*)
- You must pay me for the car before Friday. Otherwise, I will offer it to someone else.
  (i.e., *If you do not pay me for the car before Friday, I will offer it to someone else.*)

473. **otherwise**: When used to mean *if not*, *otherwise* should normally be used to start a new sentence. It should not be used in the middle of a sentence to join two clauses.

wrong	I may meet you at the party tonight, otherwise I will see you tomorrow.
right	I may see you at the party tonight. Otherwise, I will see you tomorrow.

WORDS USED TO SHOW DEGREE OR EXTENT

for the most part	to some extent
so ... that	too ... for ... to
such ... that	to some degree
to a certain extent	

So ... that

474. **so ... that**: When separated from each other by an adjective or adverb, these two words express degree or extent, answering questions such as *How far ...?, How big ...?, How much ...?*. Examples:

- How fat is he? He is so fat that he cannot see his feet.
- How large is Canada? It is so large that you need about six days to drive across it.

So ... that is the only combination of words that can be used in this way; it is wrong to say "very fat that ..." or "too large that," just as it is wrong to leave out the word *so* and simply use *that* in such sentences.

wrong	She was very late for dinner that there was no food left for her.
right	She was so late for dinner that there was no food left for her.
wrong	Dominic speaks quickly that it is often difficult to understand him.
right	Dominic speaks so quickly that it is often difficult to understand him.

Such ... that

475. **such ... that**: Like *so ... that*, the expression *such ... that* is used to express degree or extent, answering questions such as, *How big ...?, How long ...?, How fast ...?*. Notice the difference in the way the two are used.

right	How far is it? It is <u>such</u> a long way <u>that</u> you would never be able to get there walking.
or	It is <u>so</u> far <u>that</u> you would never be able to reach there walking.
right	How fat is he? He is <u>such</u> a fat man <u>that</u> his trousers need to be made specially for him.
or	He is <u>so</u> fat <u>that</u> his trousers need to be made specially for him.

The difference between the two is of course that only one word is normally used between *so* and *that*, whereas two or three words (usually an article, an adjective, and a noun) are used between *such* and *that*. Be careful not to confuse the two, or to leave out *such*.

| *wrong* | It was a hot day that nobody could stay outside for long. |
| *right* | It was such a hot day that nobody could stay outside for long. |

That, which

476. **that/which**: It is correct to use *that* in restrictive clauses and *which* in non-restrictive clauses.

needs checking	The only store which sells this brand is now closed.
revised	The only store that sells this brand is now closed.
needs checking	The position which Marx adopted owed much to the philosophy of Hegel.
revised	The position that Marx adopted owed much to the philosophy of Hegel.

Although the use of the word *which* in any restrictive clause provokes a violent reaction among some English instructors, there are some instances in which one is quite justified in using *which* in this way. Such is the case when the writer is already using at least one *that* in the sentence:

| *needs checking* | He told me that the radio that he had bought was defective. |
| *revised* | He told me that the radio which he had bought was defective. |

Better yet, in many cases, is to avoid the use of a second relative pronoun by rephrasing:

right   He told me that the radio he had bought was defective.

Indeed, instructors who object to *which* point out that rephrasing can often make the sentence shorter and crisper:

fair   The ending, which comes as a surprise to most readers, is profoundly unsettling.

better   The ending is both surprising and unsettling.

fair   The 2002 campaign, which had been carefully planned, was an enormous success.

better   The carefully-planned 2002 campaign was an enormous success.

But *which* is not a special case in this regard. *That, who,* and *whose* can often be fruitfully removed in the same way:

fair   The surplus that we now project for 2003 will probably be exceeded in 2004.

better   The projected 2003 surplus will probably be exceeded in 2004.

fair   Eisenhower hired as his personal driver a woman who turned into a long-term friend.

better   Eisenhower and his driver became close friends.

The vice, then, is not *which* per se, but wordiness in general. Those who focus their attention on the one word and rail that "witches ride on broomsticks" might do better to treat the excessive use of *which* as a symptom of a much broader disease.

WORDS USED TO MAKE COMPARISONS

by comparison	on the one hand ...
in contrast	... on the other hand

OTHER JOINING WORDS AND EXPRESSIONS

as illustrated above/below	in other words
as mentioned above/below	in the event of
as we can see/we can see that	in the light of
assuming that	in this respect/in some respects
as shown in the diagram	above/below
in that	firstly/in the first place
these findings indicate that	secondly/in the second place
to begin with	for one thing
whereby	

PUNCTUATION

The Period •

The most important mark of punctuation is the full stop (or period), which is used to separate one sentence from another, and the most common punctuation mistakes involve the use of the period. The first of these is the run-on sentence: a sentence that continues running on and on instead of being broken up into two or more sentences. (Where a comma has been used instead of a period, the term *comma splice* is often used to denote a run-on sentence.) The second is the incomplete sentence (or *sentence fragment*): a group of words that has been written as if it were a full sentence, but that needs something else to make it complete.

477. **run-on sentence/comma splice**: The basic idea of a sentence is that it expresses one complete idea. Often, remembering this simple fact will be enough to keep run-on sentences at bay, particularly if one reads work over to oneself (aloud, if it's not too embarrassing) and notices where one pauses naturally.

wrong	Early last Thursday we were walking in the woods it was a bright and clear morning.
right	Early last Thursday we were walking in the woods. It was a bright and clear morning.

In the above example it should be quite clear that there are two separate ideas, and that these should be put into two separate sentences. Sometimes, though, it is not so simple. In particular, certain words may be used to join two clauses into one sentence, while other words should not be used in this way. We have already seen (in our survey of joining words) some examples of words that cause problems of this sort. Here is a review:

and: The appearance of more than one *and* in a sentence is often a sign that the ideas would be better rephrased.

wrong	Beaverbrook effectively mobilized the resources of the country to serve the war effort overseas and he later was knighted and he is also well-known for creating a media empire.
right	Beaverbrook effectively mobilized the resources of the country to serve the war effort—an accomplishment for which

he later was knighted. He is also well-known for creating a media empire.

or   Beaverbrook, who had created a vast media empire before the war, then distinguished himself by effectively mobilizing the resources of the country to serve the war effort. It was in recognition of this service that he was knighted.

or   Beaverbrook, who had created a vast media empire before the war, then distinguished himself by effectively mobilizing the resources of the country to serve the war effort; it was in recognition of this service that he was knighted.

hence:

wrong   With the exception of identical twins no two people have exactly the same genetic makeup hence it is impossible for two people to look exactly the same.

right   With the exception of identical twins no two people have exactly the same genetic makeup. Hence, it is impossible for two people to look exactly the same.

however:

wrong   During the rainy season more water flows over Victoria Falls than over any other falls in the world however several other falls are higher than Victoria.

right   During the rainy season more water flows over Victoria Falls than over any other falls in the world. However, several other falls are higher than Victoria.

or   During the rainy season more water flows over Victoria Falls than over any other falls in the world; several other falls, however, are higher than Victoria.

otherwise:

wrong   You had better leave now otherwise we will call the police.
right   You had better leave now. Otherwise, we will call the police.
or   You had better leave now; otherwise, we will call the police.

therefore:

wrong   Money was tight and jobs were scarce, therefore she decided to stay in a job she did not like.

right   Money was tight and jobs were scarce; therefore she decided to stay in a job she did not like.

Notice in the above cases that one way to correct a comma splice is often to use a semi-colon. Unlike a comma, a semi-colon may be used as a connector between clauses. (The discussion on pages **172–173** may be helpful in this connection.)

478. **then**: An even more common cause of run-on sentences than any of the above is the word *then*. Unlike *when, then* should not be used to join two clauses together into one sentence. *And then* may be used, or a semi-colon, or a new sentence may be begun.

wrong	We applied the solution to the surface of the leaves then we made observations at half-hour intervals over the next twelve hours.
right	We applied the solution to the surface of the leaves. Then we made observations at half-hour intervals over the next twelve hours.
or	We applied the solution to the surface of the leaves; then we made observations at half-hour intervals over the next twelve hours.
or	We applied the solution to the surface of the leaves and then we made observations at half-hour intervals over the next twelve hours.
wrong	On June 10, 1999, Yugoslav troops began withdrawing, then the NATO bombing was suspended and the war in Kosovo ended.
right	On June 10, 1999, Yugoslav troops began withdrawing. Then the NATO bombing was suspended and the war in Kosovo ended.
wrong	The Montreal Canadiens produced vital late-period goals then they wrapped their iron defence around the Calgary Flames to take an upper hand in the game.
right	The Montreal Canadiens produced vital late-period goals and then wrapped their iron defence around the Calgary Flames to take an upper hand in the game.

479. **abbreviations**: The period is also used to form abbreviations. If in any doubt about whether or not to use a period in an abbreviation, or where to put it, think of (or look up) the full form of what is being abbreviated.

wrong	Jones, Smithers et. al. will be there in person.
right	Jones, Smithers et al. will be there in person.
	(*Et al.* is short for the latin *et alia*, meaning *and other*.)

480. **incomplete sentences**: A good writer always asks herself as she checks her work if each sentence is complete in itself; in this way the more obvious errors will almost always be caught. For example, if

When the meeting ends tomorrow is in the rough draft as a complete sentence, re-reading will probably lead to the realization that the idea is not complete; the group of words needs another group of words to finish it (e.g., *When the meeting ends tomorrow we should have a comprehensive agreement.*). Be particularly careful with longer sentences to make sure they are complete. For example, the group of words *Marina walked to the sea* is a complete sentence, but the following sentence is incomplete, even though it is much longer; it lacks a main clause that tells us what happened when she was walking:

wrong	While Marina was walking to the sea and thinking of her father and the sound of a woodthrush.
right	While Marina was walking to the sea she heard the sound of a woodthrush and thought of her father.
wrong	Unemployment was a serious problem in Britain in the early 1990s. In fact, throughout the world.
right	Unemployment was a serious problem in the early 1990s, both in North America and in Europe.
wrong	So long as you have a place to live and enough to eat.
right	So long as you have a place to live and enough to eat, you have some reason to be thankful.

The three words which most frequently lead students to write incomplete sentences are *and, because,* and *so.*

481. **and**: Although there are certain cases in which it is possible to begin a sentence with *and*, these are extremely difficult to sense. It is usually better for all except professional writers not to begin sentences with *and* if they wish to avoid incomplete sentences.

worth checking	To make this crop grow well you should add Compound 'D' fertilizer to the soil. And you should add top dressing a few months later.
right	To make this crop grow well you should add Compound 'D' fertilizer to the soil, and top dressing a few months later.

482. **because**: In order to prevent young children who have difficulty in writing long sentences from writing incomplete sentences, many primary school teachers wisely tell their pupils not to begin sentences with *because*. In fact it is not incorrect to begin with *because*, so long as the sentence is complete. The rule to remember is that any sentence with *because* in it must mention <u>both</u> the cause <u>and</u> the result. Whether

the word *because* comes at the beginning or in the middle of the sentence does not matter; what is important is that the sentence has two parts.

wrong	In the early 1980s Sandinista leaders told their people to be ready for war. Because the United States had been trying to destabilize Nicaragua.
right	In the early 1980s Sandinista leaders told their people to be ready for war, because the United States had been trying to destabilize Nicaragua.
wrong	Because of the cold and wet weather which affected the whole area. Many people were desperately trying to find more firewood.
right	Because of the cold and wet weather which affected the whole area many people were desperately trying to find more firewood.

483. **so**: This word is probably the biggest single cause of incomplete sentences. As is the case with *and*, there are certain situations in which professional writers manage to get away with beginning sentences with *so*, but normally this should not be attempted. *So* should be used to join ideas together into one sentence, not to separate them by starting a new sentence.

wrong	I did not know what was happening. So my friends explained the procedure to me.
right	I did not know what was happening, so my friends explained the procedure to me.
wrong	The meat was too heavily spiced. So most of it had to be thrown away.
right	The meat was too heavily spiced, so most of it had to be thrown away.

The Ellipsis •••

Three dots are used to indicate the omission of one or more words needed to complete a sentence or other grammatical construction.

484. **ellipsis**: Note that when used in quotation an ellipsis comes <u>inside</u> the quotation marks, and that when an ellipsis precedes a period the sentence should end with <u>four</u> dots.

wrong	Harris shows more than a trace of paranoia in her book; she speaks, for example, of "the elements trying to subvert the

essence of liberal society, of tolerance, of goodwill ... They are all around us."

right   Harris shows more than a trace of paranoia in her book; she speaks, for example, of "the elements trying to subvert the essence of liberal society, of tolerance, of goodwill .... They are all around us."

The Comma   ,

Although the omission or wrong use of a comma sounds like a small mistake, it can be very important. The following group of words, for example, forms a sentence only if a comma is included:

wrong   Because of the work that we had done before we were ready to hand in the assignment.
right   Because of the work that we had done before, we were ready to hand in the assignment.

The omission or addition of a comma can also completely alter the meaning of a sentence—as it did in the Queen's University Alumni letter that spoke of the warm emotions still felt by alumni for "our friends, who are dead" (rather than "our friends who are dead"). The second would have been merely a polite remembrance of those alumni who have died; the first suggests that <u>all</u> the friends of the reader are dead.

485. omission of commas: Commas very commonly come in pairs, and it is wrong to omit the second comma in a pair. Be particularly careful when putting commas around a name, or around an adjectival subordinate clause.

wrong   My sister Caroline, has done very well this year in her studies.
right   My sister, Caroline, has done very well this year in her studies.
wrong   The snake which had been killed the day before, was, already half-eaten by ants.
right   The snake, which had been killed the day before, was already half-eaten by ants.

486. extra comma: Writers often add a comma when they feel a sentence is getting long, regardless of whether one is needed or is appropriate.

wrong   The ever-increasing gravitational pull of the global economy, is drawing almost every area of the earth into its orbit.

right   The ever-increasing gravitational pull of the global economy
            is drawing almost every area of the earth into its orbit.

487. serial comma: An important use of commas is to separate the
entries in lists. Many authorities feel that a comma need not appear
between the last and second-last entries in a list, since these are usually
separated already by the word *and*. Omitting the last comma in a
series will occasionally lead to ambiguity, though; when in doubt,
include the serial comma. And when the list includes items that have
commas within them, use a semi-colon to separate the items in the
list.

wrong   This book is dedicated to my parents, Ayn Rand and God.
right   This book is dedicated to my parents, Ayn Rand, and God.
wrong   The three firms involved were McCarthy and Walters, Har-
            ris, Jones, and Engleby, and Cassells and Wirtz.
right   The three firms involved were McCarthy and Walters; Har-
            ris, Jones, and Engleby; and Cassells and Wirtz.

The Question Mark   **?**

488. question mark: All students know that a question should be
followed by a question mark, but it is easy to forget, particularly if one
is writing quickly or if the question mark should appear within other
punctuation.

wrong   Would Britain benefit from closer ties with Europe. Almost
            30 years after the UK joined the EC, the question continues
            to bedevil British political life.
right   Would Britain benefit from closer ties with Europe? Almost
            30 years after the UK joined the EC, the question continues
            to bedevil British political life.

The Exclamation Mark   **!**

This mark is used to give extremely strong emphasis to a statement. It
should be used very sparingly, if at all, in formal written work; most
good writers avoid it completely, since they realize that it does not
lend any additional impact to what they are saying.

The Semi-Colon   **;**

This mark is used to separate ideas that are closely related to each
other. In most cases a period could be used instead; the semi-colon
simply signals to the reader the close relationship between the two

ideas. In the following example the second sentence reinforces the statement of the first; a semi-colon is thus appropriate, although a period is also correct:

- This book is both exciting and profound. It is one of the best books I have read.
- This book is both exciting and profound; it is one of the best books I have read.

Similarly in the following example the second sentence gives evidence supporting the statement made in the first sentence. Again, a semi-colon is appropriate:

- The team is not as good as it used to be. It has lost four of its past five games.
- The team is not as good as it used to be; it has lost four of its last five games.

The semi-colon is also used occasionally to divide items in a series that includes other punctuation:

- The following were told to report to the coach after practice: Jackson, Form 2B; Marshall, Form 3A; Gladys, Form 1B.

THE COLON :

This mark is often believed to be virtually the same as the semi-colon in the way it is used. In fact, there are some important differences. The most common uses of the colon are as follows:

- in headings, to announce that more is to follow, or that the writer is about to list a series of things.
- to introduce a quotation.
- between two clauses, to indicate that the second one provides an explanation of what was stated in the first.

This last use is very similar to the main use of the semi-colon. The subtle differences are that the semi-colon can be used in such situations when the ideas are not quite so closely related, and the colon asks the reader to pause for a slightly longer period. Note that a colon must be preceded by an independent clause; what comes before it, in other words, could be a full sentence on its own. Here are some examples:

- UNQUIET UNION: A Study of the Federation of Rhodesia and Nyasaland.
- In the last four weeks he has visited five countries: Mexico, Venezuela, Panama, Haiti, and Belize.
- The theory of the Communists may be summed up in a single phrase: abolition of private property.

489. **colon**: Be sure to use a colon to introduce a list.

wrong	The operation in Toronto has supplied Mr. Bomersbach with four luxury cars, two Cadillacs, a Mercedes, and a Jaguar.
right	The operation in Toronto has supplied Mr. Bomersbach with four luxury cars: two Cadillacs, a Mercedes, and a Jaguar.

THE HYPHEN ▬

This mark may be used to separate two parts of a compound word (e.g., *tax-free*, *hand-operated*). Notice that many such word combinations are hyphenated only if the combination acts as an adjective:

- No change is planned for the short term.
  (*Term* acts here as a noun. with the adjective *short* modifying it.)
- This is only a short-term plan.
  (Here the compound acts as a single adjective, modifying the noun *plan*.)

Hyphens are also used to break a word at the end of a line if there is not enough space.

490. **hyphen**: A hyphen should never be used to break up proper nouns, and should be used to break up other words only when it is placed between syllables. Any noun beginning with a capital letter (e.g., *Halifax, Blair, January, Harriet*) is a proper noun.

wrong	Thomas Huxley coined the word *agnostic* to refer to someone who does not believe in the existence of God, but is not prepared to rule out the possibility either.
right	Thomas Huxley coined the word *agnostic* to refer to someone who does not believe in the existence of God, but is not prepared to rule out the possibility either.

Whenever one is uncertain about whether or not to use a hyphen, the easy solution is to put the entire word on the next line.

THE DASH ▬▬

Dashes are often used in much the same way as parentheses, to set off an idea within a sentence. Dashes, however, call attention to the set-off idea in a way that parentheses do not:

- Peterborough (home of Broadview Press) is a pleasant city of 70,000.
- Peterborough—home of Broadview Press—is a pleasant city of 70,000.

A dash may also be used in place of a colon to set off a word or phrase at the end of a sentence:

- He fainted when he heard how much he had won: one million dollars.
- He fainted when he heard how much he had won—one million dollars.

em—dashes and en–dashes: The above applies to what is known as the em dash—so-called because in most typefaces it is about the same length as the letter *m*. There is also a slightly shorted form of dash—known as the en dash—which fulfils a different function. Whereas an em dash is used to separate groups of words, an en dash is used to separate numbers, as in these examples:

- Richard Harris (1930–2002) was both a singer and a noted actor.
- The street numbers are as follows: in the first block west of Main Street, 1–100; in the second block, 100–200; and so on.

Although it is standard to use the en dash in such circumstances in published work, the en dash does not appear on most keyboards, and the hyphen is usually used in its stead in everyday work. Most keyboards also lack em dashes; in such circumstances use -- (instead of -) to distinguish a dash from a hyphen.

wrong	Malaysia's Petronas Towers-the tallest buildings in the world-were completed in 1997. A tower in Shanghai is expected to surpass the record early in the present century.
right	Malaysia's Petronas Towers—the tallest buildings in the world—were completed in 1997. A tower in Shanghai is expected to surpass the record early in the present century.

Parentheses ( )

Parentheses are used to set off an interruption in the middle of a sentence, or to make a point which is not part of the main flow of the sentence. They are frequently used to give examples, or to express something in other words using the abbreviation *i.e.* Example:

- Several world leaders of the 1980s (Deng in China, Reagan in the US, etc.) were very old men.

SQUARE BRACKETS   [ ]

Square brackets are used for parentheses within parentheses, or to show that the words within the parentheses are added by another person.

- Lentricchia claims that "in reading James' Preface [to *What Maisie Knew*] one is struck as much by what is omitted as by what is revealed."

THE APOSTROPHE   ,

The two main uses of the apostrophe are to show possession (e.g., *Peter's book*) and to shorten certain common word combinations. The shortened forms (e.g., *can't, shouldn't, he's*) are known as *contractions*.

491. **contractions**: Contractions are used frequently in this book, which is relatively informal in its style. Contractions, however, should not be used in more formal written work. Use *cannot*, <u>not</u> *can't*; *do not*, <u>not</u> *don't*; and so on.

informal	The experiment wasn't a success, because we'd heated the solution to too high a temperature.
more formal	The experiment was not a success, because we had heated the solution to too high a temperature.

492. **possession**: The correct placing of the apostrophe to show possession can be a tricky matter. When the noun is singular, the apostrophe must come before the *s* (e.g., *Peter's, George's, Canada's*), whereas when the noun is plural and ends in an *s* already, add the apostrophe after the *s*.

wrong	We have been asked to dinner by Harriets mother.
right	We have been asked to dinner by Harriet's mother.
worth checking	His parent's house is filled with antiques.
right	His parents' house is filled with antiques.
wrong	All three groups of parents attended their infant's one-month pediatric checkup, and observations were made of father's interactions with their infants.

right	All three groups of parents attended their infants' one-month pediatric checkup, and observations were made of fathers' interactions with their infants.

When a singular noun already ends in *s*, authorities differ as to whether or not a second s should be added after the apostrophe:

correct	Ray Charles' music has been very influential.
correct	Ray Charles's music has been very influential.

Whichever convention a writer chooses, he should be consistent. And be sure in such cases not to put the apostrophe before the first *s*.

wrong	Shield's novel is finely, yet delicately constructed. (concerning novelist Carol Shields)
right	Shields' novel is finely, yet delicately constructed. (or *Shields's novel*)

Quotation Marks " "

The main use of quotation marks is to show that the words are repeated exactly as they were originally spoken or written. For a discussion of difficulties associated with this use see the chapter on direct and indirect speech immediately following.

According to different conventions, words that are being mentioned in a grammatical sense, rather than used to convey meaning, may be set off by quotation marks, single quotation marks, or italics:

- The words "except" and "accept" are sometimes confused.
- The words 'except' and 'accept' are sometimes confused.
- The words *except* and *accept* are sometimes confused.

Quotation marks (or single quotation marks) are sometimes used to indicate that the writer does not endorse the quoted statement, claim, or description. Quotation marks are usually used in this way only with a word or a brief phrase. When they are so used they have the connotation of *supposed* or *so-called*; they suggest that the quoted word or phrase is either euphemistic or downright false:

- After a violent workout the weightlifters would each consume a "snack" of a steak sandwich, a half-dozen eggs, several pieces of bread and butter, and a quart of tomato juice.

In the following two versions of the same report, the more sparing use of quotation marks in the second version signals clearly to the reader the writer's scepticism as to the honesty of the quoted claim, and may be taken to imply that the former Russian President indulged his legendary fondness for alcohol during the flight.

- President Yeltsin appeared to stagger as he left the plane. "The President is feeling tired and emotional," his Press Secretary later reported.
- A "tired and emotional" President Yeltsin appeared to stagger as he left the plane.

493. **misuse of quotation marks to indicate emphasis**: Quotation marks (unlike italics, bold letters, capital letters, or underlining) should never be used to try to lend emphasis to a particular word or phrase. Because quotation marks may be used to convey the sense *supposed* or *so-called* (see above), the common misuse of quotation marks to try to lend emphasis often creates ludicrous effects.

wrong	All our bagels are served "fresh" daily.
	(The unintended suggestion here is that the claim of freshness is a dubious one.)
right	All our bagels are served fresh daily.
or	All our bagels are served **fresh** daily.
	(if emphasis is required in an advertisement)
wrong	Dogs must be "leashed." (BC ferries sign)
right	Dogs must be leashed.

Single Quotation Marks   ‘ ’

In North America the main use of single quotation marks is to mark quotations within quotations:

- According to Clinton's Press Secretary, "When the President said, 'I never inhaled,' he meant it."

Depending on convention, single quotation marks may also be used to show that a word or phrase is being mentioned rather than used (see above).

In the United Kingdom and some other countries, quotation marks and single quotation marks are used for direct speech in precisely the opposite way that North Americans use them; single quotation marks (or inverted commas, as they are sometimes called) are used for direct speech, and double marks are used for quotations within quotations. Here is the correct British version of the above sentence:

- According to Clinton's Press Secretary, 'When the President said, "I never inhaled", he meant it.'

Note here that UK usage also places the comma outside the quotation mark.

DIRECT AND INDIRECT SPEECH

DIRECT SPEECH

Direct speech is a written record of the exact words used by the person speaking. The main rules for writing direct speech in English are as follows:

- The exact words spoken—and no other words—must be surrounded by quotation marks.
- A comma should precede a quotation, but according to American convention other punctuation should be placed inside the quotation marks. Examples:

> He said, "I think I can help you."
>> (The period after *you* comes before the quotation marks.)

> "Drive slowly," she said, "and be very careful."
>> (The comma after *slowly* and period after *careful* both come inside the quotation marks.)

With each change in speaker a new paragraph should begin. Example:

> "Let's go fishing this weekend," Mary suggested. "It should be nice and cool by the water."
> "Good idea," agreed Faith. "I'll meet you by the store early Saturday morning."

British convention, however, places the punctuation *outside* the quotation marks:

- 'An iron curtain is descending across Europe', declared Winston Churchill in 1946.

Canadian usage allows writers either to follow the American convention or to make an exception when the punctuation clearly pertains only to the structure of the surrounding sentence and not to the quoted word or phrase:

- "An iron curtain is descending across Europe," declared Winston Churchill in 1946.
- Was it Churchill who described the post-war divide between newly Communist Eastern Europe and the West as "an iron curtain"?

The most common difficulties experienced when recording direct speech are as follows:

494. omission of quotation marks: This happens particularly frequently at the end of a quotation.

wrong	She said, "I will try to come to see you tomorrow. Then she left.
right	She said, "I will try to come to see you tomorrow." Then she left.

495. placing punctuation outside the quotation marks:

wrong	He shouted, "The house is on fire"!
right	He shouted, "The house is on fire!"

496. including the word *that* before direct speech: *That* is used before passages of indirect speech, <u>not</u> before passages of direct speech.

wrong	My brother said that, "I think I have acted stupidly."
right	My brother said, "I think I have acted stupidly."
or	My brother said that he thought he had acted stupidly.
wrong	The official indicated that, "we are not prepared to allow galloping inflation."
right	The official said, "We are not prepared to allow galloping inflation."
or	The official indicated that his government was not prepared to allow galloping inflation.

497. when to indent: In a formal essay, any quotation longer than three lines should normally be single-spaced and indented to set it off from the body of the text. Any quotation of more than a single line from a poem should also be single-spaced and indented. Quotations set off from the body of the text in this way should not be preceded or followed by quotation marks.

wrong	Larkin's last great poem, 'Au bade,' is haunted by the fear of death: "Not to be here, Not to be anywhere, And soon; nothing more terrible, nothing more true." Some have called the vision of the poem unremittingly grim, but it is filled with subtle shadings.
right	Larkin's last great poem, 'Au bade,' is haunted by the fear of death:

> *Not to be here,*
> *Not to be anywhere,*
> *And soon; nothing more terrible, nothing more true.*

Some have called the vision of the poem unremittingly grim, but it is filled with subtle shadings.

See under Sequence of Tenses (page 30) and Writing About Literature (page 238) for discussions of other difficulties in using quotations.

INDIRECT SPEECH

Indirect speech reports what was said without using the same words that were used by the speaker. The rules for writing indirect speech are as follows:

- Do not use quotation marks.
- Introduce statements with the word *that*, and do not put a comma after *that*. Questions should be introduced with the appropriate question word (*what, why, whether, if, how, when,* etc.).
- Change first person pronouns and adjectives (e.g., *I, me, we, us, my, our*) to third person (*he, she, they, him, her, them, his, hers,* etc.).

  > "I am not happy with our team's performance," said Paul.
  > Paul said that he was not happy with his team's performance.

- Second person pronouns must also sometimes be changed.
- Change the tenses of the verbs to agree with the main verb of the sentence. Usually this involves moving the verbs one step back into the past from the tenses that were used by the speaker in direct speech. Notice in the above example, for instance, that the present tense *am* has been changed to the past tense *was* in indirect speech. Here are other examples:

  > "We will do everything we can," he assured me.
  > He assured me that they would do everything they could.
  >   (*Will* and *can* change to *would* and *could.*)
  > "You went to school near Brandon, didn't you?" he asked me.
  > He asked me if I had gone to school near Brandon.
  >   (*Went* changes to *had gone.*)

- Change expressions having to do with time. This is made necessary by the changes in verbs discussed above. For example, *today* in direct speech normally becomes *on that day* in indirect speech, *yesterday* becomes *on the day before, tomorrow* becomes *the next day,* and so on.

The most common problems made when indirect speech is being used are as follows:

498. confusion of pronouns: Many writers do not remember to change all the necessary pronouns when shifting from direct to indirect speech.

- When I met him he said, "You have cheated me." (direct speech)

wrong   When I met him he said that you had cheated me.
right   When I met him he said that I had cheated him.

- He will probably say to you, "I am poor. I need money."

wrong   He will probably tell you that he is poor and that I need money.
right   He will probably tell you that he is poor and that he needs money.

499. verb tenses: Remember to shift the tenses of the verbs one step back into the past when changing something into indirect speech.

- She said, "I will check my tires tomorrow."

wrong   She said that she will check her tires the next day.
right   She said that she would check her tires the next day.

- "Can I go with you later this afternoon?" he asked.

wrong   He asked if he can go with us later that afternoon.
right   He asked if he could go with us later that afternoon.

PARAGRAPHING

500. error in paragraphing: There is a degree of flexibility when it comes to the matter of where and how often to start new paragraphs. Sometimes a subtle point in an argument will require a paragraph of almost an entire page to elaborate; occasionally a single sentence can form an effective paragraph. Yet separating ideas into paragraphs remains an important aid to the processes of both reading and writing. Here are some guidelines as to when it is appropriate to begin a new paragraph:

IN NARRATION:

- whenever the story changes direction.
  (This was the moment Paul Martin had been waiting for ..., When Napoleon left Elba he ....)
- when there is a gap in time in the story.
  (Two weeks later the issue was raised again in cabinet ....)

IN DESCRIPTION:

- whenever you switch from describing one place, person, or thing to describing another.
  (Even such a brief description as this has been is enough to give some sense of the city and its pretensions. Much more interesting in many ways are some of British Columbia's smaller cities and towns ....)

IN PERSUASION OR ARGUMENT:

- when a new topic is introduced.
  (There can be little doubt that Austen's asides on the literary conventions of her time provide an amusing counterpoint to her story. But does this running commentary detract from the primary imaginative experience of Northanger Abbey?)
- when there is a change in direction of the argument.
  (To this point we have been looking only at the advantages of a guaranteed annual income. We should also ask, however, whether or not it would be practical to implement.)

WHEN CHANGING FROM ONE MODE TO ANOTHER:

- Description, narration, and argument are commonly blended together in writing. If, for example, a text moves from describing an experiment to analysing its significance, it's a good time to start a new paragraph. If it moves from telling where Napoleon went and what he did to discussing why events unravelled in this way, the same holds true.

GENERALIZATION, ABSTRACTION, JARGON, AND DOUBLESPEAK

Generalization is the process of moving from an observation or conclusion about a single thing or a small number of things to a conclusion about all or most of that group. Abstraction, on the other hand, is at its most basic level the isolation of some particular quality of a thing from the rest of its properties—the consideration of the colour of a particular object, for example.

Many people are a bit hazy on the difference between abstraction and generalization—not surprisingly, since the two are related activities that we often perform simultaneously. Perhaps the best way of keeping them straight is to remember that the opposite of *general* is *particular,* while the opposite of *abstract* is *concrete*:

- *Emotions* is a broad general category; *love* and *hate* are particular emotions.
    (None is a concrete thing.)
- The greenness of the Brazilian flag is an abstraction; the flag itself is a concrete thing.
    (We may also, of course, speak of one particular Brazilian flag or of the Brazilian flag in general, or of all flags in general; there can be numerous levels of both abstraction and generalization.)

A great deal of writing involves shifts not only from the general to the particular and back again but also from one level of generalization to another:

- An article on Chippendale chairs would probably refer to particular examples from the eighteenth century studio of Thomas Chippendale himself, generalize about all chairs of that type, generalize further about the furniture of the period, and perhaps generalize at one higher level about how and why such designs suited the overall sensibilities of eighteenth century England.
- An English literature essay might make a general claim about Jane Austen's use of irony. It might then descend one level of generality to discuss the differences in the degree to which the generalization applies in the various novels. It might then move to a lower level of generality, distinguishing between the scenes in *Northanger Abbey* that are suffused with the characteristic Austen sense of irony and those (apparently remaining from the first draft of the novel) that are almost pure melodrama with no irony to them whatsoever. Finally, the essay would doubtless give particular examples—quote sentences or paragraphs that exemplify an ironic tone and a melodramatic one.

Both abstraction and generalization are important mental processes for any writer; they help us, as Janet Giltrow puts it, to "name and manage otherwise unruly details." But writers have to learn to use them with care. As a rule, generalizations must be supported by evidence. (Generalizations that are commonplace may be made without support; one does not need to provide evidence in support of the generalization that dogs have four legs or that war is a terrible thing.) And they should be precise. *Most Canadians voted against the Free Trade Agreement in the 1988 election* is an imprecise generalization. *In the 1988 election most Canadians voted for parties that opposed the Free Trade Agreement* is more accurate. Such concern for precision may seem like pedantry; is there any difference between the two? Yes, there is. In that election, many Canadians who opposed Free Trade nevertheless voted for the Conservatives, just as many Canadians who supported Free Trade voted for the Liberals or the NDP. Free Trade was the most contentious issue in the campaign, but not the only one; it was an election, not a referendum. Being careful about such distinctions is an important element of good writing.

501. mixed levels of abstraction or generalization: When a comparison is being drawn or an extended argument is being shaped, the levels of abstraction or generalization should be kept consistent.

wrong	Ethnicity, like the aged, women, and others, is believed by some scholars to be best understood within a broad context of inequality, and outside of any specific "cultural" argument.
right	Ethnicity, like age, gender, and other categories on the basis of which discrimination may occur, is believed by some scholars to be best understood within a broad context of inequality, and outside of any specific "cultural" argument.

502. excessive abstraction: Almost any combination of abstract words can create fuzziness of meaning unless the writer exercises extreme care. Look at the following passage, for example:

- There are two features of Nyerere's later view of the transition to socialism which distinguish it from his earlier view. First, the trends in Tanzanian society which he felt would soon greatly increase the strength of the opposition to socialism led him in the years after the Arusha Declaration to a greater sense of urgency about the need seriously to set in train the transition to socialism. Second, he had by his mid-forties a much clearer perception than he had had as a younger man of the initiatives the government should take to achieve an effective transition to socialism.

> This new perception of the transition to socialism owed much, of course, to the character of the socialist society which Nyerere finally hoped to achieve. It was, however, very much shaped as well by his understanding of the political realities of Tanzania at the time.
>
> It was Nyerere's ideas on the transition to socialism rather than his vision of a transformed Tanzania which had a direct and major impact upon policy and politics in the years after the Arusha Declaration. (Cranford Pratt, *The Critical Phase in Tanzania*)

This is the sort of thing English instructors have in mind when they tell their students to use concrete words rather than abstractions. By itself there is nothing wrong with any of the words *features, transition, socialism, distinguish, trends, opposition, perception, initiatives, character, socialist society, understanding, political realities, ideas, vision, transformed, impact,* or *policy.* But put them together in a string like this—unbroken by any words like dog, box, tree, or paper—and you have writing that puts even the most determined reader to sleep. Moreover, the writer who consistently uses such words is likely to find herself circling round and round in a fog. (It should not be inferred that Cranford Pratt is such a writer; the point of including a passage from a book by this distinguished professor is rather that even the best writers must be wary of such problems.) Let's try the first paragraph again:

- By the time of the Arusha Declaration Nyerere had realized how deeply and strongly the currents of opposition to socialism flowed; he would have to move fast. But he had also realized much more clearly by this time what the government could do to speed up the process.

Some academics might complain that this version is too journalistic, but at least it has the virtue of clarity. What about the rest? Pratt seems to be saying something like this:

- How much did Nyerere's vision of socialism itself have to do with the change in his view of how it should be achieved? Some, of course, but not much. It was his concept of how the vision should be achieved rather than the vision itself that shaped Tanzanian politics in the years after the Arusha Declaration.

Does this in fact say anything of importance? Not really; it might be best to cut the entire paragraph. But until one trims some of the verbal foliage away, it is difficult to see how little is being said.

503. **jargon:** Every academic discipline and indeed every area of human life has its own jargon; it is no fault in English to use jargon

appropriate to one's subject matter and audience. But it is easy to overdo the use of jargon, and all too easy to write in ways that may be appreciated by only a small number when one's subject justifies aiming for a larger audience.

The excessive use of jargon may be as much a problem of psychology as it is of English grammar and usage. It often comes from people being more concerned with making themselves sound knowledgeable and intellectual than with acquiring knowledge or developing their intelligence; more concerned with making their ideas sound important than with thinking them through and expressing them clearly. The best way to guard against excessive jargon is always to ask yourself if you are saying what you mean in the simplest possible way. Let us look at some examples:

- The very fact that these articles criticizing the government had been published in the state-controlled newspaper told the reader something of consequence. It indicated that these were the parameters within which debate had been sanctioned by the Central Committee of the ruling party.

The jargon word here is of course *parameters*. This word has a very specific technical meaning in mathematics, and should not be used in other contexts. It gained currency out of a confusion with *perimeter* (the boundary of a closed area), and out of people's desire to use words that sound impressive but are clearly understood by neither writer nor reader. *Sanction* is another troublesome word in the passage—it would be a perfectly good word if it had not come to take on two diametrically opposed meanings. Here one presumes it means to *approve of*, but it is possible that it means to *restrict* instead. Because of such ambiguity the word is best avoided. The more general question is whether this writer has expressed his or her meaning in the clearest and most concise way possible. Let's try again:

- The very fact that these articles criticizing the government had been published in the state-controlled newspaper told the reader that the Central Committee of the ruling party had allowed debate in these areas.

Notice the other changes we have made: cutting the wordy "told the reader something of consequence," and changing from a passive verb (*had been sanctioned*) to an active one (*had allowed*). This change puts the subject (*the Central Committee*) at the beginning of the second clause, and allows us to cut "It indicated."

The final result is a sentence that is a good deal simpler and shorter. One cannot be fooled into thinking it says anything particularly profound, but one needn't waste any time in puzzling out what the writer means.

jargon	The plan is more philosophical than operational in terms of framework.
clear	The plan is still only an idea; it hasn't yet been tried, and it may not work.
jargon	This paper argues that by interrogating the author's constructions of difference we may more nearly approach the critical taxonomy by which she de-centers and indeed subverts the tropes of race and of gender.
clear	How does the author construct difference? What categories does she see things falling into? This paper argues that she de-centers and indeed subverts the tropes through which race and gender have traditionally been presented.
	(Note that the clearer version here is created more by re-phrasing than by removing jargon.)
jargon	The great interfaces across the entire spectrum of Canadian-American relations are in order.
clear	Canada and the United States are on good terms.

Here is a list of commonly used jargon words and expressions; if you find yourself using them a good deal, think about whether you might better re-phrase:

access	commence
enhance	impact on
implement	interface
optimal	opt for
parameter	point in time
previous to	prior to
prioritize	specificity
structure	totality
utilize	viable
-wise (money-wise, sales-wise, weather-wise, etc.)	

504. **doublespeak**: George Orwell coined the word *doublespeak* in his novel *1984* to describe the use of language to disguise one's true meaning. This is a variant of jargon that one should try particularly hard to avoid. Here are a few humorous but saddening examples:

poor	The government must deal with the issue of revenue enhancement.

better   The government will have to raise taxes.

poor   Our guest rooms feature the most prestigious body cleaning systems.

better   We have good bathtubs.

poor   We provide outplacement consulting to companies involved in downsizing their operations.

better   We advise companies on how best to fire people.

(These examples are taken from the *Quarterly Review of Doublespeak*, which is published by the National Council of Teachers of English, 1111 Kenyon Rd., Urbana, Ill. 61801.)

BIAS-FREE LANGUAGE

505. **gender:** The healthy revolution in attitudes towards gender roles in the last generation has created some awkwardness in English usage—though not nearly so much as some have claimed. *Chair* is a simple non-sexist replacement for *chairman*, as is *business people* for *businessmen*. Nor is one forced into *garbageperson* or *policeperson*; *police officer* and *garbage collector* are entirely unobjectionable even to the linguistic purist. *Fisher* is a quite delightful replacement for *fisherman*; here again, there is no need for the *-person* suffix.

The use of *mankind* to mean *humanity*, and of *man* to mean *human being*, have for some years been rightly frowned upon. (Ironically enough, *man* originally had *human being* as its only meaning; in Old English a *werman* was a male adult human being, a *wifman* a female.) A remarkable number of adults still cling to sexist usages, however, and even still try to convince themselves that it is possible to use *man* in a gender-neutral fashion. Among them are the editors of *The Economist*, who posed the question, "What is Man?" in the lead article of their September 14, 1996, issue. "To what extent are men's actions determined by their genes?" the article asked, and clearly did not intend the answer to apply to only one-half the human race.

Well, why can't *man* be gender neutral? To start with, because of the historical baggage such usage carries with it. Here, for example, is what the best-selling novelist Grant Allen had to say on the topic in a magazine called *Forum* in 1889:

- In man, I would confidently assert, as biological fact, the males are the race; the females are merely the sex told off to recruit and reproduce it. All that is distinctly human is man—the field, the ship, the mine, the workshop; all that is truly woman is merely reproductive—the home, the nursery, the schoolroom.

But the baggage is not merely historical; much of the problem remains embedded in the language today. As it happens, a useful litmus test appeared in the same issue of *The Economist*. Further on in the magazine this sentence appears:

- One of the most basic distinctions in human experience—that between men and women—is getting blurrier and blurrier.

Now let's try the same sentence using *man's* instead of *human*:

- One of the most basic distinctions in man's experience—that between men and women—is getting blurrier and blurrier.

In this sort of context we are all forced to sense that something is amiss. We have to realise when we see such examples that *man* and *he* and even *mankind* inevitably carry with them some whiff of maleness; they can never fully and fairly represent all of humanity. (If they didn't carry with them some scent of maleness it wouldn't be possible to make a joke about the difficulty of turning *men* into *human beings*.) Most contexts are of course more subtle than this, and it is thus often easy for humans—but especially for men—not to notice that the male terms always carry with them connotations that are not gender-neutral. *Humanity, humans, people*—these words are not in any way awkward or jargon-ridden; let's use them.

To replace *man* with *humanity* is not inherently awkward to even a slight degree. But the pronouns are more difficult. Clearly the consistent use of *he* to represent both sexes is unacceptable. Yet *he/she, s/he*, and *he or she* are undeniably awkward. *S/he* is quite functional on the printed page, but defies translation into oral English. Another solution is to avoid the singular pronoun as much as possible either by repeating nouns (*An architect should be aware of the architect's clients' budgets as well as the architect's grand schemes*) or by switching to the plural (*Architects should be aware of their clients' budgets as well as of their own grand schemes*). Of these two the second is obviously preferable. In longer works some prefer a third strategy that eliminates awkwardness entirely: to alternate between the masculine pronoun *he* and the feminine pronoun *she* when referring to a single, generic member of a group. Using *she* to refer to, say, an architect, or a professor, or a sports star, or a prime minister can have the salutary effect of reminding readers or listeners that there is nothing inherently male in these occupations. In a short piece of writing, however, it can be distracting to the reader if there are several bounces back and forth between female and male in the same paragraph. And a cautionary note should accompany this strategy even when it may conveniently be employed: be very careful not to assign *he* to all the professors, executives, or doctors; and *she* to all the students, secretaries, or nurses.

pronouns: Undoubtedly the most troublesome questions for those who are concerned both about gender equality and about good English arise over situations involving singular pronouns such as *everyone, anyone, anybody, somebody, someone, no one, each, either, neither*. It can be difficult enough to re-cast sentences involving such words so that everything agrees even before the issue of gender enters the picture.

- Everybody felt that the film was better than any other they had seen that year.

According to the rules most of us have been taught, that sentence is wrong; *everybody* is singular, and *they* must therefore be changed:

- Everybody felt that the film was better than any other she had seen that year.
- Everybody felt that the film was better than any other he had seen that year.
- Everybody felt that the film was better than any other she or he had seen that year.

But, as Robertson Cochrane has pointed out ("Sex and the Single Pronoun," *The Globe and Mail*, May 1992), the insistence on the singularity of such pronouns is a relatively recent phenomenon, dating from the codification of English grammar that took root in the eighteenth century. Before that time Chaucer, Shakespeare, Swift, and the rest had no qualms about using *they* or *their* to refer to *anyone* and *everyone*. Cochrane persuasively argues that returning to the ways of Chaucer and Shakespeare in this respect is better than constantly trying "to write around the pronoun problem, and [it is] certainly less offensive than arrogantly and 'properly' applying masculine labels to all of humankind."

inappropriate	Mankind cannot bear too much reality.
gender neutral	Human kind cannot bear too much reality.
inappropriate	Everyone will have a chance to express his views
(*though "correct"*)	before the meeting is over.
gender neutral	Everyone will have a chance to express their views
(*though "incorrect"*)	before the meeting is over.

Of course issues of gender are not confined to the right word choice. Consider the following descriptions of political candidates with essentially the same backgrounds:

- Carla Jenkins, a lawyer and a School Board Trustee, is also the mother of three lovely daughters.
- George Kaplan, a lawyer and a School Board Trustee, has a long record of public service in the region.

- George Kaplan, a lawyer and a School Board Trustee, is also the father of three lovely daughters.
- Carla Jenkins, a lawyer and a School Board Trustee, has a long record of public service in the region.

The impression left in many minds by such phrasings is that the person described as having a long record of public service is well suited to public office, while the person whose parenting is emphasized may be better suited to staying at home.

Some may feel that parenthood is relevant in such cases; if you do, be sure to mention it both for women and for men. The general rule should be that parenting (and physical appearance) should not be mentioned unless you feel them relevant to the point(s) you are making.

Before leaving the issue of gender and language, let me raise the issue of the attitude we bring with us when we read or write. Some writers seem to <u>prefer</u> to think of gender-neutral language as inherently awkward or absurd. Here's an example of what I mean, taken from a widely-adopted textbook:

Maintaining Objectivity

Avoiding discriminating language is important. Just as important, however, is avoiding a witch hunt. Taken to extremes, political correctness will weaken your writing. Middleman, for example, is a perfectly legitimate term, widely understood. There is no point in confusing readers by substituting distributional intermediary merely to avoid the suffix -*man*. Little is gained by referring to a stripper as an ecdysiast when most readers will not recognise the euphemism. And no one is going to take seriously a writer who calls short people vertically challenged. Remember, the point of considerate language is to be fair and polite, not to be obscure or silly. (Bonnie Carter & Craig Skates, *The Rinehart Guide to Grammar and Style*. Fort Worth: Rinehart, 4/e 1996)

Think about this for only a moment, and it may seem quite unexceptionable—entirely reasonable, even. Think again. The tip-off here is the way that the question of the word *middleman* has been approached. Not as the occasion for an interesting, if possibly difficult search for ways of expressing ourselves that will avoid both awkwardness and bias, but rather as a matter that will inevitably involve a choice between the two. The authors here seem more interested in finding reasons to ridicule the struggle for fairness than in joining in the effort to improve things.

Let's approach the word in a different frame of mind. To start with, the fair comparison is not between *distributional intermediary* and *middleman* but between *intermediary* and *middleman*. Perhaps the former is more awkward, but it is not obviously so:

- One of the reasons for high prices in this industry is that there are too many middlemen.
- One of the reasons for high prices in this industry is that there are too many intermediaries.

Alternatives in different circumstances may include *wholesalers, distributors, go-betweens*—none of them obscure, confusing, or laughable. Ecdysiast is indeed a laughable euphemism, but not one that is needed to circumvent biased usages. (*He's a male stripper* suffers from the same defect as *He's a male nurse*, but *stripper* in itself is gender-neutral.) And, though there is indeed a societal bias against short people, no one seriously suggests euphemism as a solution.

For many years now "politically correct" has been used with quotation marks around it to mean *aesthetically distasteful and ethically wrong-headed*—and we are often meant to be left with the suggestion that those who criticise the "politically correct" do not themselves have a political agenda; they are "maintaining objectivity." It is telling in this connection that the authors of *The Rinehart Guide* couch the matter as an issue of etiquette rather than one of equity: "the point of considerate language is to be fair and polite." To be sure, it is a virtue to be polite and considerate. But unquestioning politeness to those in positions of power and privilege may sometimes entail an acceptance of terms of reference that are anything but fair. Sometimes one may have to choose beween being fair and being polite. And the point of searching for bias-free ways of expressing oneself is in fact not to be polite, but to be fair. Sometimes it comes to a choice; language can be an instrument of positive change, or an instrument of repression. In that context we can probably never avoid being biased in one direction or the other, and we are wise to remember that complete objectivity is impossible.

None of this should be taken to suggest that there are not awkwardnesses to struggle with in the search for bias-free coinages. (*Statesman* and *manned spaceflight*, for example, resist easy substitutions.) But these are surprisingly few. In most cases one need not resort to the oft-lampooned *person* suffix. *Chair* and *flight attendant* felt a little odd at first (in language as in the rest of life it may take a while to get used to new things), but no one is bothered by them now. *First-year student* still feels odd to many Americans, but not in Canada, where it has always been used. And the process continues. *Snowbody* is a wonderful word that my daughter and a friend of hers helped me make up, but I suspect it will be years before *snowman* begins to sound as clunky as *stewardess*. Try it, though—and try to smile in fun rather than in derision. Put the accent on the first syllable. And remember, there are few things more gender-neutral than a body made up of three spheres of snow.

race, culture, and sexual orientation: Although gender is the most contentious issue in the struggle for bias-free language, it is not the only one. Almost everyone is aware that one should avoid various terms for particular racial or cultural groups (see the list below), and it is just as important to avoid language that conveys derogatory implications on the basis of sexual orientation. The most appropriate terms to use do not stay constant, however; everything hinges on connotation, and since connotations may change over time, so does appropriate usage. The best principle to follow here is to pay attention to how members of particular groups prefer to be described.

A few racial and cultural terms are so deeply encoded in the language that people may use them without being aware of their underlying meaning.

offensive	I'm convinced that the shopkeeper tried to gyp me.
	(*Gyp* originated in the prejudice that Roma were congenital cheats.)
bias-free	I'm convinced that the shopkeeper tried to cheat me.

Another example of a widely-used expression that is strongly if more subtly coloured with bias is the expression *white trash*. The implications of the expression are brought forward in the following passage:

- The [Jerry Lee] Lewis and [Jimmy] Swaggart clans were, in the harsh modern parlance, white trash. They lived in the black part of town, and had close relations with blacks. Mr. Swaggart's preaching and Mr. Lewis's music were strongly influenced by black culture. "Jimmy Swaggart was as black as a white man can be," said black elders in Ferriday. (*The Economist*, April 15, 2000)

This passage brings out the implication of the expression; the "trashiness" that is the exception for white people is implicitly regarded as the norm for black people.

Given the generally high level of awareness in Western society of the evils of anti-Semitism it is extraordinary that *jew* is still sometimes used in casual conversation as a verb in the same way that *gyp* is used. It is a use that should never be allowed to go unchallenged—and when such usages are challenged speakers will often realise they have been unthinkingly using a coinage learnt in childhood—and will change.

Less obviously offensive but still objectionable is the use of unnecessary racial or gender or religious identifiers. Mentioning a person's race or gender or religion in connection with occupation is a common habit, but one that reinforces stereotypes as to what sort of person one would naturally expect to be a lawyer or a doctor or a nurse. Unless race or gender or religion is in some way relevant to the conversation, there is no need to refer to someone as a *male nurse*, or a *Jewish doctor*, or a *Native lawyer*.

In one important respect the issue of bias-free usage differs from every other issue discussed in this book. Throughout, our focus has been on formal writing, and it has frequently been emphasized that many informal and colloquial usages that are inappropriate to formal writing may be quite unexceptional in other forms of writing, or in speech. The same cannot be said of the difference between biased and bias-free language. It is no less damaging to use sexist, racist, or homophobic language in speech than it is in writing; indeed, it may even be more so. The cumulative repetition in speech of colloquial expressions—including such "innocent" expressions as the contemptuous use of *that's so gay*—probably does considerably more to reinforce human prejudice than does the written word.

Bias-free Vocabulary: A Short List

actress	actor
alderman	councillor
bad guy	villain
bellboy	bellhop
bogeyman	bogey monster
businessman	businessperson, entrepreneur
caveman	cave-dweller
chairman	chair
clergyman	minister, member of the clergy
congressman	representative
con-man	con-artist
draftsman	drafter
Eskimo	Inuit

NB Some Alaskan groups still prefer *Eskimo*.

fireman	firefighter

fisherman	fisher
foreman	manager, supervisor
freshman	first-year student
garbageman	garbage collector
gunman	shooter
gyp	cheat, con
Gypsies	Roma
henchmen	thugs
Indian	Native, First Nations

NB As with *Eskimo/Inuit* and *African American/black*, the key consideration is sensitivity to audience. If you do not belong to the group but you know that the people you are writing about prefer a particular designation, that is the one to use.

infantryman	footsoldier
layman	layperson
longshoreman	shiploader, stevedore
maid	housekeeper
mailman	letter carrier, mail carrier
male nurse	nurse
man	humanity
man (an exhibit)	staff
man (a barricade)	fortify, occupy
man (a ship)	crew
manhandle	rough-up, maul
manhole	sewer hole, access hole, street hole
manhole cover	sewer cover, street hole cover
mankind	human kind, people, humanity, humans
manly	self-confident, courageous, straightforward
manmade	handmade, human-made, constructed
middleman	intermediary
negro	black, African American

NB In the United States *African-American* is generally preferred; in Canada *black* is often the preferred term.

policeman	police officer
postman	letter carrier, mail carrier
salesman	salesperson
snowman	snowbody (rhymes with *nobody*)
sportsman	sportsperson
stewardess	flight attendant
unsportsmanlike	unsporting
waitress	server

weatherman	weather forecaster
womanly	warm, tender, nurturing, sympathetic
workman	worker, labourer

NB A much more complete guide is Rosalie Maggio's *Talking About People: A Guide to Fair and Accurate Language* (Oryx Press, 3/e 1997).

METAPHOR AND MEANING

Metaphors may either enliven prose or deaden it; it is all in how you use them. In that sentence there are two metaphors; the verbs *enliven* and *deaden* both implicitly compare writing to a living thing. As this suggests, a metaphor is a comparison of one thing to another made through the use of a word or words that do not apply literally. *My love is a red, red rose* is a metaphor. *My love is <u>like</u> a red, red rose* is a simile—a type of metaphor that uses the word *like*. We do not often use poetic metaphors like this in prose, but nevertheless our writing is likely to be strongly laced with metaphorical language. Phrases such as the following are all too familiar to us:

- That will be the acid test.
- The United States has always been a melting pot.
- He is barking up the wrong tree.
- I threw caution to the winds.
- This reorganization lays the foundation for future change.
- We were told that we would have to bite the bullet.
- The government's move has paved the way for a resumption of talks.
- We are opening up new horizons.
- The university was then a hotbed of unrest.

For the most part these are what are known as dead metaphors— metaphors that have been used so frequently that they no longer conjure up any physical image in the minds of those who hear or read them. When we hear the phrase *miss the boat* we do not think of a boat, any more than we think of pavement when we hear the expression *paved the way for*. It is a moot point whether a dead metaphor is better than no metaphor at all, but certainly a fresh metaphor is far better than either. Instead of *paved the way*, for example, what about *blazed a path*? Instead of a *hotbed* try a *cauldron*. Instead of *nipping something in the bud*, try *digging up the seedlings*. It may take a little longer, but the improvement in one's writing is worth it.

So many people have been using metaphors for so long that it is extremely difficult to find fresh ones for every idea you wish to express. One useful compromise is to try to bring dead metaphors to life by using them in new ways. For example, no one thinks of a wave if you say, *The Mayor has been riding a wave of popular support since his election*. Mention the wave again in a slightly different way, however, and it becomes water again to the reader:

- The Mayor has been riding a wave of popular support since the election. The question now is when that wave will crest.
- The company wanted to nip in the bud the spreading unrest among its employees before it became a tangled, snake-infested jungle.

506. mixed metaphors: A dead metaphor all too often becomes a mixed metaphor as well. Mixed metaphors occur when we are not really thinking of the meaning of the words we use. *If we bite the bullet we have to be careful not to throw the baby out with the bathwater; We will leave no stone unturned as we search for an avenue through which the issue may be resolved.* As soon as one really thinks about such sentences one realizes that the bullet is really better off out of the baby's bathwater, and that the best way to search for an avenue is not to turn stones over.

wrong	Now Chretien is out on a limb because his colleagues pulled the rug out from under him.
right	Now Chretien is out on a limb and some of his colleagues are preparing to saw it off.
wrong	The man in the street has trouble keeping his head above water.
right	The average person today has trouble keeping his head above water.

SLANG AND INFORMAL ENGLISH

507. slang/informal English: The following words and expressions are often used in conversation, but not in formal English. The more formal word is listed afterwards. The most frequently troublesome entries are given a separate number:

anyways	anyway
anywheres, anyplace	anywhere
awful	poor, miserable, sick
awfully	very, extremely

> Some authorities continue to hold that *awful* should retain its original meaning of *filled with or inspiring awe*. In any case, a better replacement can always be found. The same is even more true of the use of the adverb *awfully* as an intensifier to mean *very* (*awfully good, awfully small*, etc.).

boss	manager, supervisor
bunch	group
(except for grapes, bananas, etc.)	
buy	bargain
(as a noun—*a good buy*, etc.)	
kid	child, girl, boy
kind of, sort of	rather, in some respects
let's us	let us
lots of	a great deal of
mad	angry
(unless the meaning is insane)	

All contractions (*it's, he's, there's, we're*, etc.) should be avoided in formal writing, as should conversational markers such as *Well, ...*

508. could care less/couldn't care less: In the early 1990s people started to say sarcastically *I could care less* to mean the opposite—that they *couldn't* care less. For some time *I could care less* seemed to be taking over, regardless of the tone of voice used, and the meaning of the words themselves seemed in danger of being lost. In recent years *couldn't care less* has made something of a comeback.

wrong	Most of the time most people could care less about what their elected representatives are doing.
right	Most of the time most people couldn't care less about what their elected representatives are doing.

509. get: should not be used to mean *come, go, be,* or *become*

| *wrong* | Henry and Jane Seymour got married in 1536, only ten days after the death of Anne Boleyn. |
| *right* | Henry and Jane Seymour were married in 1536, only ten days after the death of Anne Boleyn. |

510. go (to mean *say*)

| *wrong* | He goes, "What do you mean?" |
| *right* | He said, "What do you mean?" |

511. have got (to mean *have*)

| *less formal* | He has got two houses and three cars. |
| *more formal* | He has two houses and three cars. |

In conversational English *got* has become widely used as an auxilliary verb, probably because of the awkwardness of pronouncing certain combinations involving common contractions. Thus we would never shorten *I have you covered* to *I've you covered*; instead we would say, *I've got you covered*. *Have got* is also an informal synonym for *have* in the sense of *possess*. Both these uses of *got* are usually to be avoided in formal writing.

512. let's say: This expression should be omitted entirely from writing.

| *wrong* | Let's say for example a relative dies, a poor family will have to deal with financial worries as well as with grief. |
| *right* | If a relative dies a poor family will have to deal with financial worries as well as with grief. |

513. like (to mean *say* or *indicate through gesture*): An expressive idiom, but one to be avoided in writing.

| *conversation* | She's like, "Why do we have to be here?" and I'm like, "Duh!" |
| *formal* | She wondered why we had to be there; to me it was obvious. |

514. off (to mean *from*)

| *wrong* | I got it off him for two dollars. |
| *right* | I bought it from him for two dollars. |

515. put across, get across (one's point): express, convince

wrong   He could not get his point across.
right   He could not persuade us he was right.

516. well: In conversation *well* is often added to sentences while you are thinking of what to say. Do not do this in writing.

wrong   Well, at the end of the war there was some doubt within the Cabinet as to which course to take.
right   At the end of the war there was some doubt within the Cabinet as to which course to take.

517. when you get right down to it: usually best omitted; use *otherwise, indeed,* or *in fact.*

THE WRITING PROCESS

What are the most important things to think of when writing? First, that you have something to say. And second, that you keep in mind whom you are writing for.

Though some of the finest essays are narrative or descriptive, most of the extended writing that adults are expected to do—whether as students, business people, bureaucrats, or academics—is structured in order to persuade. This is true even of most writing that is not "argumentative" in any narrow sense. It may through analysis try to persuade the reader of the validity or usefulness of a particular approach; it may employ description or narration in the service of persuasion. But normally it will have as a central purpose a desire to persuade the reader of something. To persuade us through description that St. John's, Newfoundland, is the most entertaining town in North America. To persuade us through selective narration that the Americans were or were not justified in dropping the atomic bomb on Japan in 1945. To persuade us through analysis of the narrative structure of *The Remains of the Day* that Ishiguro's novel leads the reader to invest emotional energy in the character of Stevens. To persuade us through argument that high housing densities are necessary to vibrant urban life, or that wind-power is the most cost-effective method of generating electricity over the long term.

Almost every book about writing will tell you of the importance of the thesis, and of the thesis statement. And there is no doubt that it is as helpful to the writer to try to ensure that the main idea of an essay or report can be expressed concisely and directly as it is helpful to the reader to have it so expressed (see examples on next page). Often, though, what one begins with as the main thing one wants to say will be modified or qualified during the research and writing process— and occasionally it may be entirely reversed; one may become convinced that the precise opposite of what one began by trying to demonstrate is in fact the case. Writing an essay or a report is in this respect not unlike conducting an experiment. One begins with a hypothesis. The hypothesis is tested during the process of research, writing, and revision. Refined into the thesis, it is the central thread of the essay or report.

518. poor thesis or thesis statement:

poor   Art is important to society in many ways, and I will talk about them in this essay. One of the artists I will focus on is Robert Mapplethorpe, the subject of much controversy over many years.

> (Yawn. The statement is too general and too vague to have significance.)

better   The art of Robert Mapplethorpe deserves to be exhibited— and at public expense—even if most people find it abhorrent.

> (This statement is more precise, more limited, more interesting.)

poor   In this paper I will examine various reasons for launching the war in Kosovo in 1999.

> (This is a statement of topic rather than of thesis. It's also wordy.)

better   The moral case for the US and its allies to wage a bombing-only war against Yugoslavia in 1999 was stronger than the strategic one; air attacks alone had never before been enough to win a war.

> (Suddenly there is an argument being made.)

poor   The purpose of this essay is to explore the interplay between poetry and the novel. I will prove that good poets don't usually write good novels and vice versa.

> (Full points for ambition, but it's the subject for a book, not a term paper. At most, a short paper might justifiably speculate about such a large question in its conclusion; the main focus should be much narrower. Also, the statement is far too bold in its generalization. "What about Thomas Hardy?" the professor will ask. "What about Boris Pasternak?")

better   Ondaatje's characters seem thin and unreal to the reader— alternately brittle and transparent. Paradoxically, however, it may be precisely these qualities that allow the poetic power of his prose—at once brutal and fragile—to strike the reader with full force.

> (A much narrower but still controversial thesis exploring the connections between poetry and prose.)

Books about writing also often emphasize the importance of having a plan for any essay or report. And rightly so; it is very useful to draw up a point-form summary of the idea, laid out to show the flow of ideas, and the way in which they should flow together as paragraphs. Any such plan should usually include headings grouping the ideas:

- three reasons why Alberta has in the past chosen coal rather than wind for generating electricity.
- two false assumptions on which many of the arguments in favour of dropping the bomb are based.

- examples of the ways in which Ishiguro's syntactical structures support his narrative techniques.
- examples of the ways in which the spareness of his descriptions does the same.

And so on. But if it is important to have a plan, it is equally important to be willing to change it. To be able to recognise halfway through the writing process that in fact the whole section on the general historical context in which something happened would better go before the direct presentation of the arguments as to why it happened, and that the rebuttal of the arguments of Jones should not be introduced until after Smith's contentions have been thoroughly discussed. To be able to cut large chunks, no matter how interesting, if they turn out not to be relevant to the main point. To be able to add sections that will provide necessary qualification for one's thesis. And to pay attention to the ideas that one is likely to have *while one is writing*; interesting and original ideas are as likely to surface during the process of writing as during the process of reading and researching.

Last but far from least, it is important to let the writing process have several stages. The first of these (and for many people the most difficult) is simply to get words onto paper, or onto a screen and into a computer memory. At this stage it may be fruitful to remember that nothing is at stake where a first draft is concerned; no one but yourself need see it or see the flaws that will be an inevitable part of it. Get something on paper first—and then worry about improving it.

Part of overcoming writer's block, then, is often an acceptance by the writer that the writing process will have several stages—and that at least two of these will be stages not of planning or of writing but of revising. That too may end up requiring a good deal of often unexpected writing. And at a minimum it should involve not only a willingness but a determination to improve the writing throughout rather than merely to correct obvious errors. Too many students—not to mention people in business and bureaucrats—feel that they have essentially finished the job when they have completed a first draft. The checklist below is intended largely to help writers think through the revising process. But the essential first stage is psychological—the recognition of the value of taking the time to do two, three, or more drafts. As Ian Cameron of Carleton University recommends in *For All Practical Purposes*:

- A few students feel that they are as likely to make more mistakes in checking and correcting their work as they are to correct the mistakes they have already made, but in fact almost every student is able to improve his or her work at least fifteen per cent by checking it slowly and carefully. Remember, you are not checking simply for details such as spelling; you should be trying to replace words, to re-arrange paragraphs, to cut entire sections, to alter almost every sentence.

By its very nature, revising is likely to lead to more cuts than additions. Might this not cause damage? "Aren't I more likely to do well," some may ask themselves, "if I've written more than has been asked for?" If the instructor has asked for 1,000 words, they feel they should write 1,500; if 2,500 words are requested, they are sure to top 3,000. Experienced writers have learnt that quantity matters much less than quality; unless an essay or report is well below the requested number of words the only thing that matters is what it says, and how well it says it.

Advice on the writing process may also be found elsewhere in these pages. In particular, it may be helpful to consult the chapters on Putting Ideas Together, Paragraphing, and Writing With Computers.

Essay Checklist

- Does this piece of writing have a clear purpose? Have I made that purpose clear to the reader?
- What audience is this written for? Is the tone suited to the intended audience throughout?
- Of what am I trying to persuade my audience? Is this made completely clear near the beginning (whether in a formal thesis statement or otherwise)? Is it again made clear near the conclusion?
- Does the essay follow a clear path? Are there too many digressions? Is there any extraneous material that should be cut, or transferred out of the body of the text and into a note?
- Is the structure of the argument signalled by the paragraphing?
- Does the paragraph remain the unit of composition throughout?
- Does the point I am making remain clear in every paragraph? In every sentence?
- Is there some variety in sentence structure? Have I avoided awkward sentence constructions? And run-on sentences?
- Are most verbs in the active voice?
- Do the verbs always agree with the subjects?
- Do I use concrete and specific language wherever possible? Do I avoid excessive use of jargon or unnecessarily obscure language?
- Am I careful in my use of qualifiers, avoiding statements that are too bald or extreme, but not qualifying all the strength or interest out of my argument?
- Is my writing ever wordy? Where could I still trim?

- Did I revise (from hard copy) and rewrite the essay thoroughly?
- Did I proofread after I had revised?
- Have I checked the punctuation carefully throughout?
- Have I proofread as well as used a computer spell-check?
- Have I used the correct system of documentation? Do the references follow this system consistently throughout?
- Have I given appropriate acknowledgment to all the sources I used? Is there any point at which I might have been guilty of plagiarism by paraphrasing without acknowledgment?
- Does the format (spacing, margins, etc.) follow specifications?
- Have I answered all the above questions honestly?

EXAMINATIONS

Even those who realize the value of taking the time to revise an essay or report have a natural—and understandable—tendency to assume that entirely different principles apply to examinations. There are differences, of course, but the basic similarities should also be kept in mind. Time allocation involves greater pressure in this context, but planning and revision are just as important; again, quantity matters less than quality. If at all possible, then, avoid writing madly to the last moment of the exam. A well-written short answer is almost invariably better received than a sloppy, long-winded one, and even a few moments spent on checking and revising will almost always be of enormous value. Here are two additional pointers:

- Take your time in reading the examination questions; many a student has done a marvelous job answering a question that wasn't asked, where a few extra moments of calm reflection while reading the examination would have made all the difference.
- For long essay questions take the time to make even the roughest of plans for your answer. Not only will this help you to remember the points you wish to make; it will also lead to a better-structured answer.

Note: An excellent guide to the peculiarities of exam-writing is *Making Your Mark* by Catherine Taylor et al., published by Trent University.

WRITING BY COMPUTER

COMPUTERS AND THE WRITING PROCESS

No one born later than, say, 1950 needs to be convinced of the advantages of computers for writing. But many of us need to remind ourselves periodically of some of the pitfalls of word-processed writing. Some problems are readily avoided if one retains the habit of careful proofreading: the perils of spell-check, for example (see below) or the dangers of search and replace. It is all too easy to come to rely on the computer a little too heavily in such contexts—as I found myself doing recently when I instructed my computer to do a search and replace on a contract, replacing all occurrences of *author* in the contract with the words *senior editor*. What need could there be to confirm? The contract was almost in the mail before *senior editorization* and *senior editority* caught my eye. I certainly had not *senior editorized* the change, but my computer had no way of stopping once I had unleashed its search and replace engine.

Proofreading may be enough to check some of the bad cognitive habits that computers breed in many writers who work only on screen; it certainly will not eliminate them all. For some of us computers can be wonderful facilitators of flow; many people find it easier to get a lot of ideas out of their heads and "on paper" by using a computer than by using a pen and paper. But the same habits of scrolling that can facilitate flow in writing and in reading can distort our ability to arrange ideas in an ordered fashion so as to best present an argument. Though researchers are far from understanding why, they have now assembled a considerable body of evidence suggesting that seeing a succession of printed pages enables one to combine and connect ideas in ways that are not always evident if one restricts oneself to scrolling text on the screen. This is why it is vitally important to work with paper as well as on screen. It is ironic that the very means by which the re-ordering of blocks of text has become a matter of effortlessly keyboarding (rather than of laboriously cutting, pasting, and retyping) also acts to dull the cognitive processes that are required for humans to re-order those blocks most effectively. But that is the reality all writers must come to terms with.

If computer technology may facilitate the sort of writing flow that is the best tonic for writer's block, the speed with which that technology changes may also sometimes give us an excuse not to write. It is all too easy to decide that it will be impossible to finish a thesis or complete a report unless and until one upgrades software, replaces that old hard drive, or acquires a faster machine. In almost all cases this is really just a way of trying to avoid the hard job of getting down to writing. We should all make it a firm rule not to let our fascination with technology get in the way of our writing.

A Note on Spell-Check

Commonly used words are also commonly misspelled words—and not only because they occur frequently. Most of us have the sense when we use a word such as *surreptitiously* to check the spelling in a dictionary, or with the spell-check mechanism on our computer. But words such as *its* and *it's*, or *than* and *then*, or *compliment* and *complement* we tend to use without thinking—and no computer spell-check will tell us if we have had a mental lapse and used the wrong one. (It would be difficult for me to count the times as a publisher that I have received manuscripts that began with a *Forward* rather than a *Foreword*.) It is worth remembering that no computer can be a substitute for careful proofreading.

The Internet

In 1992 the media was full of references to the need to create an "electronic highway." But within a year almost everyone had realized that one had already been created. The Internet had originally been the product of the American Defence Department's desire to build diffuse lines of communication as a defence against attacks on the country's infrastructure. Made available for use by academics in the 1980s, it had quietly developed by the early 1990s into an extraordinarily efficient and inexpensive means of communication. And as Web technology has developed, its potential has continued to grow.

Technology that can be used in so many ways can of course also be misused in many ways. Given the pace of change—and the complexity of the topic—it would be unwise in a book of this size to attempt any comprehensive treatment of how to use the Internet as a resource tool for writing. But some general guidelines may be useful.

Research Using the Internet

The Internet may seem like a goldmine when it comes to research. But if so, the likeness is to a vein of ore that is not always sufficiently concentrated as to make the mining of it economic. Sometimes the most difficult thing is to decide when it is worth one's while to commit one's resources to the mining operation. Search engines are likely to turn up vast amounts of material on almost any topic. But often much of it will be unreliable—and it is extraordinarily difficult for the novice to tell what is likely to be reliable and what isn't.

At one end of the spectrum, many refereed scholarly journals are available on-line—and some are available only on the Internet. The best way to consult reference works that are constantly updated (such as the *Oxford English Dictionary*) is through the Internet. And some academic disciplines are now turning to publication via the Internet for scholarly monographs. (The historian Robert Darnton, for example, has led an initiative by the American Historical Association and Columbia University Press to publish through the Internet monographs which are of real importance but of very specialized academic interest.)

At the other end of the spectrum are countless materials that have not been reviewed either by academic authorities or by publishers. How is one to gauge the reliability of such material? Should one just stick to established sources in the library? How is it possible to avoid spending a large amount of time merely to amass a large quantity of unreliable source material?

There are no easy answers to these questions, and the best strategies are likely to vary depending on the sort of research one is doing. The most important thing for the novice may be simply to consult one's instructor on the issue of what sources—whether in the library or on the Internet—may be most appropriate to use for a given assignment.

Some other research principles may be helpful. Think of the credentials of the author; is he or she an academic at a respected institution; and has he or she published widely on the topic? How new is the material? (Obviously some premium is to be placed on more recent research, though often the most important works on a topic will not be new.) Which works on a topic are cited most often by others? If a work is frequently cited by others, it will be one that should be taken into account. What is the point of view of the author? One key consideration in assembling the resources one will deal with is making sure that a variety of view points are represented.

You should not feel obligated, though, to give equal weight to all points of view. Particularly where material on the Web is concerned, it will sometimes be the case that implausible or downright irresponsible points of view will be more widely represented than views that deserve greater respect. Such is obviously the case with websites promulgating racist or anti-Semitic views, but it may also be the case with certain scientific matters. For some years now, for example, the vast majority of reputable scientific opinion has been in broad agreement as to the dangers of global warming. Dissenting scientific voices comprise only a small minority among the community of reputable scientists—but their views receive disproportionate space on the Web, where numerous sites are largely devoted to casting doubt on the consensus scientific view on global warming (and, not by coincidence, to preserving the status quo for the coal industry, the oil and gas industry, and so on). here such ideologically charged issues as these are concerned, it is worth paying particularly close attention to accounts that run counter to the normal ideological stance of the publication. When the right-wing magazine *The Economist* accepted a few years ago that the weight of evidence overwhelmingly supported the argument that global warming posed a real danger, or when the left-of-center British newspaper *The Guardian* concluded that despite its socialist rhetoric the Mugabe government in Zimbabwe was denying its people both economic justice and basic human rights, such views deserve special respect.

With library sources, the publisher of a work is also a helpful clue for the researcher. The experienced researcher will take account of the publisher, but not put too much stock in its reputation; the university presses of Oxford, Cambridge, Harvard, and Princeton have published a few real clunkers as well as vast amounts of first-rate scholarship. And because librarians often have standing orders from such prestigious presses as these, a clunker from them is more likely to find its way onto the shelves of the university library than a clunker from, say, Wilfrid Laurier Press or Hackett Publishing. Nevertheless, there will always be a better than average chance of work published by a highly reputable organization being of high quality. This holds true for the Web as well. Few book publishers issue works electronically, but more and more academic journals are available electronically—including a number of the most prestigious. The beginning student will often not know which journals or which book publishers have a solid track record. But it will help to be wary of self-published material, whether in book form or on the Web, and it will help as well if the researcher pays attention to such matters, and is prepared to ask questions of instructors and of fellow students.

Many of the principles of library research, then, apply to research on the Web too. Perhaps above all, it is important to note each source you consult in writing an essay, report, or thesis. (Be sure as well to mark clearly any passages or phrases that are a direct quote rather than a summary or your own commentary on what you have read, so as not to confuse your own ideas or phrasings with those of the authors you have consulted.) In the case of an Internet reference it may be more convenient to store the information on your hard drive or on a disc rather than on a card or piece of paper—but the principle of noting sources carefully remains the same.

If many of the principles are the same, the mechanisms of Web research are very different from the mechanisms of using the library, and are constantly changing. A number of good guidebooks devoted entirely to using Internet sources are now available, and are updated regularly. Referencing styles also change frequently. Some of the essential points of referencing Internet sources appear below in the chapter on referencing. The fullest and most up-to-date treatments of referencing according to particular styles, however, are to be found through the websites of the relevant organizations: the MLA, APA, and so on.

OBSERVING NETIQUETTE

"Netiquette" is a clever little pun that seems to have stuck. It neatly encapsulates the notion that standards of courtesy and consideration are as important in cyberspace as they are in other areas of human existence—and that the Internet is sufficiently different from other forms of communication as to make some new guidelines advisable.

Anyone who has used e-mail has probably sensed that the medium lends itself to a higher degree of informality (for both sender and recipient) than does the sending of a letter printed on corporate or departmental letterhead. The combination of distance, informality, and invisibility that electronic communication embodies seems to encourage the spontaneous expression of emotion in ways that might otherwise not feel appropriate. It often seems to foster a breeziness that is as friendly as it is efficient. But it also seems to lend itself to the venting of certain sorts of anger, in ways that other media of communication do not. And sometimes it leads people to divulge personal information that on reflection they might rather have kept to themselves. These tendencies of e-mail—to foster sometimes unexpected degrees of intimacy, and to facilitate the unbridled expression of anger—argue for the wisdom of taking the time to edit and proof any electronic message, checking its tone quite as much as its grammar.

The increasing use of electronic communication in a wide variety of contexts continues to raise issues of appropriate tone and of level of formality. For the most part, no one expects e-mails to conform to all the conventions of more formal communications; it would be foolish to worry about a typo or two in an e-mail dashed off to a friend. But any e-mail should be clear, unambiguous, and written in an appropriate tone; again, it is wise to edit and proofread carefully any message you send. And if you are using e-mail as a convenient way to convey a more formal document, that document should indeed conform to the conventions of standard usage. A proposal submitted electronically or a memo circulated electronically should be phrased, proofed, and presented as carefully as you would the same document in hard copy form. As with writing, faxing, or phoning, then, the context and the expectations of your audience are always important.

Privacy issues are at least as important with electronic communications as they are with other forms of communication. As a recipient, consider the feelings of the sender; unless it is obviously appropriate to forward a message, for example, ask the permission of the sender before you pass it on. And as a sender, it is worth remembering that electronic communication can often end up being less private than regular mail. Since recipients are not always as considerate as one might wish (and since errors in filing and forwarding can occur) it is wise to consider whether the potential recipients of a message may be a much larger group than intended—and word the message accordingly.

POINT-FORM NETIQUETTE

- keep messages clear and brief.
- edit/proof all messages before sending—for tone as well as form.
- use clear subject headings.
- make the text as easy to read as possible; leave a line between paragraphs (rather than indent); use italics—or place an underscore mark before and after the relevant word(s) as a substitute for italics; use only well-known abbreviations.
- when quoting from a previous message, quote only the necessary passage(s).
- address the message carefully.
- attachments: be aware that some recipients may have difficulty downloading attachments, and be prepared to use alternative means in such circumstances.
- visuals: remember that (s)he may not have the same technology you do. Think twice, for example, before sending a large file of graphic information that may take the recipient an inordinate amount of time to download—if indeed (s)he has the capacity to do so.
- listservs/chatgroups/newsgroups/bulletin boards: There are a variety of Internet mechanisms for sharing information among many individuals with a common interest. Conventions may vary with each group; it makes sense to pay attention to the procedures followed

and the tone adopted by established users before you start to play an active role yourself. And if in any doubt as to appropriate procedures, ask the listowner/bulletin board organizer.

- post only information that is likely to be of interest to others—and as with e-mail, be as clear and as brief as possible.
- be particularly sensitive to the demands you may be making on the time of others. If, for example, you are sending an "information-only" e-mail to a department head who may deal with a hundred e-mails a day, make it clear in the heading or at the beginning of the message that this is for information only, and that no reply is required.
- the overriding principle: always show consideration for your reader(s).

PLAGIARISM, COPYRIGHT, AND THE WEB

Keeping careful track of your sources—and clearly indicating for your own reference what is a quotation and what is your own comment on a work you have consulted—not only saves time; it also prevents unintentional plagiarism.

Although the possibilities both for unintended and for intentional plagiarism are vastly greater with the Web than they were when hard copy materials were the only resources, the mechanisms for detection have expanded as well; search engines can often confirm for an instructor in seconds that a particular string of words in a student essay has been lifted unacknowledged from another source.

Copyright rules for written materials apply to the Internet just as they do to books or articles; written work is under copyright protection for many years after it is published. In the United States the 1998 Sonny Bono Copyright Amendment Act significantly extended copyright protection; most written material published in 1924 or later will remain in copyright for many years to come; in the UK and other European countries work is in copyright for 70 years after the death of the author (or translator); in Canada and Australia work is in copyright for 50 years after the death of the author or translator.

Except for quoting brief passages (with the proper acknowledgment), you may not reproduce material from the Web without the permission of the copyright holder. Nor may you post copyrighted materials on the Web without permission from the copyright holders.

FORMAT AND SPELLING

519. **capitalization**: Proper nouns (naming specific persons, places, or things) should always be capitalized. Common nouns are not normally capitalized. Here are a few examples:

Proper	**Common**
June	summer
Parliament of Canada	in parliament
Mother (used as a name)	my mother
Remembrance Day	in remembrance
Memorial Day	as a memorial
National Gallery	a gallery
Director	a director
Professor	a professor
the Enlightenment	the eighteenth century
the Restoration	the restoration
(historical period in England)	(other uses of the word)
the Middle Ages	middle age
(historical period in Europe)	(a period of life between youth and old age)
God	a god
Catholic	catholic
(belonging to that particular church)	(meaning wide-ranging or universal)
a Liberal	a liberal
(belonging to the Liberal Party)	(holding liberal ideas)
a Democrat	a democrat
(belonging to the Democratic Party)	(believing in democratic ideals)

Names of academic subjects are not capitalized (unless they are names of languages). Major words in the titles of books, articles, stories, poems, films, and so on should be capitalized; articles, short prepositions, and conjunctions are not normally capitalized in titles.

needs checking	She became a Director of the company in 2002.
revised	She became a director of the company in 2002.
or	She became a member of the Board of Directors in 2002.
needs checking	Robert Boardman discusses *The Bridge On The River Kwai* extensively in his book.
revised	Robert Boardman discusses *The Bridge on the River Kwai* extensively in his book.

520. abbreviations: Abbreviations are a convenient way of presenting information in a smaller amount of space. This section discusses conventions for using abbreviations in formal writing.

521. titles: Titles are normally abbreviated when used immediately before or after a person's full name.

> Mr. Isaiah Thomas
> Sammy Davis Jr.
> Dr. Jane Phelps
> Marcia Gibbs, MD

When using a title together with the last name only, the full title should be written out.

> Prof. Marc Ereshefsky
> Professor Ereshefsky
> Sen. Keith Davey
> Senator Davey

522. academic and business terms: Common abbreviations are acceptable in formal writing so long as they are likely to be readily understood. Otherwise, the full name should be written out when first used and the abbreviation given in parentheses. Thereafter, the abbreviation may be used on its own.

- The Atomic Energy Commission (AEC) has broad ranging regulatory authority.
- The American Philosophical Association (APA) holds three large regional meetings annually.

523. Latin abbreviations: Several abbreviations of Latin terms are common in formal academic writing:

> | | |
> |---|---|
> | cf. | compare (Latin *confer*) |
> | e.g. | for example (Latin *exempli gratia*) |
> | et al. | and others (Latin *et alia*) |
> | etc. | and so on (Latin *et cetera*) |
> | i.e. | that is (Latin *id est*) |
> | NB | note well (Latin *nota bene*) |

524. numbers: Numbers of one or two words should be written out. Use figures for all other numbers.

needs checking	The building is 72 storeys tall.
revised	The building is seventy-two storeys tall.

The same principle applies for dollar figures (or figures in other currencies).

needs checking	She lent her brother 10 dollars.
revised	She lent her brother ten dollars.

It is acceptable to combine figures and words for very large numbers:

• The government is projecting a $200 billion deficit.

In general, figures should be used in addresses, in dates, to give percentages, and to report scores or statistics.

needs checking	In the third game of the tournament, Canada and the Czech Republic tied three three.
revised	In the third game of the tournament, Canada and the Czech Republic tied 3–3.

525. **italics**: Italics may be represented in hand written or typed papers by underlining. Italics serve several functions. While short stories, poems, and other works are set off by quotation marks, longer works and the names of newspapers, magazines, and so on should appear in italics:

> "The Dead"
> "Burnt Norton"
> "Budget Controversy Continues"
> "Smells Like Teen Spirit"
> *Dubliners*
> *Four Quartets*
> *The Economist*
> *Nevermind*

Italics are used for the names of paintings and sculptures, television series, and software. Italics are also used for words or phrases from other languages in written English.

needs checking	The play ends with an appearance of a deus ex machina.
revised	The play ends with an appearance of a *deus ex machina*.

Either italics or quotation marks may be used to indicate that words are mentioned rather than used. (See the chapter on punctuation, under quotation marks.) Finally, italics are often used to provide special emphasis that is not otherwise clear from the context or the structure of the sentence.

526. **spelling**: The wittiest example of the illogic of English spelling remains Bernard Shaw's famous spelling of *fish* as *ghoti*. The *gh* sounds like the *gh* in *enough*; the *o* sounds like the *o* in *women* (once spelled *wimmen*, incidentally); and the *ti* sounds like the *ti* in *nation* or *station*. Shaw passionately advocated a rationalization of English spelling; it still has not happened, and probably never will. Perhaps the best way to learn correct spelling is to be tested by someone else, or to test yourself every week or so on a different group of words. For example, you might learn the words from the list below beginning with *a* and *b* one week, the words beginning with *c* and *d* the next week, and so on.

527. **spell-check:** No computer can be a substitute for careful proofreading. Spell check is wonderful, but it cannot tell if it is your friend or your fiend, or if you have signed off a letter with best wishes or beast wishes.

528. **spelling and sound**: Many spelling mistakes result from similarities in the pronunciation of words with very different meanings. These are covered in the list below. Other words that cause spelling difficulties are listed separately.

absent (adjective)	absence (noun)
absorb	absorption
accept	except
access (entry)	excess (too much)
advice (noun)	advise (verb)
affect (to influence)	effect (result)
allowed (permitted)	aloud
alter (change)	altar (in a church)
appraise (value)	apprise (inform)
bitten	beaten
base (foundation)	bass (in music)
bath (noun)	bathe (verb)
berry (fruit)	bury (the dead)
beside (by the side of)	besides (as well as)
birth	berth (bed)
bizarre (strange)	bazaar (market)
bloc (political grouping)	block

breath (noun)	breathe (verb)
buoy (in the water)	boy
buy (purchase)	by
cash	cache (hiding place)
casual (informal)	causal (to do with causes)
cause	case
ceased (stopped)	seized (grabbed)
ceiling (above you)	sealing
chick	cheek
chose (past tense)	choose (present tense)
cite (make reference to)	sight/site
climatic (climate)	climactic (climax)
cloths (fabric)	clothes
coma (unconscious)	comma (punctuation)
compliment (praise)	complement (make complete)
conscious (aware)	conscience (sense of right)
contract	construct
conventional (usual)	convectional (transfer of heat)
conversation	conservation/concentration
cord (rope)	chord (music)
convinced	convicted (of a crime)
council (group)	counsel (advice)
course	coarse (rough)
credible (believable)	creditable (deserving credit)
critic (one who criticizes)	critique (piece of criticism)
defer (show respect)	differ
deference (respect)	difference
deprecate (criticize)	depreciate (reduce in value)
desert (dry place)	dessert (sweet)
device (thing)	devise (to plan)
died/had died	dead/was dead
dissent (protest)	descent (downward motion)
distant (adjective)	distance (noun)
edition (of a book, etc.)	addition (something added)
emigrant	immigrant
envelop (verb)	envelope (noun)
except	expect
fear	fair/fare (payment)
feeling	filling
fell	feel/fill
flaunt (display)	flout (disobey)
formally	formerly (previously)
forth (forward)	fourth (after third)
forward	foreword (in a book)
foul	fowl (birds)
future	feature

genus (biological type)	genius (creative intelligence)
greet	great/grate (scrape)
guerrillas	gorillas
guided (led)	guarded (protected)
had	heard/head
heat	heart/hate
heir (inheritor)	air
human	humane (kind)
illicit (not permitted)	elicit (bring forth)
illusion (unreal image)	allusion (reference)
immigrate	emigrate
independent (adjective)	independence (noun)
inhabit (live in)	inhibit (retard)
instance (occurrence)	instants (moments)
intense (concentrating)	intents (purposes)
isle (island)	aisle (to walk in)
know	no/now
kernel	colonel
lack	lake
later	latter/letter
lath (piece of wood)	lathe (machine)
lead (heavy element)	led
leave	leaf
leave	live
leaving	living
lessen (reduce)	lesson
let	late
lightning (from clouds)	lightening (becoming lighter)
lose (be unable to find)	loose (not tight)
mad (insane)	maid (servant)
man	men
martial (to do with fighting)	marshal
mental	metal
merry	marry
met	meet/mate
minor (underage)	miner (underground)
mist (light fog)	missed
moral (ethical)	morale (spirit)
mourning (after death)	morning
new	knew
of	off
on	own
ones	once
pain	pane (of glass)
patients (sick people)	patience (ability to wait)
peer (look closely)	pier (wharf)

perpetrate (be guilty of)	perpetuate (cause to continue)
perquisite (privilege)	prerequisite (requirement)
personal (private)	personnel (employees)
perspective (vision)	prospective (anticipated)
poor	pour (liquid)/pore
precede (go before)	proceed (continue)
precedent	president
price (cost)	prize (reward)
prostate (gland)	prostrate (lying down)
quay (wharf; pronounced *key*)	key
quite	quiet (not noisy)
rein (to control animals)	rain/reign
release (let go)	realize (discover)
relieve (verb)	relief (noun)
response (noun)	responds (verb)
rid	ride
ridden	written
rise	rice
rite (ritual)	right/write
rod	rode/reared
rote (repetition)	wrote
saved	served
scene (location)	seen
saw	seen
saw	so/sew
seam (in clothes)	seem (appear)
secret	sacred (holy)
sell (verb)	sail (boat)
senses	census (population count)
shed	shade
shone	shown
shot	short
sit	sat/set
smell	smile
snake	snack (small meal)
soar	sore (hurt)
sole (single)	soul (spirit)
sort (type or kind)	sought (looked for)
steal (present tense)	stole (past tense)
straight (not crooked)	strait (of water)
striped (e.g. a zebra)	stripped (uncovered)
suite (rooms or music)	suit/sweet
super	supper (meal)
suppose	supposed to
sympathies (noun)	sympathize (verb)
tale (story)	tail

talk	took
tap	tape
than	then
they	there/their
thing	think
this	these
throw	threw (past tense)
tied	tired
urban (in cities)	urbane (sophisticated)
vanish (disappear)	varnish
vein (to carry blood)	vain
waist (your middle)	waste
wait	weight (heaviness)
waive (give up)	wave
wants	once
weak (not strong)	week
weather (sunny, wet, etc.)	whether (or not)
wedding	weeding
were	where
wholly (completely)	holy (sacred)/holly
woman	women
won	worn
yoke (for animals)	yolk (of an egg)

529. American spelling, British spelling, Canadian spelling: A number of words that cause spelling difficulties are spelled differently in different countries. In the following list the British spelling is on the right, the American on the left. Either is correct in Canada, so long as the writer is consistent:

American	British
behavior	behaviour
center	centre
cigaret	cigarette
color	colour
defence	defence
favor	favour
favorite	favourite
fulfill	fulfil
humor	humour
likable	likeable
maneuver	manoeuvre
marvelous	marvellous
neighbor	neighbour
omelet	omelette

program	programme
Shakespearian	Shakespearean
skillful	skilful
skeptical	sceptical
theater	theatre
traveling	travelling

530. Other spelling mistakes: Following is a list of some other commonly misspelled words:

abbreviation	argument	colleague
absence	arsonist	colonel
accelerator	arteriosclerosis	colossal
accident	artillery	column
accidentally	asinine	commitment
accommodation	author	committee
achieve	auxiliary	comparative
acknowledge	bacteria	competition
acquire	basically	competitor
acquisition	battery	complexion
acquit	beautiful	conceive
acre	beginning	condemn
across	believe	conjunction
address	boast	connoisseur
adjacent	boastful	consensus
advertisement	breakfast	consistent
affidavit	bulletin	controller
ambulance	burglar	convenience
amoeba	burial	cooperation
among	buried	cooperative
ammonia	business	courteous
amortize	candidate	courtesy
amount	capillary	creator
anachronism	cappuccino	creature
analogous	Caribbean	criticism
analysis	carpentry	cyst
anchor	cautious	decisive
androgynous	ceiling	definite
annihilate	changeable	delicious
antecedent	character	description
anti-Semitic	chlorophyll	desirable
anxious	choir	despair
apocalypse	cholesterol	despise
apparatus	chrome	destroy
apparently	chromosome	develop
appreciate	chronological	diesel
approach	chrysalis	different
architect	chrysanthemum	dilemma
arguable	coincidence	dining

disappear
disappoint
disastrous
discrimination
disease
disintegrate
dissatisfied
dominate
dormitory
double
doubtful
drunkard
drunkenness
duchess
due
dying
eclipse
effective
efficient
eighth
embarrass
employee
encourage
enemy
enmity
enormous
entertain
enthusiasm
entitle
entrepreneur
environment
enzyme
epidermis
epididymis
erroneous
esophagus
especially
espresso
essential
exaggerate
excessive
excite
exercise
exhilaration
existence
existent
experience
extraordinary
Fahrenheit
faithful

faithfully
farinaceous
fault
financial
foreigner
foretell
forty
fourth
gauge
gamete
germination
government
grammar
grateful
gruesome
guarantee
guerrillas
guilty
happened
happiest
hatred
hectare
helpful
hyena
hypothesis
ichthyology
idiosyncratic
imaginary
imagine
immigration
immersible
impeccable
importance
impresario
inchoate
incomprehensible
indigenous
independent
indestructible
indispensable
ineffable
infinitesimal
inoculate
insufferable
intention, intentional
interrupt
irrelevant
irresponsible
isosceles
isthmus

itinerary
jealous
jeopardy
journalist
jump
junction
kneel
knowledge
knowledgeable
laboratories
laboratory
language
lazy, laziness
ledger
leisure
liaise
liberation
library
licence
lieutenant
liquid, liquefy
literature
lying
medicine
medieval
membrane
merciful
mermaid
millennia
millennium
millionaire
mischief
mischievous
modern
naked
naughty
necessary
necessity
noticeable
nuclear
nucleus
obscene
obsolescent
obsolete
occasion
occasional
occupy
occur
occurred
occurrence

omit
ourselves
paid
parallel
parliament
parliamentary
party
permissible
permission
perpendicular
perseverance
photosynthesis
playful
possess
possession
poultry
predictable
pregnancy
pregnant
prerogative
prescription
privilege
properly
psychiatric
psychological
punctuation
pursue
questionnaire
really
receipt
recommend
referee
reference
regret
repeat
repetition
replies
reply
residence (place)
residents (people)
restaurant
revolutionary
rheumatism

rhododendron
rhombus
rhubarb
rhyme
rhythm
saddest
sandals
scene
schedule
schizophrenic
science
scintillate
scissors
scream
scrumptious
search
seize
sense
separate
shining
shotgun
sigh
significant
simultaneous
sincerely
slippery
slogan
smart
solemn
spaghetti
speech
spongy
sponsor
stale
stingy
stomach
stubborn
studious
studying
stupefy
stupid
subordinate
subpoena

substitute
subtle, subtlety
suburbs
succeed
success, successful
sue, suing
summary
surprised
surreptitious
surrounded
survive
symbol
talkative
tarred
television
temperature
tendency
theoretical
theory
title
tough
tragedy
trophy
truly
unique
until
vacancy
vacillate
valuable
vegetable
vehicle
vicious
visitor
volume
voluntary
Wednesday
welcome
whisper
writer
writing
written
yield

VOCABULARY:
SOME NATIONAL VARIATIONS

The following list of variants from some nations in which English is a primary first language does not include slang or idioms.

Australia	Canada
announcer/host/presenter	announcer/host
attic/loft	attic
autumn	fall/autumn
award rate	minimum wage
baby carriage/pram	baby carriage
back yard	back yard/garden
back bacon	back bacon
baked potato/jacket potato	baked potato
bangs (hair)	bangs
bathers/cozzy	bathing suit/swimsuit
beanie	toque
billion	billion
biscuit	cookie
bitumen road	paved road
block of land	plot of land
bowser	gas pump
brew (tea)	steep
bus/coach (inter-city)	bus
cake (layer)	cake (layer)
can/tin (of food)	can/tin
car (rail passenger)	car
chemist	drugstore/pharmacy
chips (potato)/crisps	chips
Cludo	Clue (board game)
coloured pencil	pencil crayon
concrete block	concrete block
constituency	riding/constituency
(House of Representatives)	(House of Commons)
contraceptive	condom/safe/rubber
corn starch/corn flour	corn starch
dam (human-made)	pond/lake
dessert/pudding	dessert
diaper/nappy	diaper
different from/to	different from
drapes	curtains/drapes

Say What?

"How many railway sleepers are there in the pile?"
"Put on your toque; it's cold."
"Pull over on the verge, please."
"She never drinks soda; it's too sweet for her."
"Do you sell university calendars here?"

England	United States
presenter/host	host/announcer
loft	attic
autumn	fall/autumn
minimum wage	minimum wage
pram	babycarriage
back garden	back yard
back bacon	Canadian bacon
jacket potato	baked potato
fringe	bangs
swimming costume	swimsuit
woolly hat	wool hat
thousand million	billion
biscuit	cookie
metalled road	paved road
plot of land	plot of land
petrol pump	gas pump
brew	steep
coach	bus
gateau	cake (layer)
tin	can
carriage	car
chemist	drugstore
crisps	chips
Cludo	Clue
pencil crayon	colored pencil
breeze block/concrete block	concrete block
constituency	district
(House of Commons)	(House of Representatives)
condom/rubber	condom/safe
corn flour	corn starch
pond/lake	pond/lake
sweet/pudding	dessert
nappy	diaper
different from/to	different from/than
curtains	drapes/curtains

Australia	Canada
dumpster	dumpster
editorial/leader	editorial
eggplant/aubergine	eggplant
electrical cord/flex	electrical cord
elevator/lift	elevator
engaged (phone)	busy
eraser	rubber/eraser
escalator/moving staircase	escalator
extension cord/lead	extension cord
fire plug	fire hydrant
fire station/fire hall	fire station
fire engine	fire engine
first-year student	first-year student
fish fingers	fish sticks
fizzy drink	soft drink/pop
flashlight/torch	flashlight
fly (trousers)	fly
frankfurt	hotdog/wiener
freeway/motorway	expressway/freeway
gas/petrol (for a car)	gas
general store	grocery store
generator/dynamo	generator
get a rise (in pay)	get a raise
give (someone) a bell	a call/ring
globe (light)	bulb
grazier	farmer
green beans	green beans
grumble	grumble
gum boots	rubber boots
hamburger (prepared)/mince	hamburger/ground beef
half-mast (flag)	half-mast
hang up/ring off	hang up
hood/bonnet (of a car)	hood
hot water bag	hot water bottle
hot-water service	hot water heater
house for sale	house for sale
house for let	house for rent
icing (cake)	icing
in the post	in the mail/by post
intersection	intersection
invigilate (exam)	invigilate
kerosene/paraffin	kerosene
latex paint/emulsion paint	latex paint
lima beans/broad beans	lima beans
locked/shut tight	locked/shut tight
lollies	candies
match/game	game
Mother's Day	Mother's Day
(Father's Day is the same in all cases)	
moving company	van line
muffler/silencer (of a car)	muffler
nature strip	shoulder

England	United States
rubbish skip	dumpster
leader	editorial
aubergine	eggplant
flex	electrical cord
lift	elevator
engaged	busy
eraser	rubber
moving staircase	escalator
lead	extension cord
fire hydrant	fire hydrant
fire hall	fire station
fire truck	fire engine
first-year student	freshman
fish fingers	fish sticks
fizzy drink	soda
torch	flashlight
flies	fly
frankfurter	frank/wiener/hotdog
dual carriageway/motorway	freeway/thruway
petrol	gas
grocer	grocery store
dynamo	generator
get a rise	get a raise
a ring	a call
bulb	bulb
farmer	farmer
runner beans	green beans
grouse/grumble	grumble
wellingtons	rubber boots/rainboots
beefburger/mince	hamburger
half-mast	half-staff
ring off	hang up
bonnet	hood
hot water bottle	hot water bottle
immersion heater	hot water heater
house under offer	house for sale
house for let	house for rent
frosting	icing
in the post/by the post	in the mail/by mail
junction	intersection
proctor	invigilate
paraffin	kerosene
emulsion paint	latex paint
broad beans	lima beans
made fast/locked	locked/shut tight
sweets	candies
fixture/match	game
Mothering Sunday	Mother's Day
removals	van line
silencer	muffler
verge	shoulder

Australia

Canada

Australia	Canada
odometer/milometer	odometer
outbuildings (at a farm)	outbuildings
outside toilet	outhouse
oval/sports field	sports field
pacifier	pacifier/soother
paddock	field
parka	rain jacket/windbreaker/raincoat/parka
phone cord	phone cord
pie/flan	pie
post box	post box/mail box
prawns	shrimps
prospectus (university)	calendar
public holiday	public holiday
railway/railroad	railway/railroad
car hire/rental	car rental
ring off (phone)	hang up
row boat	row boat
rubbish tin	wastebasket/garbage can
rubbish tip/tip	garbage dump
run (for election)	run
runners	track shoes/runners/sneakers
sailboat/sailing boat	sailboat
sand shoes	running shoes/canvas shoes
scrap yard/car breaker	scrap yard (car)
second floor	second floor
semi-(trailer)	semi-/transport trailer
(road train—more than one trailer)	
shallots	green onions/spring onions/scallions
skirting board	baseboard
skivvy	turtleneck
sleepers	ties (railway)
standings (sports)	standings
station (sheep or cattle)	ranch/farm
sticky tape	scotch tape
stockyard	stockyard
stretcher	cot
stroller	stroller
study/revise (for a test)	study
subway/underground	subway
sun bake	sunbathe
surgery	doctor's office
sweater/jumper	sweater
take away (food)	take-out
taxi-truck	rent-a-truck
thongs (footwear)	flip-flops/thongs
traffic circle	traffic circle
trailer/caravan	trailer/camper
trousers	pants/trousers/slacks
truck/lorry	truck
ute (utility vehicle)	pick-up truck

England	United States
milometer/trip meter	odometer
outhouses	outbuildings
outdoor privy	outhouse
pitch/sports field	sports field
dummy	pacifier/soother
field	field
anorak/mac	windbreaker/rainjacket
phone lead	phone cord
flan	pie
pillar box	mail box
prawns	shrimps
prospectus	catalog
bank holiday	public holiday
railway	railroad
car hire	car rental
ring off	hang up
rowing boat	rowboat
waste paper basket	wastebasket
rubbish tip/refuse tip/tip	garbage dump
stand	run
trainers	track shoes
sailing boat	sailboat
plimsoles	sneakers/tennis shoes
car breaker	scrap yard
third floor	second floor
articulated lorry	eighteen wheeler
spring onions	green onions
skirting board	baseboard
polo-neck top	turtleneck shirt
sleepers	ties
tables	standings
farm	ranch
sellotape	scotch tape
cattle pen	stockyard
camp bed	cot
push chair/pusher	stroller
revise (for a test)	study
underground/tube	subway
sunbathe	sunbathe
surgery	doctor's office
jumper	sweater
take away	take out
van hire service	rent-a truck
thongs	thongs
roundabout	traffic circle
caravan	trailer
trousers	slacks/pants
lorry	truck
pick-up	truck

Australia	Canada
trucks (railway)	freight cars (railway)
trunk/boot (of a car)	trunk
turf/sods	turf
underground walkway	underground walkway
vacuum/hoover	vacuum
vest	vest/waistcoat
wait on	wait for
wake up (someone else)	wake up
washcloth/flannel	washcloth
washing-up liquid	dish detergent
winery	vineyard
woolgrower	sheepfarmer
zillion	zillion

England	United States
trucks	freight cars
boot	trunk
sods	turf
subway/underpass	underground walkway
hoover	vacuum
waistcoat	vest
wait for	wait for
knock up/wake up	wake up
flannel	washcloth
washing-up liquid	dish detergent
vineyard	vineyard
sheepfarmer	sheepfarmer
billion	zillion

SPECIAL WRITING SITUATIONS

ACADEMIC WRITING

Academic writing often depends upon the use of jargon—namely, the specialized language of any scholarly field. Inevitably, such language will sometimes present challenges, and communication is always made easier to the extent that the writer is able to express ideas in the most straightforward manner possible. The goal is to balance the requirements of the academic discipline with those of communication—to write in a varied and flexible style, one that utilizes simple words wherever possible without becoming simplistic.

The tone of academic writing is typically one of careful argument. The aim is to persuade the reader through logic and through the marshalling of evidence (rather than, for example, through attempting to exhort or entertain the reader). It is thus always important when writing in an academic context to provide support for whatever claims you make, and to be careful in how you phrase those claims. Almost all academic writers rely heavily on words in phrases such as *for the most part, mainly, tends to ...,* and so on, in order to ensure that the claims they are making allow for some exceptions. Conversely, they tend to avoid words such as *always* and *never,* which would leave their arguments open to being refuted through a single exception.

Most academic essays are formal pieces of writing, and should be approached as such. Readers expect a calm and disinterested tone, free of extreme emotion and of slang or conversational usage. That should not be taken to imply that thinking rigorously about a topic precludes feeling strongly about it—or conveying to the reader how the writer feels. But usually it is advisable to try to do this without employing first-person singular pronouns; most academic writers use *I* or *me* infrequently, if at all. Most academic writers aim to succeed in persuading their readers by letting the evidence speak for itself. Thus, many instructors advise their students to avoid entirely the use of first-person pronouns.

As with all guidelines to style and tone, though, this one should not be regarded as written in stone. George Orwell, often praised as the finest essayist of the twentieth century, uses *I* and *me* frequently.

BUSINESS WRITING

Tone may be the most important aspect of business writing. The adjective *businesslike* conjures up images of efficaciousness and professional distance, and certainly it is appropriate to convey those qualities in most business reports, memos, and correspondence. In a great deal of business writing, however, it is also desirable to convey a warm personal tone; striking the right balance between the personal and the professionally distanced is at the heart of the art of business writing. A few guidelines:

(a) Consult your colleagues. Circulate a draft of any important document to others and ask their opinion. Is the tone too cold and formal? Is it too gushy and enthusiastic? Is it too direct? Or not direct enough?

(b) Be careful about suggesting you are speaking for your entire organization. Unless you are sure, you are well advised to qualify any extreme statements.

needs checking	Our organization wants to underprice every competitor.
revised	In my experience our prices are lower than those of major competitors.
needs checking	There is no way we would ever cut back on research and development.
revised	As an organization we have a strong commitment to research and development.

Given that business communication operates within a hierarchical power structure, it is particularly important to foreground consideration in business, memos, letters, and e-mails. Avoid direct commands wherever possible; give credit to others when things go right; and take responsibility and apologize when things go wrong.

needs checking	Here is the material we spoke of. Send the report in by the end of the month to my attention.
revised	I enclose the material we spoke of. If you could send in the report by the end of the month to my attention, I'd be very grateful.
needs checking	I am writing in response to your complaint. We carry a large number of products with similar titles, and sometimes errors in shipping occur. Please in future specify the ISBN of the item you are ordering, as that will help keep errors to a minimum.
revised	Thank you for your letter—and my sincere apologies on behalf of our company for our mistake. As you may know, we carry a large number of products with similar titles, and (particularly in cases

where our customer service department is not able to double check against an ISBN) errors do sometimes occur. But that is an explanation rather than an excuse; I do apologize, and I have asked that the correct item be shipped to you immediately. Thank you for drawing this matter to my attention.

Writing About Literature

All subject areas have their own conventions and specialized vocabulary. Writing about literature is singled out here for special treatment not because its practices are inherently more important than those of other disciplines, but because its conventions present fundamental problems for the student at the level of sentence structure.

verb tense: The past tense is, of course, normally used to name actions which happened in the past. But when one is writing about what happens in a work of literature, convention decrees that we use the simple present tense.

needs checking	Romeo fell in love with Juliet as soon as he saw her.
revised	Romeo falls in love with Juliet as soon as he sees her.
needs checking	In her short stories, Alice Munro explored both the outer and the inner worlds of small town life.
revised	In her short stories, Alice Munro explores both the outer and the inner worlds of small town life.

quotations: When writing about history or politics—in the past tense—one is likely to find difficulty with quotations in the present or future tenses. When writing about literature the problem is the reverse; one is writing in the present tense, but many of the quotations one usually wishes to use are in the past tense. Often it is necessary to rephrase and/or adjust the length of the quotation in order to preserve grammatical consistency.

needs checking	Emma Bovary lives largely through memory and fantasy. She daydreams frequently, and as she reads, "the memory of the Vicomte kept her happy."
revised	Emma Bovary lives largely through memory and fantasy. She daydreams frequently, and as she reads, "the memory of the Vicomte" keeps her happy.

DOCUMENTATION

There are two chief concerns when it comes to citing and documenting material: accuracy and consistency. Whatever system of citation is used, a research writer must follow it closely and consistently. Four of the most commonly used systems of citation are summarized in these pages—MLA style, APA style, Chicago style, and CBE style. It may also be helpful to consult exemplary essays. (A selection of these may be found on the Broadview Press website in the pages providing adjunct material to this and other Broadview writing texts; go to www.broadviewpress.com, and click on links.)

CITATION AND PLAGIARISM

To take the words or ideas of another without properly acknowledging them is to commit plagiarism—a serious form of dishonesty. Plagiarism is subject to serious penalties at all academic institutions; these may range from a failing grade being assigned for the relevant course to outright expulsion from the institution.

The avoidance of plagiarism begins with careful research so as to remove any chance of your confusing someone else's words for your own during the writing process. Judgment of the crime of plagiarism, incidentally, makes no provision for malice aforethought; whether or not a writer is wilfully deceptive makes no difference. Therefore competent writers are extremely careful. They keep thorough and well organized notes while reading and researching—notes that clearly indicate where each idea comes from and when the exact words used by another writer are being jotted down.

If you summarize or paraphrase someone else's work without using the exact words that they use, you do not need to use quotation marks—but you must still cite the work.

> Researchers have shown that the model of genetic mapping first advanced by Crick and Watson leaves many questions unanswered (Commoner 42).

Do you need a citation for everything? No. Obviously citations are not needed when you are putting forward your own original ideas. Nor are they necessary when you are touching on common knowledge. If you refer to the population of China or the date when the North American Free Trade Agreement was signed, you do not need to provide any citation, since such information is generally available and widely known.

If you quote the exact words of a source, rather than summarize or paraphrase, it is important to integrate the quotation into the body of your writing. To this end, phrases such as the following are very useful:

- As Smith and Jones have demonstrated,
- In the words of one researcher,
- As Nussbaum observes,
- Kendal suggests that "...
- Murphy and other scholars have rejected these claims, arguing that "...
- Morgan has emphasized this point in her recent research: "...
- As Sayeed puts it, "...

Phrases such as these are known as signal phrases: they signal to the reader that the research of another is being referred to.

It may be helpful to consult the sections above on the use of quotation marks and other punctuation as well as the information below on various documentation styles.

MLA Style

The most prevalent style of documentation in the Humanities is that of the Modern Language Association (MLA); this is the most widely recommended style in disciplines such as English, comparative literature, rhetoric, and film studies. Sample essays using MLA style appear on the Broadview website. A summary of some main elements appears below.

parenthetical referencing: Under the MLA system a quotation or specific reference to another work is followed by a parenthetical page reference:

> Bonnycastle refers to "the true and lively spirit of opposition" with which Marxist literary criticism invigorates the discipline (204).

The book is then listed under "Works Cited" at the end of the essay:

> Bonnycastle, Stephen. *In Search of Authority: An Introductory Guide to Literary Theory.* 2nd ed. Peterborough: Broadview, 1996.

placing of parenthetical reference: The parenthetical reference comes before the period or comma in the surrounding sentence. (If the quotation ends with punctuation other than a period or comma, then this should precede the end of the quotation, and a period or comma should still follow the parenthetical reference.)

> Ricks refuted this point early on (16), but the claim has continued to be made in recent years.

parenthetical reference when text is in parentheses: If a parenthetical reference occurs within text in parentheses, square brackets are used for the reference.

> The development of a mass literary culture (or a "print culture," to use Williams' expression [88]) took several hundred years in Britain.

author not named in a signal phrase: If the context does not make it clear who the author is, that must be added to the parenthetical reference:

> Even in recent years some have continued to believe that Marxist literary criticism invigorates the discipline with a "true and lively spirit of opposition" (Bonnycastle 204).

two authors/three authors: In these cases all authors should be named either in the signal phrase or in the parenthetical reference.

> Chambliss and Best argue that the importance of this novel is primarily historical (233).
> Two distinguished scholars have recently argued that the importance of this novel is primarily historical (Chambliss and Best 233).

four authors/more authors: In the parenthetical reference use only the first author's name, followed by et al. (short for the Latin *et alia*, "and others").

author unknown/corporate author: Be sure to refer to the relevant organization and/or the title of the piece so as to make the reference clear.

> As the *New York Times* reported in one of its several December 2 articles on the Florida recount, Vice-President Gore looked tired and strained as he answered questions (Gore Press Conference A16).
> According to the *Columbia Encyclopaedia*, in the 1990s Sao Paulo began to rapidly overtake Mexico City as the world's most polluted city ("air pollution" 21).

multi-volume works: Note the volume you are referring to, followed by a colon, before noting the page number.

> Towards the end of *In Darkest Africa* Stanley refers to the Victoria Nyanza (2:387).

parenthetical references to electronic sources: The same rules as for print sources apply, but very frequently electronic sources lack page numbers. In that case refer if possible to paragraph or section number.

> In "The American Scholar" Emerson asserts that America's long apprenticeship to the learning of other lands is drawing to a close (par. 1).

If the author of the electronic source is not given, it may be identified in the parenthetical reference by a short form of the title.

> During the campaign the New Democratic Party's web page for the candidate mentioned his leading role in the protests in Seattle in 2000 (Robinson).

two or more authors with the same last name: If the Works Cited list includes two or more authors with the same last name, the parenthetical reference should supply both first and last names:

> One of the leading economists of the time advocated wage and price controls (Harry Johnston 197).

Shakespeare, the Bible: The Bible and works of drama available in many editions should be cited in a way that enables the reader to check the reference in any edition. Here are parenthetical references for Shakespeare's *The Merchant of Venice*, Act 2, Scene 3, lines 8-13; and for Genesis, Chapter 2, verse 14:

> (MV 2.3 8-13)   (Gen. 2.14)

novels, plays, poems, etc.: The basic principles of the parenthetical reference system are the same regardless of whether one is citing a book, an article in a journal or a magazine, a newspaper, a book review, or a literary work. For poems one cites line numbers rather than page numbers, however, and for any novel available in more than one edition or format it is advisable to include chapter number as well as page number.

works in an anthology or book of readings: In the parenthetical reference for a work in an anthology, use the name of the author of the work, not that of the editor of the anthology. The page number, however, should be that found in the anthology.

> The following citation refers to an article by Fredrik Gleach in an anthology edited by Jennifer Brown and Elizabeth Vibert.

> One of the essays in Brown and Vibert's fine collection argues that we should rethink the Pocahontas myth (Gleach 48).

Following is a sample of text with citations in MLA style:

Urban renewal is as much a matter of psychology as it is of bricks and mortar. As Paul Goldberger has described, there have been many plans to revitalize Havana (50-61). But both that city and the community of Cuban exiles in Florida remain haunted by a sense of absence and separation. As Lourdes Casal reminds us,

> Exile
> is living where there is no house whatever
> in which we were ever children;   (1-3)

The psychology of outsiders also makes a difference. Part of the reason Americans have not much noticed the dire plight of their fifth-largest city is that it does not stir the national imagination (Rybczynski 12). Conversely, there has been far more concern over the state of cities such as New Orleans and Quebec, whose history and architecture excite the romantic imagination. As Nora Phelps has discussed, the past is in itself a key trigger for romantic notions, and it is no doubt inevitable that cities whose history is particularly visible will engender passionate attachments. And as Stephanie Wright and Carole King have detailed in an important case study, almost all French-speaking Quebecers feel their heritage to be bound up with that of Quebec City (2: 171-74). (Richard Ford's character Frank Bascombe has suggested that "New Orleans defeats itself" by longing for "a mystery it doesn't have and never will, if it ever did" [48; ch. 3] but this remains a minority view.)

Georgiana Gibson is also among those who have investigated the interplay between urban psychology and urban reality (Cities 64-89). Gibson's personal website now includes the first of a set of working models she is developing in an attempt to represent the effects of various psychological schema on the landscape.

The above references connect to Works Cited as follows:

Works Cited

Casal, Lourdes. "Definition." Trans. Elizabeth Macklin. *New Yorker* 26 Jan. 1998: 79.

Ford, Richard. *The Sportswriter*. 1986. New York, Random House, 2nd Vintage Edition, 1995.

Gibson, Georgiana. *Cities in the Twentieth Century*. Boston: Beacon, 1997.

———.Homepage.10June1999.30July1999<http:www.geography.byu.edu/gibson/personal.htm>.

———. "The Mind and the City." *Urban Myths: A History*. Ed. Brian Earn and Shelagh Towson. San Francisco: Harbor, 1993. 176–84.

Goldberger, Paul. "Annals of Preservation: Bringing Back Havana." *New Yorker* 26 Jan. 1998: 50–62.

Phelps, Nora. "Pastness and the foundations of romanticism." *Romanticism on the Net* 11 Aug. 1998. 6 July 1999 <http://users.ox.ac.uk/~st0385/phelpmws.html>.

Rybczynski, Witold. "The Fifth City." Rev. of *A Prayer for the City*, by Buzz Bissinger. *New York Review of Books* 5 Feb. 1998: 12–14.

Wright, Stephanie, and Carole King. *Quebec: A History*. Montreal: McGill-Queen's UP, 1998. 2 vols.

Among the details to notice here:

- All important words in titles are capitalized.
- The date appears in Works Cited only.
- When a work has appeared in an edited collection, information on the editors must be included in the reference.
- Only the first author's first and last names are reversed in the list of Works Cited.
- If a book review or film review has a title, that should appear under Works Cited, which should also indicate the title of the book or film being reviewed.
- Translators should be included under Works Cited.
- Publisher as well as city of publication should be given.
- UP is the abbreviation used for University Press.
- Online citations include the date of publication or of last revision followed by the date of access.
- Where two or more works by the same author are included in Works Cited, second and subsequent entries substitute three hyphens and a period for the author name.

OTHER POINTS ABOUT WORKS CITED

scholarly articles: For scholarly journals the Works Cited listing should include issue number and page numbers:

Raedts, Peter. "The Children's Crusade of 1212." *Journal of Medieval History* 3.4 (1977): 279–325.

Hurka, T.M. "Improving on Perfectionism." *Philosophical Review* 99 (1996): 462–73.

newspapers and magazines: Unsigned articles in newspapers and magazines are listed by title:

"Clash over Nobel Cash." *Washington Post* 11 Feb. 1998: A14.

"Getting Hip to Squareness: We Want Our Virginity Back." *The Atlantic Monthly* Feb. 2002: 20–21.

books with no author: Books with no author should be alphabetized by title, except where you have referred to only one entry in an encyclopedia or dictionary:

"Artificial." *Oxford English Dictionary* 2nd edition. Oxford: Oxford UP: 1989.

selections from anthologies or collections of readings: A selection from a book of readings or anthologies should be listed as follows:

Gleach, Frederic W. "Controlled Speculation: Interpreting the Saga of Pocahontas and Captain John Smith." *Reading Beyond Words: Contexts for Native History*. Ed. Jennifer S.H. Brown and Elizabeth Vibert. Peterborough: Broadview, 1996. 21–42.

If you are listing two or more items from the same anthology, use the following format:

Cruikshank, Julie. "Discovery of Gold on the Klondike: Perspectives from Oral Tradition." Brown and Vibert 433–59.

Brown, Jennifer S.H., and Elizabeth Vibert. *Reading Beyond Words: Contexts for Native History*. Peterborough: Broadview, 1996.

Gleach, Frederic W. "Controlled Speculation: Interpreting the Saga of Pocahontas and Captain John Smith." Brown and Vibert 21–42.

material from prefaces, introductions, etc.: If you refer to something from a preface, introduction, or foreword, the reference under Works Cited should begin with the name of the author of that preface, introduction, or foreword:

Warkentin, Germaine. Introduction. *Set in Authority*. By Sara Jeannette Duncan. Peterborough: Broadview, 1996. 9–51.

films, programs, performances, etc.: Films, radio or television programs, interviews, dramatic performances, musical recordings, and paintings should be listed as follows:

Wag the Dog. Dir. Barry Levinson. With Robert DeNiro, Dustin Hoffman. Alliance, 1997.

Twitch City. With Don MacIvor. CBC TV, 13 Jan. 1998.

Bellow, Saul. Interview. *Books in Canada*. Sept. 1996: 2–6.

Counts, Dorothy Ayers, and David R. Counts. Interview. Pamela Wallin Live. CBC Newsworld. 26 Nov. 1997.

Rosengarten, Herbert. Personal interview. 21 Jan. 1998.

A Doll's House. By Henrik Ibsen. Dir. Anthony Page. With Janet McTeer and Owen Teale. Belasco, New York. 22 May 1997.

Dylan, Bob. "Out of Love." Time Out of Mind. Columbia, 1997.

Housser, Yvonne McKague. Cobalt. 1931. National Gallery of Canada, Ottawa.

electronic sources—reference data base or scholarly project: Begin with the author (if any) and title of the source. You should also include the name of any organization sponsoring the site, and include your date of access as well as the electronic address.

Emerson, Ralph Waldo. The American Scholar. (1837) Literary Works of American Transcendentalism. Ed. Ann Woodlief. 1999. Virginia Commonwealth U. 16 Mar. 2001 <http://www.vcu.edu/engweb/transweb/litlist.htm>.

Statistics Canada. "University Enrolment, full-time and part-time, by sex." 24 March 2002. <http://statcan.ca/english/Pgdb/People/Education/educ03a.htm>.

NB In an address listing for an electronic source, do not use a hyphen to break the address at the end of a line; if it must be broken, do so after a slash.

electronic sources—books and periodical articles online: As much as possible, follow the guidelines for in-print books and articles; if the book or article is not paginated, include whatever information is available as to paragraphs or sections. Include both date of access and website address.

Gladwell, Malcolm. "The Art of Failure: Why Some People Choke and Others Panic." *The New Yorker* 21 Aug. 2000: 5 secs. <http://www.gladwell.com/2000_08_21_a_choking.htm>.

electronic sources—CD-ROM: List the source as you would a book, but include CD-ROM before the publication information.

Milne, David. *The Canadian Encyclopedia*. CD-ROM. Toronto: McClelland & Stewart, 2002.

further information: More complete information on changes to MLA style regarding electronic sources may be found at http://www.mla.org.

APA STYLE

APA citation system: The documentation system of the American Psychological Association is commonly used in many social sciences. The APA system emphasizes the date of publication, which must appear within an in-text citation:

> Bonnycastle (1996) refers to "the true and lively spirit of opposition" (p. 204) with which Marxist literary criticism invigorates the discipline.

If the reference does not involve a quotation (as it commonly does not in social science papers) only the date need be given as an in-text citation, providing the author's name appears in the signal phrase:

> Bonnycastle (1996) argues that the oppositional tone of Marxist literary criticism invigorates the discipline.

The reference under "References" at the end of the paper would in either of the above cases be as follows:

Bonnycastle, Stephen (1996). *In search of authority: A guide to literary theory* (2nd ed.). Peterborough: Broadview Press.

If the context does not make clear who the author is, that must be added to the in-text citation.

> Even in recent years some have continued to believe that Marxist literary criticism invigorates the discipline with a "true and lively spirit of opposition" (Bonnycastle, 1996, p. 204).

The basic principles of the in-text citation and reference system are the same regardless of whether one is citing a book, an article in a journal or a magazine, a newspaper, a multi-volume work, a book review, or a literary work (though literary works are rarely cited in papers that follow APA style):

> Urban renewal is as much a matter of psychology as it is of bricks and mortar. As Goldberger (1998) has described, there have been many

plans to revitalize Havana. But both that city and the community of Cuban exiles in Florida remain haunted by a sense of absence and separation. As Lourdes Casal (1998) reminds us,

Exile
is living where there is no house whatever
in which we were ever children;   (1. 1-3)

The psychology of outsiders also makes a difference. Part of the reason Americans have not much noticed the dire plight of their fifth-largest city is that it does not "stir the national imagination" (Rybczynski, 1998, p. 12). Conversely, there has been far more concern over the state of cities such as New Orleans and Quebec, whose history and architecture excite the romantic imagination. As Nora Phelps (1998) has discussed, the past is in itself a key trigger for romantic notions, and it is no doubt inevitable that cities whose history is particularly visible will engender passionate attachments. And as Stephanie Wright and Carole King (1998) have detailed in an important case study, almost all French-speaking Quebecers feel their heritage to be bound up with that of Quebec City. (Richard Ford's character Frank Bascombe has suggested that "New Orleans defeats itself" by longing "for a mystery it doesn't have and never will, if it ever did" [Ford, 1986, 48] but this remains a minority view.)

Georgiana Gibson (1997) is also among those who have investigated the interplay between urban psychology and urban reality. Gibson's personal website (1999) now includes the first of a set of working models she is developing in an attempt to represent the effects of psychological schema on the landscape.

The in-text citations above would connect to References as follows:

References

Casal, L. (1998, January 26). Definition. (Elizabeth Macklin, Trans.) *New Yorker*, 79.

Ford, R. (1986, 2nd Vintage ed. 1995). *The sportswriter*. New York: Random House.

Gibson, G. (1993). The mind and the city. In B. Earn & S. Towson (Eds.), *Urban myths: A history* (pp. 176-84). San Francisco: Harbor.

Gibson, G. (1997). *Cities in the twentieth century*. Boston: Beacon.

Gibson, G. (1999, June 10). Homepage. <http:www.geography.byu.edu/ GIBSON/personal.htm> (1999, July 30).

Goldberger, P. (1998, January 26). Annals of preservation: Bringing back Havana. *New Yorker* 50-62.

Phelps, N. (1998). Pastness and the foundations of romanticism. *Romanticism on the Net*, 11. <http://users.ox.ac.uk/~scat0385/phelpsmws.htm> (1999, July 6).

Rybczynski, W. (1998, February 5). The fifth city. [Review of the book *A prayer for the city*], *New York review of books*, 12-14.

Wright, S. & King, C. (1998). *Quebec: A history* (Vols. 1-2). Montreal: McGill-Queen's University Press.

Among the details to notice in this reference system:

- Where two or more works by the same author are included in References, they are ordered by date of publication.
- APA style prefers author initials rather than first names.
- Only the first words of titles and subtitles are capitalized, except for proper nouns.
- The date appears in brackets at the beginning of each entry in References.
- The in-text citation comes before the period or comma in the surrounding sentence.
- If an in-text citation occurs within text in parentheses, square brackets are used for the reference.
- When a work has appeared in an edited collection, information on the editors must be included in the reference.
- Authors' first and last names are reversed; note the use of the ampersand (&) between author names.
- Translators should be included under Works Cited.
- Publisher as well as city of publication should be given.
- Months and publisher names are not abbreviated; the day of the month follows the name of the month.
- Online references include the date of publication or of last revision in parentheses immediately after the author's name, and date of access, also in parentheses, at the end of the entry.

scholarly articles: For scholarly journals the References listing should include volume number, issue number, and page numbers:

Raedts, Peter (1977). The children's crusade of 1212. *Journal of medieval history* 3, (4), 279–325.

Hurka, T.M. (1996) Improving on perfectionism. *Philosophical review 99*, 462–73.

Unsigned articles in newspapers and magazines are listed by title:

Clash over Nobel cash. (1998, February 11). *Washington post*, A14.

books with no authors: Books with an unknown author should be alphabetized in the References list by title or publisher name:

Oxford English dictionary (2nd ed.). (1989). Oxford: Oxford University Press.

two or more authors with the last same name: If the References list includes two or more authors with the same last name, the signal phrase before the in-text citation should supply first name (or initials):

> One of the leading economists of the time, H. Johnston (1977), advocated wage and price controls.

three to five authors: For works with three to five authors, identify all authors in the signal phrase or the parentheses the first time the source is cited, but thereafter use only the first author's name followed by "et al."

CHICAGO STYLE

Chicago Style citation system: The Chicago Manual of Style sets out guideines for an author-date system of documentation that is comonly used in social sciences such as political science. As with the APA system, this style requires that the date of publication appear within an in-text citation:

> Bonnycastle refers to "the true and lively spirit of opposition" with which Marxist literary criticism invigorates the discipline (Bonnycastle 1996, 204).

If the reference does not involve a quotation (as it commonly does not in social science papers) only the date need be given as an in-text citation, providing the author's name appears in the signal phrase:

> Bonnycastle (1996) argues that the oppositional tone of Marxist literary criticism invigorates the discipline.

The reference under "Bibliography" at the end of the paper would in either of the above cases be as follows:

> Bonnycastle, S. 1996. *In search of authority: An introductory guide to literary theory* 2nd ed. Peterborough: Broadview Press.

The basic principles of the in-text citation and reference system are the same regardless of whether one is citing a book, an article in a journal or a magazine, a newspaper, a multi-volume work, a book review, or a literary work (though literary works are rarely cited in papers that follow Chicago style):

> Urban renewal is as much a matter of psychology as it is of bricks and mortar. As Goldberger (1998) has described, there have been many plans to revitalize Havana. But both that city and the community of Cuban exiles in Florida remain haunted by a sense of absence and separation. As Lourdes Casal (1998) reminds us,

> Exile
> is living where there is no house whatever
> in which we were ever children;   (lines 1-3)

> The psychology of outsiders also makes a difference. Part of the reason Americans have not much noticed the dire plight of their fifth-largest city is that it does not "stir the national imagination" (Rybczynski, 1998, 12). Conversely, there has been far more concern over the state of cities such as New Orleans and Quebec, whose history and architecture excite the romantic imagination. As Nora Phelps (1998) has discussed, the past is in itself a key trigger for romantic notions, and it is no doubt inevitable that cities whose history is particularly visible will engender passionate attachments. And as Stephanie Wright and Carole King (1998) have detailed in an important case study, almost all French-speaking Quebecers feel their heritage to be bound up with that of Quebec City. (Richard Ford's character Frank Bascombe has suggested that "New Orleans defeats itself" by longing "for a mystery it doesn't have and never will, if it ever did" [Ford, 1986, 48] but this remains a minority view.)

> Georgiana Gibson (1997) is also among those who have investigated the interplay between urban psychology and urban reality. Gibson's personal website (1999) now includes the first of a set of working models she is developing in an attempt to represent the effects of psychological schema on the landscape.

The in-text citations above would connect to the Bibliography as follows:

Bibliography

Casal, Lourdes. 1998. Definition. (trans. E. Macklin, Trans.) *New Yorker*, 26 January, 79.

Ford, Richard. 1986. *The sportswriter*. 2nd Vintage ed. 1995. New York, Random House.

Gibson, Georgiana. 1993. The mind and the city. In *Urban myths: A history* edited by Brian Earn & Shelagh Towson. San Francisco: Harbor, 1993.

Gibson, Georgiana. 1997. *Cities in the twentieth century*. Boston: Beacon.

Gibson, Georgiana. 1999. Homepage. 10 June, 1999. <http:www.geography.by/u.edu/GIBSON/personal.htm> (30 July, 1999).

Goldberger, Paul. 1998. Annals of preservation: Bringing back Havana. *New Yorker* 26 January, 50-62.

Phelps, Nora. 1998. Pastness and the foundations of romanticism. *Romanticism on the net* 11, (May 1999) <http://users.ox.ac.uk/~scat0385/phelpsmws.htm> (6 July, 1999).

Rybczynski, Witold. 1998. Review of *A prayer for the city* by D.B. Smith. *New York review of books,* 5 February, 12-14.

Wright, Stephanie & Carole King. 1998. *Quebec: A history* Vols. 1-2. Montreal: McGill-Queen's University Press.

Among the details to notice in this reference system:

- Where two or more works by the same author are included in the Bibliography, they are ordered by date of publication.
- Only the first words of titles and subtitles are capitalized, except for proper nouns.
- The date appears at the beginning of each entry in the Bibliography.
- There is no punctuation between author and date in the in-text citation.
- When a work has appeared in an edited collection information on the editors must be included in the reference.
- Authors' first and last names are reversed except for second authors.
- Translators should be included in the bibliographic reference.
- Publisher as well as city of publication should be given.
- Months and publisher names are not abbreviated.
- The day of the month precedes the name of the month.
- Online references include the year of publication after the author's name, and the date of access in parentheses at the end of the entry.

scholarly articles: For scholarly journals the Bibliography should include volume number, issue number, and page numbers:

Raedts, Peter. 1977. The children's crusade of 1212. *Journal of medieval history* 3 (4): 279-325.

Hurka, T.M. 1996. Improving on perfectionism. *Philosophical review*. 99: 462-73.

newspaper articles: Newspaper items are rarely listed separately. Instead, the name of the paper and the relevant run of dates may be given.

books with no author: Books with no specific or known author should be alphabetized in the Bibliography by title:

Oxford English dictionary. 1989. 2d ed. Oxford: Oxford University Press.

two or more authors with the same name: If the Bibliography includes two or more authors with the same last name, the signal phrase before the in-text citation should supply first name (or initials):

> One of the leading economists of the time, H. Johnston (1977), advocated wage and price controls.

unpublished works: Unpublished material is treated much as are journal articles:

Perkins, B. 1988. An investigation of voting patterns in the 1993 Canadian election. Ph.D. diss., University of Alberta, Edmonton.

Canada. House of Commons. Debates, 17 March 1997.

Canada. Senate. Special Committee on Election Spending. Interim report. 1988.

U.S. Congress. House Committee on Ways and Means. Hearings on Extension of North American Free Trade Agreement. 99th Cong., 1st sess., 1997. Vol. 1.

U.S. Congress. House Committee on Ways and Means. Subcommittee on Trade. Hearing #105-32 on Free Trade Area of the Americas. 105th Congress. 10 August 1997.<http://frwebgate.access.gpo.gov/cgi-bin/getdoc.cgidbname=_house_hearings&/docid=f:50672.wais> (22 July 1999).

CBE STYLE

CBE citation system: The Council of Biology Editors style of documentation is commonly used in the natural sciences and the physical sciences. Guidelines are set out in *Scientific Style and Format: The CBE Manual for Authors, Editors, and Publishers.*

in-text citation: Citations in CBE style may follow alternative formats. In one format, superscript numbers are inserted after any mention of a source:

1. In-text citation by using citation-sequence superscript format

> Gibson[1] argues that the variables have not been sufficiently well controlled for in this type of experiment.

This system also requires a superscript [1] for any other citations of the same work.

2. In-text citation by name-year format

An alternative system is to cite the author name and year of publication in brackets:

> Gibson argues that the variables have not been sufficiently well controlled for this type of experiment (Gibson 2000).

> The key contributions to the study of variables in the 1990s (Soames 1993; Zelinsky 1997) have both been strongly challenged in recent years.

CBE style list of references: Citations in CBE style must correspond to items in a "List of References." In the citation-sequence superscript format, the references are listed in the sequence in which they have been cited in the text:

1 Soames G. Variables in large data-base experiments. Natural history 1999 Mar: 144-51.
2 Zelinsky KL. The study of variables: an overview. New York: Academic; 1994. 216 p.

In the name-year format, the references are listed alphabetically:

Soames, G. 1999 Mar. Variables in large data-base experiments. Natural history: 144-51.
Zelinsky KL. 1994. The study of variables: an overview. New York: Academic. 216 p.

The basic principles of the system are the same regardless of whether one is citing a book, an article in a journal or magazine, a newspaper article, or an electronic document.

Here is a sample using citation-sequence format:

> Over the centuries scientific study has evolved into several distinct disciplines. Physics, chemistry, and biology were established early on; in the nineteenth and twentieth centuries they were joined by others, such as geology and ecology. Much as the disciplines have their separate spheres, the sphere of each overlaps those of others. This may be most obvious in the case of ecology, which some have claimed to be a discipline that makes a holistic approach to science respectable.[1] In the case of geology, as soon as it became clear in the nineteenth century that the fossil record of geological life would be central to the future of geology, the importance of connecting with the work of

biologists became recognised.[2] Nowadays it is not surprising to have geological research conducted jointly by biologists and geologists (e.g. the work of Newton and Trewman[3]). And, with the acceptance of "continental drift" theories in the 1960s and 1970s, physics came to be increasingly relied on for input into discussions of such topics as collision tectonics (e.g. Pfiffton, Earn, and Brome[4]).

The growth of the subdiscipline of biochemistry at the point of overlap between biology and chemistry is well-known, but many are unaware that the scope of biological physics is almost as broad; Frauenfrommer[5] provides a helpful survey. Nowadays it is not uncommon, indeed, to see research such as the recent study by Corel, Marks, and Hutner,[6] or that by Balmberg, Passano, and Proule,[7] both of which draw on biology, chemistry, and physics simultaneously.

Interdisciplinary scientific exploration has also been spurred by the growth of connections between the pure sciences and applied sciences such as meteorology, as even a glance in the direction of recent research into such topics as precipitation[8] or crating[9] confirms. But to the extent that science is driven by the applied, will it inextricably become more and more driven by commercial concerns? Christopher Haupt-Lehmann[10] thinks not.

The citations above would connect to References as follows:

References

1 Branmer A. Ecology in the twentieth century: a history. New Haven; Yale UP; 1989. 320 p.
2 Lyell C. Principles of geology. London; John Murray; 1830. 588 p.
3 Newton MJ, Trewman NH, Elser S. A new jawless invertebrate from the Middle Devonian. Paleontology 2001; 44 (1):43–52.
4 Pfiffton QA, Earn PK, Brome C. Collision tectonics and dynamic modelling. Tectonics 2000; 19(6):1065–1094.
5 Frauenfrommer H. Introduction. Frauenfrommer H, Hum G, Glazer RG, editors. Biological physics third international symposium; 1998 Mar 8-9; Santa Fe NM [Melville, NY]: American Institute of Physics. 386 p.
6 Corel B, Marks VJ, Hutner H. The modelling effect of Elpasolites. Chemical Sciences 2000; 55(10):935–8.
7 Balmberg NJ, Passano C, Proule AB. The Lorenz-Fermi-Pasta-Ulam experiment. Physica D: Nonlinear phenomena [serial online] 2000; 138(1):1–43. Available at www.elseviere.com/locate/phys. (Accessed March 21, 2001).
8 Caine JS, Gross SM, Baldwin G. Melting effect as a factor in precipitation-type forecasting. Weather and forecasting 2000; 15(6):700–14.

9 Pendleton AJ. Gawler cration. Regional geology 2001; 11:999–1016.

10 Haupt-Lehmann C. Money and science: the latest word. New York times 2001 Mar 23; Sect D:22 (col 2).

Among the details to notice in this reference system:

- The entries in References are listed in the order they first appear in the text.
- Unpunctuated initials rather than first names are used in References.
- The date appears near the end of the reference, before any page reference.
- Only the first words of titles are capitalized (except for proper nouns).
- When a work has appeared in an edited collection the names of the editor(s) as well as the author(s) must appear in the reference.
- "and" is used for in-text citations of works with more than one author — but not in the corresponding reference.
- Publisher as well as city of publication should be given.
- Months and journal names are generally abbreviated.
- References to electronic publications include the date of access as well as date of publication or latest revision.
- Names of articles appear with no surrounding quotation marks; names of books appear with no italics.

Here is the same passage with the CBE name-year format used:

Over the centuries scientific study has evolved into several distinct disciplines. Physics, chemistry, and biology were established early on; in the nineteenth and twentieth centuries they were joined by others, such as geology and ecology. Much as the disciplines have their separate spheres, the sphere of each overlaps those of others. This may be most obvious in the case of ecology, which some have claimed to be a discipline that makes a holistic approach to science respectable (Branmer 1989). In the case of geology, as soon as it became clear in the nineteenth century that the fossil record of geological life would be central to the future of geology, the importance of connecting with the work of biologists became recognised (Lyell 1830). Nowadays it is not surprising to have geological research conducted jointly by biologists and geologists (e.g. Newton, Trewman, and Elser 2001). And, with the acceptance of "continental drift" theories in the 1960s and 1970s, physics came to be increasingly relied on for input into discussions of such topics as collision tectonics (e.g. Pfiffton, Earn, and Brome 2000).

The growth of the subdiscipline of biochemistry at the point of overlap between biology and chemistry is well-known, but many are unaware that the scope of biological physics is almost as broad; Frauenfrommer, Hum, and Glazer (1998) provide a helpful survey. Nowadays it is not uncommon, indeed, to see research such as the recent study by Corel, Marks, and Hutner (2001) or that by Balmberg, Passano, and Proule (2000), both of which draw on biology, chemistry, and physics simultaneously.

Interdisciplinary scientific exploration has also been spurred by the growth of connections between the pure sciences and applied sciences such as meteorology, as even a glance in the direction of recent research into such topics as precipitation (Caine, Gross, and Baldwin 2000) or crating (Pendleton 2001) confirms. But to the extent that science is driven by the applied, will it inextricably become more and more driven by commercial concerns? Christopher Haupt-Lehmann (2001) thinks not.

The citations above would connect to References as follows:

References

Branmer A. 1989. Ecology in the twentieth century: a history. New Haven; Yale UP; 320 p.

Balmberg NJ, Passano C, Proule AB. The Lorenz-Fermi-Pasta-Ulam experiment. Physica D: Nonlinear phenomena [serial online] 2000; 138(1):1-43. Available at www.elseviere.com/locate/phys. (Accessed March 21, 2001).

Caine JS, Gross SM, Baldwin G. Melting effect as a factor in precipitation-type forecasting. Weather and Forecasting 2000; 15(6):700-14.

Corel B, Marks VJ, Hutner H. The modelling effect of Elpasolites. Chemical Sciences 2000; 55(10):935-8.

Frauenfrommer H. Introduction. Frauenfrommer H, Hum G, Glazer RG, editors. Biological physics third international symposium; 1998 Mar 8-9; Santa Fe NM. [Melville, NY]: American Institute of Physics. 386 p.

Haupt-Lehmann C. Money and science: the latest word. New York times 2001 Mar 23; Sect D:22 (col 2).

Lyell C. 1830. Principles of geology. London; John Murray. 588 p.

Newton MJ, Trewman NH, Elser S. A new jawless invertebrate from the Middle Devonian. Peleontology 2001; 44 (1):43-52.

Pendleton AJ. Gawler cration. Regional geology 2001; 11:999-1016.

Pfiffton QA, Earn PK, Brome C. Collision tectonics and dynamic modelling. Tectonics 2000; 19(6):1065-1094.

Among the details to notice in this reference system:

- The entries in References are listed in alphabetical order by author.
- Unpunctuated initials rather than first names are used in References.

- The date appears immediately after author name(s) at the beginning of the reference, before any page reference.
- The in-text citation comes before the period or comma in the surrounding sentence.
- Only the first words of titles are capitalized (except for proper nouns).
- When a work has appeared in an edited collection the names of the editor(s) as well as the author(s) must appear in the reference.
- "and" is used for in-text citations of works with more than one author—but not in the corresponding reference.
- Publisher as well as city of publication should be given.
- Months and journal names are generally abbreviated.
- References to electronic publications include the date of access as well as date of publication or latest revision.
- Names of articles appear with no surrounding quotation marks; names of books, journals, etc. appear with no italics.

Style Manuals in Various Disciplines

This book includes coverage of four commonly used documentation systems. Following is information on practices in a wider variety of disciplines:

Biology: Council of Biology Editors. *CBE Style Manual: A Guide for Authors, Editors, and Publishers in the Biological Sciences*. 5th ed. Bethesda: Council of Biology Editors, 1983.

Chemistry: American Chemical Society. *American Chemical Society Style Guide: A Manual for Authors and Editors*. 2nd ed. Washington: American Chemical Society Publishing, 1986.

English/Modern Languages: Gibaldi, Joseph, and Walter S. Achtert. *MLA Handbook for Writers of Research Papers*. 3rd ed. New York: Modern Languages Assn. of America, 1988.

Geology: Bates, Robert L., Rex Buchanan, and Marla Adkins-Heljeson, eds. *Geowriting: A Guide to Writing, Editing, and Printing in Earth Science*. 5th ed. Alexandria: American Geological Inst., 1992.

History: There is no universally accepted style of documentation for history. Many journals use some variety of Chicago Style; many use traditional footnotes or endnotes. For students the most important guideline is thus to follow whatever instructions each instructor may give you.

Law: Columbia Law Review. *A Uniform System of Citation*. 15th ed. Cambridge: Harvard Law Review, 1991.

Linguistics: Linguistic Society of America. "LSA Style Sheet." Published annually in the December issue of the LSA *Bulletin*.

Mathematics: American Mathematical Society. *A Manual for Authors of Mathematical Papers*. 8th ed. Providence: American Mathematical Society, 1984.

Medicine: International Steering Committee of Medical Editors. "Uniform Requirements for Manuscripts Submitted to Biomedical Journals." *Annals of Internal Medicine* 90 (Jan. 1979): 95-99.

Physics: American Institute of Physics. *Style Manual for Guidance in the Preparation of Papers*. 4th ed. New York: American Inst. of Physics, 1990.

Philosophy: There is no universally accepted style of documentation for philosophy. Many journals use some variety of Chicago Style; many use traditional footnotes or endnotes. For students the most important guideline is thus to follow whatever instructions each instructor may give you.

Psychology: American Psychological Association. *Publication Manual of the American Psychological Association*. 4th ed. Washington: American Psychological Assn., 1994.

FOR THOSE WHOSE NATIVE LANGUAGE IS NOT ENGLISH

The fact that different languages have different grammatical and syntactical conventions creates particular problems for anyone learning a new language. This section focusses on some of the peculiarities of English that are most likely to present difficulties to those learning the language.

ARTICLES

Articles are words used to introduce nouns. Unlike many other languages, English often requires the use of articles:

needs checking	We are interested in house with garage.
revised	We are interested in a house with a garage.

There are only three articles—*a, an,* and *the*. Articles show whether or not one is drawing attention to a <u>particular</u> person or thing. For example, we would say *I stood beside a house* if we did not want to draw attention to that particular house, but *I stood beside the house that the Taylors used to live in* if we wanted to draw attention to the particular house.

A (or *an* if the noun following begins with a vowel) is an <u>indefinite</u> article—used when you do not want to be definite or specific about which thing or person you are referring to. *The* is a <u>definite</u> article, used when you do wish to call attention to the particular thing or person. Remember that if you use *the* you are suggesting that there can be only <u>one</u> of what you are referring to.

In order to use articles properly in English it is important to understand the distinction English makes between nouns naming things that are countable (*houses, books, trees,* etc.) and nouns naming things that are not countable (*milk, confusion,* etc). Some non-count nouns name things that it does seem possible to count: *sugar, grass, furniture,* etc. In such cases counting must in English be done indirectly: *a grain of sugar, two grains of sugar, three blades of grass, four pieces of furniture,* and so on.

Distinguishing between count and non-count nouns is inevitably a challenge for those whose first language is not English. A dictionary such as *The Oxford Advanced Learner's Dictionary* can be very helpful; unlike most dictionaries it indicates whether or not each noun is a count noun.

needs checking	They bought a nice furniture for the living room.
revised	They bought a nice piece of furniture for the living room.

Frequently Used Non-Count Nouns

abstractions: advice, anger, beauty, confidence, courage, employment, fun, happiness, hate, health, honesty, information, intelligence, knowledge, love, poverty, truth, wealth, wisdom.

to eat and drink: bacon, beef, beer, bread, broccoli, butter, cabbage, candy, cauliflower, celery, cereal, cheese, chicken, chocolate, coffee, corn, cream, fish, flour, fruit, ice, ice cream, lettuce, margarine, meat, milk, oil, pasta, pepper, rice, salt, spinach, sugar, tea, water, wine, yogurt.

other substances: air, cement, clothing, coal, dirt, equipment, furniture, gas, gasoline, gold, grass, homework, jewelry, luggage, lumber, machinery, metal, mail, money, music, paper, petroleum, plastic, poetry, pollution, research, scenery, silver, snow, soap, steel, timber, traffic, transportation, violence, weather, wood, wool, work.

- NB The plural of many of these non-count nouns may be employed when you want to denote more than one type of the substance. *Breads*, for example, refers to different sorts of bread; *coffees* refers to different types of coffee, and so on.

531. **dropping the article**: Articles are not used in English to the same extent that they are used in some other languages; nouns can frequently stand alone without their article, particularly when they are being used in a general, non-specific sense. When used in this way, non-count and plural-count nouns need no article.

needs checking	If the English is to be spoken correctly, the good grammar is important.
revised	If English is to be spoken correctly, good grammar is important.
needs checking	The freedom is something everyone values.
revised	Freedom is something everyone values.

In most cases no article is necessary before a noun that is capitalized:

needs checking	They were strolling through the Stanley Park.
revised	They were strolling through Stanley Park.

Unfortunately, there are many exceptions to this rule (e.g. *the Hebrides, the Netherlands, the Dominican Republic, the United Kingdom, the Soviet Union, the United States*). A dictionary such as *The Oxford Advanced Learner's Dictionary* should be consulted in any case where you are uncertain if an article is needed.

532. **continuous verb tenses** (see also under Verb Tenses in Chapter One): In English the continuous tenses are not normally used with many verbs having to do with feelings, emotions, or senses. Some of these verbs are *to see, to hear, to understand, to believe, to hope, to know, to think* (meaning *believe*), *to trust, to comprehend, to mean, to doubt, to suppose, to wish, to want, to love, to desire, to prefer, to dislike, to hate.*

needs checking	He is not understanding what I mean.
revised	He does not understand what I mean.
needs checking	At that time he was believing that everything on Earth was created within one week.
revised	At that time he believed that everything on Earth was created within one week.

533. **omission or repetition of the subject**: With the exception of imperatives (e.g. *come here, don't stop*) where *you* is understood to be the subject, English requires that the subject of the sentence be stated. Some other languages permit the omission of the subject in various circumstances where the subject may be inferred. English does not.

needs checking	The protesters demonstrated peacefully; stood quietly outside the gates of the Prime Minister's residence.
revised	The protesters demonstrated peacefully; they stood quietly outside the gates of the Prime Minister's residence.

If the subject appears after the verb, a frequent requirement in English is for *there* or *it* to be added as an expletive before the verb *to be.*

needs checking	Is not possible to finish the job this week.
revised	It is not possible to finish the job this week.
needs checking	By the end of the century, were almost one million more people in Houston than there had been in 1980.
revised	By the end of the century, there were almost one million more people in Houston than there had been in 1980.

Within a single clause English does not permit the repetition of either the subject or the object.

needs checking	The line that is longest in a triangle it is called the hypotenuse.
revised	The line that is longest in a triangle is called the hypotenuse.
needs checking	The members of the cast loved the play that they were acting in it.
revised	The members of the cast loved the play that they were acting in.

the conditional: Those whose native language is not English often have particular difficulty with the way in which English treats conditional statements; see Chapter 1 for a full discussion of these.

APPENDIX 1: A REFERENCE GUIDE TO BASIC GRAMMAR

PARTS OF SPEECH

Nouns

Nouns are words that name people, things, places, or qualities. Some examples follow:

- names of people: boy, John, parent
- names of things: hat, spaghetti, fish
- names of places: Saskatoon, Zambia, New York
- names of qualities: silence, intelligence, anger

Nouns can be used to fill the gaps in sentences like these:

- I saw _____ at the market yesterday.
- He dropped the _____ into the gutter.
- Has she lost a lot of _____ ?
- Hamilton is a _____ with several hundred thousand people living in it.

Some nouns (e.g. *sugar, milk, confusion*) are uncountable—that is, we cannot say *a sugar, two sugars,* or *three sugars.*

Pronouns

Pronouns replace or stand for nouns. For example, instead of saying, *The man slipped on a banana peel* or *George slipped on a banana peel,* we can replace the noun *man* (or the noun *George*) with the pronoun *he* and say *He slipped on a banana peel.*

definite and indefinite pronouns: Whereas a pronoun such as *he* refers to a definite person, the words *each, every, either, neither, one, another,* and *much* are indefinite. They may be used as pronouns or as adjectives; in either case, a singular verb is needed.

- Each player wants to do his best.
    (Here the word *each* is an adjective, describing the noun *player*.)
- Each wants to do his best.
    (Here the word *each* is a pronoun, acting as the subject of the sentence.)
- Each of the players wants to do his best.
    (The word *each* is still a pronoun, this time followed by the phrase *of the players*. But it is the pronoun *each* that is the subject of the sentence; the verb must be the singular *wants*.)

possessive pronouns and adjectives: See under Adjectives below.

relative pronouns: These pronouns relate back to a noun that has been used earlier in the same sentence. Look at how repetitious these sentences sound:

- I talked to the man. The man wore a red hat.

We could of course replace the second *man* with *he*. Even better, though, is to relate or connect the second idea to the first by using a relative pronoun:

- I talked to the man who wore a red hat.
- I found the pencil. I had lost the pencil.
- I found the pencil that I had lost.

The following are all relative pronouns:

who   whose (has other uses too)
which   that (has other uses too)
whom

Try replacing the second noun in these pairs of sentences with a relative pronoun, so as to make only one sentence out of each pair:

- I polished the table. I had built the table.
- Premier Calvert is vacationing this week in Quebec's Eastern Townships. The Premier cancelled a planned holiday last fall.
- The word *other* is often used by literary theorists when speaking of a sense of strangeness in the presence of cultural difference. *Other* is usually preceded by the definite article when so used.

pronouns acting as subject and as object: We use different personal pronouns depending on whether we are using them as the subject or the object and whether they are singular or plural.

Subject pronouns:		
	I	we
	you	you
	he/she/it	they
	who, what, which	who, what, which (interrogative)

Object pronouns:		
	me	us
	you	you
	him/her/it	them
	whom, what, which	who, whom, what, which (interrogative)

- He shot the sheriff.
  (Here the pronoun *he* is the subject of the sentence.)
- The sheriff shot him.
  (Here the word *him* is the object; *the sheriff* is the subject.)
- That's the man who shot the sheriff.
  (Here the pronoun *who* is the subject of the clause *who shot the sheriff*)
- That's the man whom the sheriff shot.
  (Here the pronoun *whom* is the object; *the sheriff* is the subject.)

The distinctions between *I* and *me* and between *who* and *whom* are treated more fully under Pronoun Problems.

ARTICLES

These are words used to introduce nouns. There are only three of them: *a, an,* and *the.* Articles show whether or not one is drawing attention to a particular person or thing.

For example, we would say *I stood beside a house* if we did not want to draw attention to that particular house, but *I stood beside the house that the Taylors used to live in* if we did want to draw attention to the particular house. *A* (or *an* if the noun following begins with a vowel) is an indefinite article—used when you do not wish to be definite or specific about which thing or person you are referring to. *The* is a definite article, used when you do wish to call attention to the particular thing or person. Remember that if you use *the*, you are suggesting that there can be only one of what you are referring to.

Choose the appropriate article (*a, an,* or *the*):

- _____ moon shone brightly last night.
- She had _____ long conversation with _____ friend.
- Have you ever driven _____ car?
- Have you driven _____ car that your wife bought on Monday?

ADJECTIVES

Adjectives are words used to tell us more about (describe or modify) nouns or pronouns. Here are some examples of adjectives:

big	good	heavy
small	bad	expensive
pretty	careful	fat
quick	slow	thin

- e.g. The fat man lifted the heavy table.
  (Here the adjective *fat* describes or tells us more about the noun *man*, and the adjective *heavy* describes the noun *table*.)

- e.g. The fast runner finished ahead of the slow one.
  (*Fast* describes *runner* and *slow* describes *one*.)

Notice that adjectives usually come before the nouns that they describe. This is not always the case, however; when the verb *to be* is used, adjectives often come after the noun or pronoun, and after the verb:

- e.g. That woman is particularly careful about her finances.
  (*Careful* describes *woman*.)
- e.g. It is too difficult for me to do.
  (*Difficult* describes *it*.)

Adjectives can be used to fill the gaps in sentences like these:

- This _____ sweater was knitted by hand.
- As soon as we entered _____ the house we heard a clap of thunder.
- Those shoes are very_____.
- Derrida's argument could fairly be described as _____.

Some words can be either adjectives or pronouns, depending on how they are used. That is the case with the indefinite pronouns (see above), and also with certain possessives (words that show possession):

Possessive adjectives:	my	our
	your	your
	his/her	their
	whose	whose
Possessive pronouns:	mine	ours
	yours	yours
	his/hers	theirs
	whose	whose

- e.g. I have my cup, and he has his.
  (Here the word *his* is a pronoun, used in place of the noun *cup*.)
- e.g. He has his cup.
  (Here the word *his* is an adjective, describing the noun *cup*.)
- Whose book is this?
  (Here the word *whose* is an adjective, describing the noun *book*.)
- Whose is this?
  (Here the word *whose* is a pronoun, acting as the subject of the sentence.)

VERBS

Verbs are words that express actions or states of affairs. Most verbs can be conveniently thought of as *doing* words (e.g. *open, feel, do, carry, see, think, combine, send*), but a few verbs do not fit into this category. Indeed, the most common verb of all—*be*—expresses a state of affairs, not a particular action that is done. Verbs are used to fill gaps in sentences like these:

- I _____ very quickly, but I _____ not _____ up with my brother.
- She usually _____ to sleep at 9:30.
- Stephen _____ his breakfast very quickly.
- They _____ a large farm near Newcastle.
- There _____ many different languages that people _____ in India.

One thing that makes verbs different from other parts of speech is that verbs have tenses; in other words, they change their form depending on the time you are talking about. For example, the present tense of the verb *to be* is *I am, you are, he is*, etc., while the past tense is *I was, you were, he was*, etc. If unsure whether or not a particular word is a verb, one way to check is to ask if it has different tenses. For example, if one thought that perhaps the word *football* might be a verb, one need only ask oneself if it would be correct to say, *I footballed, I am footballing, I will football,* and so on. Obviously it would not be, so one knows that *football* is the noun that names the game, not a verb that expresses an action. See the first chapter in this book for a discussion of verb tenses.

ADVERBS

These words are usually used to tell us more about (describe or modify) verbs, although they can also be used to tell us more about adjectives or about other adverbs. They answer questions like *How...?, When...?,* and *To what extent...?,* and often they end with the letters *ly*. Here are a few examples, with some adjectives also listed for comparison:

Adjective	*Adverb*	*Adverb*
careful	carefully	today
beautiful	beautifully	often
thorough	thoroughly	very
sudden	suddenly	
slow	slowly	
easy	easily	
good	well	

- He walked carefully.
  (The adverb *carefully* tells us how he walked; it describes the verb *walked*.)

- He is a careful boy.
  (The adjective *careful* describes the noun *boy*.)
- My grandfather died suddenly last week.
  (The adverb *suddenly* tells how he died; it describes the verb *died*.)
- We were upset by the sudden death of my grandfather.
  (The adjective *sudden* describes the noun *death*.)
- She plays the game very well.
  (The adverb *well* tells us how she plays; it describes the verb *plays*. The adverb *very* describes the adverb *well*.)
- She played a good game this afternoon.
  (The adjective *good* describes the noun *game*.)
- She played a very good game.
  (The adverb *very* describes the adjective *good*, telling us how good it was.)
- According to his Press Secretary, Bush will meet Putin soon.
  (The adverb *soon* describes the verb *will meet*, telling when the action will happen.)

Choose adverbs to fill the gaps in these sentences:

- Ralph writes very _____.
- The judge spoke _____ to Milken after he had been convicted on six counts of stock manipulation and fraud.
- They were _____ late for the meeting this morning.

PREPOSITIONS

Prepositions are joining words, normally used before nouns or pronouns. Some of the most common prepositions are as follows:

about	after	across
at	before	for
from	in	into
of	on	off
over	to	until
with		

Choose prepositions to fill the gaps in these sentences:

- I will tell you _____ it _____ the morning.
- Please try to arrive _____ eight o'clock.
- He did not come back _____Toronto _____ yesterday.
- I received a letter _____ my sister.

CONJUNCTIONS

Conjunctions are normally used to join groups of words together, and in particular join clauses together. Some examples:

because	unless	after
although	until	if
and	since	or
as	before	that

- They stopped playing because they were tired.
  (The conjunction *because* joins the group of words *because they were tired* to the group of words *They stopped playing*.)
- I will give her your message if I see her.
  (The conjunction *if* introduces the second group of words and joins it to the first.)

Many conjunctions can also act as other parts of speech, depending on how they are used. Notice the difference in each of these pairs of sentences:

- He will not do anything about it until the morning.
  (Here *until* is a preposition joining the noun *morning* to the rest of the sentence.)
- He will not do anything about it until he has discussed it with his wife.
  (Here *until* is a conjunction introducing the clause *until he has discussed it with his wife*.)
- I slept for half an hour after dinner.
  (Here *after* is a preposition joining the noun *dinner* to the rest of the sentence.)
- I slept for half an hour after they had gone home.
  (Here *after* is a conjunction introducing the clause *after they had gone home*.)
- She wants to buy that dress.
  (Here *that* is an adjective describing the noun *dress*: "Which dress?" "That dress!")
- George said that he was unhappy.
  (Here *that* is a conjunction introducing the clause *that he was unhappy*.)

Choose conjunctions to fill the gaps in the following sentences:

- We believed _____ we would win.
- They sat down in the shade _____ it was hot.
- My father did not speak to me _____ he left.

PARTS OF SENTENCES

SUBJECT

The subject is the thing, person, or quality about which something is said in a clause. The subject is usually a noun or pronoun.

- The man went to town.
    (The sentence is about the man, not about the town; thus the noun *man* is the subject.)
- Groundnuts are an important crop in Nigeria.
    (The sentence is about groundnuts, not about crops or about Nigeria; thus the noun *groundnuts* is the subject.)
- Nigeria is the most populous country in Africa.
    (The sentence is about Nigeria, not about countries or about Africa; thus the noun *Nigeria* is the subject.)
- He followed me wherever I went.
    (The pronoun *He* is the subject.)

core subject: The core subject is the single noun or pronoun that forms the subject.

complete subject: The complete subject is the subject together with any adjectives or adjectival phrases modifying it.

- e.g. The lady in the huge hat went to the market to buy groceries.

The core subject is *the lady* and the complete subject is *the lady in the huge hat*.

OBJECT

An object is something or someone towards which an action or feeling is directed. In grammar an object is the thing, person, or quality affected by the action of the verb. (To put it another way, it receives the action of the verb.) Like a subject, an object normally is made up of a noun or pronoun.

direct object: The direct object is the thing, person, or quality directly affected by the action of the verb. A direct object usually answers the question *What... ?* or *Who...?* Notice that direct objects are not introduced by prepositions.

indirect object: The indirect object is the thing, person, or quality that is indirectly affected by the action of the verb. All indirect objects could be expressed differently by making them the objects of the prepositions *to* or *for*. Instead, the prepositions have been omitted. Indirect objects answer the questions, *To whom?* and *For whom?*

- McGriff hit the ball a long way.
    (What did he hit? The ball. *The ball* is the direct object of the verb *hit*.)
- She threw me her hat.

(What did she throw? Her hat. *Her hat* is the direct object. To whom did she throw it? To me. *Me* is the indirect object. Note that the sentence could be rephrased: *She threw her hat to me.*)

- They gave a watch to their father for Christmas.
  (direct object is *watch*; indirect object *father*)

PREDICATE

The predicate is everything that is said about the subject. In the example on the previous page, *went to the market to buy groceries* is the predicate. A predicate <u>always</u> includes a verb.

CLAUSE

A distinct group of words that includes both a subject and a predicate. Thus a clause always includes a verb.

PHRASE

A distinct group of words that does <u>not</u> include both a subject and a verb. Examples:

Clauses	*Phrases*
because he is strong	because of his strength (no verb)
before she comes home	before the meeting (no verb)
the professor likes me	from Halifax
a tree fell down	at lunch
who came to dinner	in the evening

TYPES OF CLAUSES

main clause: A main clause is a group of words which is, or could be, a sentence on its own.

subordinate clause: A subordinate clause is a clause which could <u>not</u> form a complete sentence on its own.

Except for *and*, *but*, and *or*, conjunctions do not introduce main clauses, so if a clause begins with a word such as *because*, *although*, *after*, or *if*, you can be confident it is a subordinate clause. Similarly, relative pronouns introduce subordinate clauses—never main clauses.

- She lives near Pittsburgh.
  (One main clause forming a complete sentence. The pronoun *She* is the subject, *lives* is the verb, and the preposition *near* and the noun *Pittsburgh* together form a phrase.)

- He danced in the street because he was feeling happy.
  main clause: He danced in the street
  subject: _____
  predicate: _____
  subordinate clause: because he was feeling happy
  subject: _____
  predicate: _____
- Mavis has married a man who is older than her father.
  main clause: Mavis has married a man
  subject: _____
  predicate: _____
  subordinate clause: who is older than her father
  subject: _____
  predicate: _____

TYPES OF SUBORDINATE CLAUSES

adjectival subordinate clause: a subordinate clause that tells us more about a noun or pronoun. Adjectival clauses begin with relative pronouns such as *who, whom, whose, which,* and *that.*

adverbial subordinate clause: a subordinate clause that tells us more about the action of the verb—telling how, when, why, or where the action occurred.

noun subordinate clause: a clause that acts like a noun to form the subject or object of a sentence.

Examples:

- He talked at length to his cousin, who quickly became bored.
  (*Who quickly became bored* is an adjectival subordinate clause, telling us more about the noun *cousin.*)
  subject of subordinate clause: the pronoun *who*
  verb in subordinate clause: _____
  subject of main clause: the pronoun *He*
  verb in main clause: _____
- My husband did not like the gift that I gave him.
  (*That I gave him* is an adjectival subordinate clause telling us more about the noun *gift.*)
  subject of subordinate clause: the pronoun *I*
  verb in subordinate clause: _____
  subject of main clause: _____
  verb in main clause: _____
- The boy whom she wants to marry is very poor.
  (*Whom she wants to marry* is an adjectival subordinate clause telling us more about the noun *boy.* Notice that here the subordinate clause appears in the middle of the main clause, *The boy is very poor.*)

subject of subordinate clause: _____
verb in subordinate clause: _____
subject of main clause: _____
verb in main clause: _____

- I felt worse after I had been to the doctor.
  (*After I had been to the doctor* is an adverbial subordinate clause telling you <u>when</u> I felt worse.)
- He could not attend because he had broken his leg.
  (*Because he had broken his leg* is an adverbial subordinate clause telling you <u>why</u> he could not attend.)
- She looked as if she had seen a ghost.
  (*As if she had seen a ghost* is an adverbial subordinate clause telling you <u>how</u> she looked.)
- What he said was very interesting.
  (*What he said* is a noun clause acting as the subject of the sentence, in the same way that the noun *conversation* acts as the subject in *The conversation was very interesting.*)
- Sue-Ellen told me that she wanted to become a lawyer.
  (*That she wanted to become a lawyer* is a noun clause acting as the object, in the same way that the noun *plans* acts as the object in *Sue-Ellen told me her plans.*)

TYPES OF PHRASES

adjectival phrase: a phrase that tells us more about a noun or pronoun.

adverbial phrase: a phrase that tells us more about the action of a verb, answering questions such as *When...?, Where...?, How...?, and Why...?*

- The boy in the new jacket got into the car.
  (*In the new jacket* is an adjectival phrase telling us more about the noun *boy.*)
- I drank from the cup with a broken handle.
  (*With a broken handle* is a phrase telling us more about the noun *cup.*)
- We went to the park.
  (*To the park* is an adverbial phrase telling <u>where</u> we went.)
- They arrived after breakfast.
  (*After breakfast* is an adverbial phrase telling <u>when</u> they arrived.)

PHRASES AND CLAUSES

- They were late because of the weather.
  (*Because of the weather* is an adverbial phrase telling us why they were late. It has no verb.)

- They were late because the weather was bad.
    (*Because the weather was bad* is an adverbial clause telling us why they were late.)
    subject: _____
    verb: _____

- The man at the corner appeared to be drunk.
    (*At the corner* is an adjectival phrase telling us more about the noun *man*.)
- The man who stood at the corner appeared to be drunk.
    (*Who stood at the corner* is an adjectival clause telling us more about the noun *man*.)
    Subject: _____
    Verb: _____

Parts of Speech and Parts of the Sentence

> *Example*: After the generous man with the big ears has bought presents, he will quickly give them to his friends.

- *Parts of speech*:

after: <u>conjunction</u>	the: <u>article</u>
generous: _____	man: _____
with: _____	the: _____
big: _____	ears: _____
has bought: _____	presents: _____
he: _____	will give: _____
quickly: _____	them: _____
to: _____	his: _____
friends: _____	

- *Parts of the sentence*:

    main clause: He will quickly give them to his friends.
    subject: _____
    predicate: _____
    verb: _____
    direct object: _____
    indirect object: _____

    subordinate clause: After the generous man with the big ears has bought presents,
    (Is this an adjectival or an adverbial subordinate clause?)
    core subject: the noun _____
    complete subject: _____
    adjectival phrase: <u>with the big ears</u>
    this phrase tells us more about the noun: _____
    predicate: _____
    direct object: _____

APPENDIX 2: CORRECTION KEY

Ab	Faulty abbreviation
Adj	Improper use of adjective
Adv	Improper use of adverb
Agr	Faulty agreement
Amb	Ambiguous
Awk	Awkward expression or construction
Cap	Faulty capitalization
D	Faulty diction
Dgl	Dangling construction
Frag	Fragment
lc	Use lowercase
Num	Error in use of numbers
‖	Lack of parallelism
P	Faulty punctuation
Ref	Unclear pronoun reference
Rep	Unnecessary repetition
R-O	Run-on
Sp	Error in spelling
SS	Faulty sentence structure
T	Wrong verb tense
tr ⌒	Transpose elements (e.g., to quickly go, recieve)
V	Wrong verb form
Wdy	Wordy
⌄	Add apostrophe or single quotation mark
⌒	Close up
⌃	Add comma
ℓ	Delete
⋏	Insert
¶	Begin a new paragraph
No ¶	Do not begin a new paragraph
⊙	Add a period
⌄ ⌄	Double quotation marks
#	Add space

EXERCISES

The numbers in the brackets that accompany most exercises correspond to the numbers assigned to errors throughout the body of the book. This is intended to make many of the exercises "self-correcting"; by referring to the relevant number in the body of the book and reading the entry, you can see if your answer is correct.

GENERAL DIAGNOSTIC OR REVIEW EXERCISE: A

Choose the correct alternatives:

1. Yesterday afternoon when he [ate/had eaten] his meal, he rushed outside. (8)
2. Not long ago much of the world was ruled by a few colonial powers. Most of Africa, indeed, was under colonial rule [until/untill] the 1960s. Now, [therefore/however], only a few countries, [for example/such as] French Guiana and the Falkland Islands, are under colonial rule. (530, 451, 470)
3. How did his criticism [affect/effect] you? (183)
4. He ran quickly [inorder/in order] to reach the bank before it closed. (390)
5. He is an intolerant person [in that/in the way that] he [believes/is believing] all Jews to be greedy. (471, 4)
6. The traffic is very heavy [everyday/every day] at this time. (390)
7. Max invited me to his cottage, where he said we [can/could] go fishing. (499)
8. My cousin [may be/maybe] coming tonight, but I [can not/cannot] be there. (390, 389)
9. [May be/Maybe] my friend will be [arriving to/arriving at/arriving] Mirabel airport soon. (389, 74)
10. [They/There] are a number of stores [near by/nearby]. (335, 389)
11. She [insisted/persisted] [in/on] finishing her work before watching television. (289)
12. Mrs. Murphy told me that she preferred [living/leaving] in Myrtle [than/to] [living/leaving] in a large city like Toronto. (528, 127)
13. He was [quite/quiet] eager to [avenge/revenge] the terrible things that had been done [to/for] him. (528, 206, 101)
14. One of the boys [is/are] responsible [for keeping/to keep] this [domitory/dormitory] tidy. (2, 64, 530)
15. If he [shoots/shot] an innocent man, a police officer would be dismissed. (10)
16. It was [wet that/so wet that/too wet that/very wet that] [they/there] was mud everywhere. (474, 335)

General Diagnostic or Review Exercise: B

Correct the error(s) in each of the following:

1. They discussed about the bilateral agreement. (99)
2. All the people who was their they were happy. (2, 335, 174)
3. Businessmen create wealth just as surely as fishermen and farmers. (505, 215)
4. The police arrived at their house quiet unexpectedly, then they arrested Mr. Svoboda. (528, 478)
5. I can not meet you later today, I have a prior engagement. (389, 477)
6. In these circumstances morale and efficiency in the organization declines. (2)
7. He had drank more than was good for him. (28)
8. He assured me that he was capable to do the work. (49)
9. Two other types of corporate concentration gives rise to concern. (2)
10. She accepted to organize the activities for Parents Day. (45, 492)
11. All of the students had good behaviors during the church service. (153)
12. The complaints against the law by the business community suggests that it must have had some affect. (2, 183)
13. Prof. Curtis unhappy with her work because he gave her an "F." (521, 385, 461)
14. In addition to the gun which was used to commit the crime, the police is also in possesion of other evidence. (476, 172, 530)
15. The airlines carry children at lower fairs than adults, even though they take up seats and generally need more attention from airline staff. (528, 178)
16. She wanted some advise on how to invest her money. (182)
17. I had been told to try and not do any mistakes. (442, 423)
18. People living in the Kalahari dessert are few, and food is short. (528, 346, 432)
19. If one believes the rate of interest will rise, it would be wise to keep ones' asset's in cash untill the rise has taken place. (492, 530)
20. For years the USSR refused to allow its "satellites" to be independent. (223)
21. Everything seem to be running satisfactory; let's let sleeping dogs lie rather than change horses in mid-stream. (2, 181, 506)
22. She asked me if I can loan her fourty cents. (206, 530)
23. Costa Rica is rather unique amoung Central American nations. (340, 530)
24. Rebecca always want to try and suceed. (2, 442)
25. Taking this into account, it becomes apparent that cost per square foot is neither the only nor the main factor that a firm such as this one should be considering. (13, 178)
26. In my opinion I think people with heavy jobs for example minors should be paid well. (371, 470, 528)

27. Instead of alternatively fighting inflation and unemployment, the goverment sometimes find that they have to fight both at the same time. (214, 2, 166)

28. On the eighteenth, too, the Canadians captured Trun, the village proposed by Montgomery for the meeting place with the Americans, who themselves were now nearing the village of Chambois just a few miles away, and yet on the night of August the nineteenth in a drizzly rain and early morning fog thousands of trapped German soldiers made their way stealthily through the narrow gap, and when the fog lifted on the morning of the twentieth the gap was still packed by the escaping army. (477)

29. To be sure, the American economy has continued to be the greatest engine for the creation of wealth and expansion of opportunity known to man, and Johnson's last vignette describes how women have conquered the professions and workplace and achieved equality. But is that all the American civic religion, the noble experiment, comes to in the end? Where does Paul Johnson come out on all this? (Walter A. McDougall, book review, *Times Literary Supplement*, November 21, 1997) (505)

GENERAL DIAGNOSTIC OR REVIEW EXERCISE: C

Correct the error(s) in each of the following:

1. In Scott Fitzgeralds' story "The Ice Palace" (which appear in the book, *Morden Short Stories*) Sally Carroll displays many sides to her character. (492, 2, 530)

2. Susan has two brothers, one of them is looking forward to start university next year, and the other one is about to start high school. (477, 57)

3. He lied that his friend had been trying to kill him. (422)

4. It was there first time at the circus, and they were so excited. (335, 434)

5. Coffee may be short this year if demand remains at it's current high level. (432, 193)

6. ABC is not more superior than any of the other detergents. (424, 140)

7. All the students talked to each other. (163)

8. None of the wheels on my bicycle turn properly. (151)

9. The doctor told him not to drink and smoke for at least six months. (395)

10. Jackson was a member of the university's security force for close to four years at the time of his death. (8)

11. Neither of these books are very well-written. (164)

12. Humanists tends to downplay the usefulness of statistics. Whereas, all too often, social scientists ignore information which cannot be quantified. (2, 480, 476)

13. Please remember all tools must be returned by 5 p.m. (385)

14. Perhaps the comparison between the moon landing and the discovery of

the Titanic is valid, but for most of us the moon landing wins for sheer drama and technological ingenuity. But then it cost billions of dollars more, so it *should* have had a bigger impact. But in long-term benefits, the two achievments may not be so different. (449)

15. We have no plans to re-introduce the legislation, there's a lot more important things to do. (477, 2)

16. The proposed movie would include Nesmith, who choose to remain at home rather than join the current Monkees reunion tour. (25)

17. The American administration wanted a free trade agreement and so did the Canadian government, which would cover almost all goods and services. (178)

18. Its important to always be careful about punctuation. (193, 1)

19. When a corporation is expanding quickly, they often experience cash-flow problems. (178)

20. She visited a doctor with a bad case of the flu. (215)

21. Travelling 1,800 feet upwards in a matter of seconds, the CN Tower seems very impressive. (13)

22. Her sister, who lives in Buffalo has been visiting her this week. (485)

23. Man is an animal that breast feeds its young. (505)

Split Infinitives (1)

Change the following split infinitives:

1. They did not want to quickly decide the issue.
2. We were asked to patiently await the decision.
3. The contractor said that the owners would have to carefully restore the house.
4. Their policy was to perpetually maintain a state of economic equilibrium.
5. The choir began to loudly sing the anthem.

Subject-verb agreement (2)

Correct the subject-verb agreement errors (and any other singular or plural errors):

1. Train in Burma usually run on time, although it sometimes take many hours to get from one place to another. The trip from Belowa to Rangoon, for example, last about eleven hour. The Railway Corporation use several different type of locomotive—steam, electric, and diesel. The newest are the electric locomotive that travel between Rangoon and Mutisa.

2. Most of the electricity that the State need come from the dam. When the water flow over the large turbine, it turn them and this produce large amount of electricity.

3. When a debate start, the Chair alway introduce the topic and then three speaker from each team argue for or against the resolution. Each speaker talk for several minute. At the end of the debate the Chair give all those in the crowd who wish to comment a chance to do so.

4. In politic as in everyday life the variation that interest us occur in two dimension. Sometime political scientist are curious about variation over time. For instance, they may ask why the number of vote received by the various parties fluctuate so much from one election to the next. At other time political scientist concentrate their attention on variation over space. They may be interested, for example, in why one nation government seem to enjoy more success than its neighbour in combatting inflation, or protecting human right.

5. Fowler (1992) pointed out that concern about the dangers of premature cognitive training and an overemphasis on personality development had delayed inordinately the recognition that the ability to talk, read, and compute increase the child's self-respect and independent functioning.

6. Canada's chances of making it to the televised finals, where the big payoff to sponsors come, are not great. (*Financial Post*, Nov. 23, 1997)

7. To make matters worse, none of the three in the Leafs training camp have much playoff experience. (*Toronto Star*, Sept. 20, 1991)

8. The technical aspect of the newspaper must also be re-evaluated. Typos, or mistakes in spelling and grammar, which makes comprehension difficult, has been made almost a thing of the past. (Editorial in the student newspaper of the State University of New York at Stony Brook, as quoted in *The New Yorker*, Jan. 12, 1992.)

9. Wall Street analysts said the tone of Mr. Greenspan's remarks to the Senate were more positive than the testimony he gave a week earlier to the House of Representatives. (*The Guardian*, March 8, 2002)

Simple Present Tense

Fill in the correct tense of the verb:

1. Every day the sun _____ [to rise] in the east and _____ [to set] in the west. Because of this, some people _____ [to think] that the sun _____ [to revolve] around the earth. In fact, the opposite _____ [to be] true; the earth _____ [to circle] the sun once a year and also spins on its axis once every day. While the sun _____ [to shine] on one side of the earth, it _____ [to be] night on the other side. (3)

2. This year she _____ [to follow] the same pattern of teaching in many lessons. As soon as she _____ [to come] into the class she _____ [to ask] several questions about the previous day's work. Then she usually _____ [to introduce] a new topic, and _____ [to talk] to us about it for several minutes. More often than not she then _____ [to assign] a written exercise to do in class. If the students _____ [to

finish] the exercise before the end of the class, she _____ [to correct] it on the board. Sometimes if there _____ [to be] a few minutes remaining she _____ [to tell] a story or asks a student to tell a story. (3)

3. Shylock _____ [to be] the most important character in Shakespeare's *The Merchant of Venice*. We _____ [to sympathize] with him despite his streak of cruelty, because we _____ [to be made] to understand his resentment of the Christians. When Shylock _____ [to accuse] Antonio in Act One of having sworn at him and spat on him merely because of his religion, Antonio—far from denying the charges— _____ [to say] that he would do the same again. Moreover, Antonio's prejudice against Jews _____ [to seem] to be shared by all the Christian characters in the play. (522)

CONDITIONAL TENSE (9, 10)

Complete the following sentences in any appropriate way:

1. If I wore no clothes at all ....
2. If the government reduces taxes ....
3. He would buy a truck if ....
4. He will buy a truck if ....
5. If an election is held next month ....
6. She will win if ....
7. She would win if ....
8. If money were abolished ....
9. Local farms would be more productive if ....
10. If he sends me the money in time ....

Fill in either the conditional tense or the simple future tense in the main clause:

> *Example*:   I _____ [to help] him if I could.
> I would help him if I could. (conditional)

1. If I found someone's wallet lying on the ground, I _____ [to return] it.
2. If I find the wallet that you have lost, I _____ [to return] it.
3. You _____ [to find] the weather extremely cold if you lived at the North Pole.
4. You _____ [to find] the weather extremely cold when you visit Canada this coming January.
5. If he gets here before three o'clock, I _____ [to take] him to see the museum.
6. If you were the Prime Minister, what _____ you _____ [to do] about the situation?

7. I _____ [to be] very happy if the company hires me as an apprentice.
8. If I were very rich, I _____ [to buy] a house in West Vancouver.

Fill in either the simple past or the simple present tense in the subordinate clause:

1. I will ask him about it if I _____ [to see] him again later today.
2. If I _____ [to win] the lottery I will buy my parents a new car.
3. If I _____ [to win] the lottery I would buy my parents a new car.
4. He would do better if he _____ [to work] harder.
5. He will do better if he _____ [to work] harder next term.
6. If a burglar _____ [to come] into your room at night, what would you do?
7. I will lend you this CD if you _____ [to promise] to take good care of it.
8. He would look much better if he _____ [to arrange] his hair differently.
9. There can no longer be any doubt that people _____ [to live] longer if they _____ [to smoke] less.

Fill in the missing verbs:

1. He _____ [to supply] our company with what we need if we _____ [to pay] him $50,000. However, we only _____ [to have] $30,000 in liquid assets.
2. If he _____ [to reply] to me quickly, as I think he will, I _____ [to be able] to make reservations for our holiday.
3. If she _____ [to believe] in God she _____ [to go] to church. However, she _____ [to be] an atheist.
4. My friend and I are thinking of going to the game this afternoon. If we _____ [to go] we probably _____ [to take] our wives with us.
5. If we _____ [to arrive] sooner, we would have been able to help him.
6. If Montcalm's most important officer _____ not _____ [to be hiding] away with his mistress, the French troops _____ [to be assembled] earlier and the British _____ [to lose] the battle on the Plains of Abraham.
7. We would have been better off if we _____ [to plant] wheat instead of cotton.
8. If you had spoken to me about it, I _____ [to do] something sooner.
9. I would have told them the truth if they _____ [to ask] me.
10. The Titanic _____ probably not _____ [to sink] if it had struck the iceberg head on.

CONDITIONAL AND PAST CONDITIONAL (9, 10, 11)

Correct the error in each of the following:

1. If we sent payment by special delivery now, it will reach her by Thursday.
2. If you would pay attention, you will understand a good deal more of what is said.
3. If they all won prizes, I'm sure some of them will still be sullen and unhappy.
4. If you would have eaten anything poisonous, there would have been some indication of trouble by now.
5. If they would have thought about it beforehand, they would not have acted so very foolishly.
6. If first baseman Eric Hinske made a play on a Scott Brotius grounder in the fourth, the Jays could have been out of the inning, trailing only 3-2.
7. If you would have come when I first called you, none of this would have happened.

Active and Passive (12)

Improve each of the following sentences by changing the verb from the passive voice to the active. You may also be able to make other improvements:

1. Legislation has been passed by the government to ensure that the rights of individuals are protected.
2. After careful deliberation, it has been decided that the application for residential zoning of the building to be changed to commercial will be approved.
3. The economy was subjected to two serious oil price shocks in the 1970s; those with cars were forced to line up for hours to obtain gasoline, and everyone was affected by inflation.
4. Research in this area was first carried out by Samuel Smith in the 1990s, and was completed after his death by a team directed by Marjorie Mullins.

A General Review of Verb Tenses

Fill in the correct tenses of the verbs:

1. This train always _____ [to leave] at exactly five o'clock. (3)
2. As he _____ [to climb] the mountain he _____ [to lose] his grip and _____ [to plunge] five hundred feet to his death.
3. After we _____ [to make] our way through the forest, we sat down to rest. (8)
4. This machinery _____ [to be] very reliable. It almost never _____ [to break] down and it _____ [to need] very little maintenance. (3)
5. He _____ [to tell] me before the meeting yesterday that they _____ [to reach] a decision already. (8)
6. The Cleveland Indians _____ [to improve] at the moment, but I

_____ [to not think] that they _____ [to be] as good as the Red Sox yet. (4)

7. The government _____ [to oppress] the people of East Timor for many years. I _____ [to hope] that it soon _____ [to be] forced to change its ways. (7)

8. _____ you ever _____ [to see] a flying saucer? (7)

9. I _____ [to tell] him what I knew if I _____ [to trust] him. Unfortunately, I don't trust him. (10)

10. If he _____ [to find out] about this he _____ [to be] very angry, but I am sure he will not find out. (10)

11. Greene's greatest novel _____ [to recount] the story of an alcoholic Mexican priest during a period in which the government _____ [to suppress] organized religion. (page 238)

DANGLING CONSTRUCTIONS (13-16)

Correct the following sentences:

1. Riding the bus to work, his wife waved at him from the sidewalk.
2. When covered with aluminum siding, we will have a much more saleable house.
3. Regarding the fiscal requirements of the government, an increase in taxes will be required if the deficit is to be reduced.
4. Looking for a moment at the implications of Smith's argument, he allows us to justify our selfish behavior.
5. Having covered the issue of stratification, the means of redistributing income will be dealt with next.
6. To obtain a sense of the density of structuralist prose, a few examples should suffice.
7. We have asked for a survey of the attitudes of consumers carried out randomly.
8. Considering all of this evidence, there is no doubt that an increased awareness of the usefulness of uniform and objectively-defined time led to the spread of clocks, and not the other way round.
9. Widely regarded as a failure by observers at the time, we can now see that Truman was a remarkably successful president.
10. To begin this essay, Faulkner's novel is written from several points of view.
11. To obtain a refund, any copies damaged in shipment must be returned promptly.
12. Having settled the issue of independence, questions of economic growth came to the fore in the public consciousness.
13. Smothered in mushrooms and lashed with HP sauce, I enjoyed the steak immensely.
14. Although redundant, the company president said the 250 workers would be offered alternative jobs.

15. To help reduce the beaver colonies, the Department of Natural Resources has even begun allowing novice trappers to learn to trap in the comfort of their own living rooms. (*The Globe and Mail*, August 12, 1991)
16. As reconstructed by police, Pfeiffer at first denied any knowledge of the Byrd murder. (*The New York Times*, reprinted in Theodore Bernstein's *Watch Your Language*)
17. The woman had moved into an apartment where she was killed a few weeks before her death. (Quoted from a Montreal newspaper in *Word Watching*, a language newsletter)
18. Remy hit an RBI single off Hass' leg, which rolled into right field. (*Webster's Dictionary of English Usage*)
19. When stewed, I like prunes.

    (Note: Numbers 13–19 of the above exercise were quoted by Robertson Cochrane in a column in *The Globe and Mail*.)

For each of the following write a complete sentence that incorporates the phrase given but does <u>not</u> allow it to dangle. Then re-write the sentence to remove the phrase:

1. Turning to Margaret Atwood's later novels ....
2. Considering the developments of the past few years in Eastern Europe ....
3. Looking at the connection between economic history and the history of ideas ....
4. Regarding the claim that women and men are intrinsically different ...
5. Having surveyed the four main theories of ....

EXERCISE: SEQUENCE OF TENSES (17–19)

Correct the following sentences:

1. The Vice President said that "We will have to improve our productivity."
2. Tennyson's Ulysses says that "I have suffered greatly, both with those/ That loved me, and alone."
3. Churchill claimed that "This is our finest hour."
4. Johnson at first believed that the Vietnam war will be over before the 1968 election.
5. For the most part the story of Chopin's *The Awakening* is narrated in a detached manner that leaves the reader to make her own inferences about the characters involved. Occasionally though, the narrative voice adopts a clear point of view. Such is the case, for example, when Mr. Pointellier "could see plainly that she was not herself. That is, he could not see that she was becoming herself and daily casting aside that fictitious self which we assume like a garment with which to appear before the world." Quite clearly, the aside concerning the "fictitious self" comes from the narrator, not from Mr. Pointellier.

Irregular verbs (20-44)

Correct whichever of the following are incorrect:

1. She can do whatever she choses.
2. The book is well-written and beautifully layed out.
3. He says that he rung me over the phone.
4. They have stole everything I own.
5. This blouse shrunk when I washed it in hot water.
6. The ship sunk in a hundred feet of water.

Fill in the simple past tense of the verbs indicated:

1. She _____ (to choose) the material that _____ (to be) least expensive.
2. Samuel _____ (to drink) too much beer last night.
3. All the pipes _____ (to burst) and water covered the floor.
4. The little baby _____ (to fall) asleep as soon as he _____ (to lie) down.
5. The soldiers _____ (to flee) as soon as they _____ (to see) the size of the opposing force.
6. As soon as I apologized, my parents _____ (to forgive) me.
7. We _____ (to grind) the seeds into a fine powder.
8. He _____ (to lay) his book down for a moment, and then he _____ (to forget) where he had put it.
9. I _____ (to lend) him five dollars yesterday.
10. The letter carrier _____ (to ring) the bell four times.
11. His whole family _____ (to seek) refuge here after leaving Guatemala.
12. The moon _____ (to shine) very brightly last night.
13. The bandits _____ (to shoot) the police officer in the back.
14. This sweater _____ (to shrink) in the wash.
15. He _____ (to sing) at the top of his voice all afternoon.
16. When the Titanic _____ (to sink), over 1,500 lives _____ (to be) lost.
17. All my food _____ (to slide) off my plate onto the floor.
18. He _____ (to spend) his entire wages on beer and cigarettes.
19. The car _____ (to spin) out of control as it _____ (to go) around the corner.
20. He _____ (to spit) in disgust on the pavement.
21. She _____ (to split) the log into two chunks easily.
22. The cougar _____ (to spring) out of the undergrowth at the deer.
23. We _____ (to swim) in the pool below the falls.
24. She _____ (to weep) for hours when she _____ (to hear) the sad news.

25. The python _____ (to wind) itself around his neck.
26. He _____ (to wring) out the wet clothing, and put it on the line.

INFINITIVE OR GERUND? (45-68)

Choose the correct alternative:

1. Mr. Carruthers accused me [to have laughed/of laughing] at him be-hind his back.
2. He has a tendency [to speak/of speaking] before he has thought about what effect his words may have.
3. Mary is certainly capable [to get/of getting] an "A" in this course.
4. He has often tried to discourage me [to try/from trying] to get into Medical School.
5. They seemed [as if they were/to be] about to attack us.
6. The Press suspected the senator [to have been involved/of having been involved] in a conflict of interest.

EXERCISE: PREPOSITIONS (69-148)

Fill in the correct preposition, or leave blank if no preposition is needed.

1. My father was very angry _____ me when I did not do what he had asked me to do.
2. We should arrive _____ Denver in time for dinner.
3. The three of them were chased _____ from school.
4. The group departed _____ Paris in the early morning.
5. We discussed _____ the problem with him for a whole afternoon.
6. We were told to continue _____ our work.
7. We must refer _____ to the first chapter to find the most important clue to the protagonist's identity.
8. The geopolitical situation in late 1938 was different _____ what it had been only a few months earlier.
9. He asked me what type _____ VCR we wanted.
10. She is convinced that this brand of detergent is superior _____ that one.

Which of the following sentences are incorrect? Correct whatever preposition mistakes you find:

1. By the time troops arrived the Russian Parliament buildings, Yeltsin and his supporters had built barricades and were prepared.
2. Chirac had intended to consult with his advisors before making a statement.
3. We must draw a different conclusion than the one we had expected.

4. Tyson departed from Las Vegas amidst a storm of controversy over the incident.
5. The controversy over whether or not special lanes for bicycles should be built along major thoroughfares centres on the issue of safety.
6. At the legislature today, a group of citizens protested against the federal government's proposal.

SINGULAR AND PLURAL (149-173)

Make the changes necessary to ensure that the parts of the sentence are in agreement:

1. Either John or his brother are responsible for causing the disturbance. (164)
2. None of the excuses we were given are satisfactory. (162)
3. Each of the members feel that the application should be rejected. (162)

Choose the correct alternative:

1. The aurora borealis is still a largely unexplained [phenomenon/phenomena]. (171)
2. There appear to be at least two [focuses/foci] in Bruegel's *Fall of Icarus*. (149)
3. There were several [Attorney Generals/Attorneys General] during the Reagan administration. (149)
4. Television is generally considered to be the most influential [media/medium]. (168)

Correct any mistakes in the following sentences:

1. The second criteria that Locke puts forward is closely connected to the first. (159)
2. The data we were shown is not sufficient to convince us. (161)
3. At the turn of the century the press was the media that affected North Americans most profoundly. (168)

PRONOUNS (176, 178)

Correct the pronoun problem in each of the following:

1. A shopkeeper's life is usually a very busy one. They often have to work at least twelve hours a day. (178)
2. Frank is not as good as Henry at the high jump. He usually jumps about five feet. (178)
3. Larson argues that the sexual stereotypes of modern Western society

will not be eradicated until the economic system alters, whereas Myers feels that a degree of stereotyping is an inevitable, if regrettable, result of genetic differences. This is important to recognize. (178)

4. Harvard must maintain the high standards that make people like Henry Rosovsky and I work twice as hard. (from an address by Harvard University president Derek Bok) (176)

Find and correct the pronoun problems:

1. Typically, a deconstructionist searches for structures that are deeply hidden, that even the author may not have been aware of. Indeed, they are often uninterested in whatever structure the author may have declared she has attempted to impose on the text.

2. Writing business letters is an important skill to learn. Normally, of course, it should begin with a salutation.

3. Ownership rights certainly protect a sphere of liberty for the rights owners, but they may also interfere with the rights of others who are no longer at liberty to use what they previously could. If this were more widely realized we might be less likely to think of liberty as an unqualified good.

WHO AND WHOM (179)

Fill in *who* or *whom*, whichever is correct:

1. _____ will be waiting for you?
2. To _____ should I address the parcel?
3. She is a writer about _____ I know very little.
4. _____ should I say is calling?
5. Andrew Johnson was the President _____ followed Lincoln.
6. Andrew Johnson was the President _____ Lincoln preceded.
7. D'Arcy McGee was the leader _____ was assassinated while John A. Macdonald was Prime Minister of Canada.
8. It was John A. Macdonald _____ said to D'Arcy McGee, "We can't afford to have two drunkards in the Cabinet; you've got to stop."
9. It was D'Arcy McGee _____ John A. Macdonald was speaking to when he said, "We can't afford to have two drunkards in this Cabinet; you've got to stop."

PART OF SPEECH CONVERSIONS (180–207)

Correct the mistake in each sentence:

1. He did not give me very good advise. (182)
2. To some extend what you say is true, but I cannot agree with you completely. (206)

3. There maybe a chance that you can still convince him to do what you want. (197)
4. She was eager to revenge what they had done to her. (206)
5. The team's four starters voted unanimous to start on four days' rest. (181)
6. I loaned him the money to buy a car. (206)
7. He was careful not to loose track of the argument. (196)
8. The above quote illustrates just how short-sighted 19th-century educators could be. (204)

LIKE AND AS (192)

Choose the correct alternative:

1. We should meet at ten o'clock [like/as] we agreed.
2. [Like/As] she said an hour ago when we began this discussion, we have to choose between the lesser of two evils.
3. [Like/As] Russia, Canada is dominated geographically by vast areas of frozen wasteland.
4. In many ways copper behaves [like/as] silver does.

DIFFICULTIES WITH MEANING (208-344)

Choose the correct word or expression:

1. Do you think your action will have any [effect/affect]? (183)
2. The shopkeeper did not want to [accept/except] a credit card. (208)
3. The tape recording [compliments/complements] the study guide. (237)
4. The [council/counsel] deliberated for seven hours before reaching a decision. (243)
5. One approach is to break down the questionnaire results by age and sex. [Alternately/Alternatively], we may study the variations among different income levels. (214)
6. He is very conservative and would never wish to [flout/flaunt] the university regulations. (273)
7. The stage can be [dissembled/disassembled] within two hours. (254)
8. The two elements must be seen as entirely [discreet/discrete]. (251)
9. She told me [definitely/definitively] that she would not support the motion. (247)
10. Britain is considering whether or not to restore [capitol/capital] punishment. (229)
11. The majority believe that theft is [amoral/immoral] in any circumstances. (217)
12. No politician is [adverse/averse] to publicity. (210)
13. They were eager to declare the amount as a [capitol/capital] gain. (229)
14. The company always purchases [stationary/stationery] in bulk. (331)

15. The book is laden with a preface, a [foreword/forward], and an intro-
    duction. (276)
16. The spokesperson [inferred/implied] that the withdrawal would be made,
    but he would not state it [explicitly/implicitly]. (284, 269)
17. The judge felt that the guilt of the accused was [mitigated/militated] by
    the manner in which he had been provoked; the victim was his supervi-
    sor at work, and had been [persecuting/prosecuting] him for years. (301,
    311)

In each of the following there is a mistake. Correct it:

1. A lot of emigrants entered Canada last year. (263)
2. Most sports stars who "write" books do it by corroborating with a professional writer. (236)
3. The experiment would of worked if we had calculated the angles correctly. (306)
4. Anyone can park here; there are no restrictions. (228)
5. The Committee is made up of imminent people from all walks of life.
   (264)
6. Like all bright young women, she is liable to succeed. (295)
7. The percent of the sample that responded to question 12 was very low.
   (428)
8. The entire town was ravished by the violent storm. (321)
9. There were to many people there; I felt claustrophobic. (337)
10. He has little or no interest in sex, but he is otherwise a very sensual
    man. (326)
11. Her writing is completely eligible; I can hardly make out a word. (262)
12. Ms. Jenkins persuaded me to invest in her business, but I decided it
    would not be a good idea. (312)

THEY, THERE, THEIR, WERE, AND *WHERE* (335, 344)

Fill in the correct choice:

1. The boys told _____ mother that they would be late.
2. _____ were many people at the political rally.
3. _____ are very happy to live in such a nice house.
4. _____ are a great many machines in that factory.
5. _____ car is old, but _____ keep it in good condition.
6. _____ are many students who have not yet handed in exercise books.
7. _____ you pleased that the Tigers won yesterday?
8. He could not tell me _____ the tools _____ kept.
9. My brother and I _____ walking to the store, _____ we hoped to
   meet several friends.
10. _____ _____ a lot of people in the audience.

OF AND *HAVE* (306)

Fill in either *of* or *have*:

1. I would _____ come if I had been able to.
2. I should _____ done more work at the beginning _____ the term.
3. The tragedy could not _____ been prevented.
4. It was very kind _____ you to write.

WORD ORDER (345–354)

Improve the word order in the following sentences:

1. This can be the result either of natural events or human actions. (349)
2. In the end, Hitler neither conquered Britain nor the Soviet Union. (349)
3. We should first ask what are the conditions under which an electronics industry is likely to flourish. (353)
4. Passions can interfere either sporadically on particular occasions, or they can be a continual influence on one's actions. (349)
5. The conclusions we draw will be largely determined by what are the assumptions we start with. (353)

In each of the following there is a word order mistake. Correct it:

1. The Tiger supporters in the crowd were few. (346)
2. The books I lent to my friend, I need them back soon. (348)
3. The men who are responsible for installing the joists, the supervisor wanted to see them. (348)
4. He neither wants pity nor charity. (349)
5. They were given sentences of between one and three years all except those who had not committed any violent offences. (350)
6. I and my friends usually spend holidays together. (351)
7. In this class there are three students only. (352)
8. I asked Faith how was she feeling. (353)
9. My father asked me what was I doing. (353)
10. They asked us what was wrong? (353)
11. I borrowed the young man's truck, who had bought it only the day before. (354)
12. You can order a complete computer system that will be delivered by telephone. (354)
13. Greville is now represented by the best of both his love poems and of his sonorous Calvinist laments. [poet Thom Gunn, writing in the *Times Literary Supplement*, August 16, 1991] (347)

Too Many or Too Few Words (355–388)

In each of the following there are either too many or too few words. Improve each sentence:

1. I myself I think that it is not wise to have more than three or four children. (372)
2. In my opinion I think men are just as intelligent as women. (371)
3. It was the general consensus of opinion that no new projects of an expensive nature should be embarked upon at that point in time. (382, 386, 379)
4. The protagonist has fallen in love a girl he met at the fair the previous weekend. (385)
5. She said that she did not to work at the factory, no matter how much she was paid. (385)
6. Insects such as moths, butterflies, fruit flies, etc. can adapt very quickly to environmental changes. (367)
7. There are several birds (penguins, ostriches and etc.) which cannot fly. (367)

Usage (391–444)

In each sentence there is one mistake. Correct it:

1. Please do not do any changes before you have asked me about them. (404)
2. There are less people in Sweden than there are in the city of New York. (421)
3. He did a lot of mistakes on his tax form. (423)
4. Hingis does not want to go to Wimbleton nor the US Open this year. (425)
5. He could not do nothing about the problems that he faced. (426)
6. The college would like to increase the places available in residence. (414)
7. A revolution is when the government changes hands as a result of a violent uprising. (418)
8. The reason the ozone layer is being destroyed is because of the effects of aerosol sprays. (431)
9. The plaintiff now intends to try and regain custody of the child. (442)

In each of the following sentences there is one mistake. Correct it:

1. According to science, it is impossible to travel faster than the speed of light. (391)
2. As he had got into the car, he turned the key in the ignition. (397)

3. The European powers wanted to colonize Africa because of the following reasons. (400)
4. He often forgets his office key at home. (410)
5. The reason she likes him is because he is a well-known personality. (431)
6. Students at this college will be substantially increased next year. (414)
7. The police did a thorough investigation, and could find no evidence of wrongdoing. (416)
8. She lied that she had not stolen any money. (422)
9. He is opposed against legalizing marijuana. (427)

PUTTING IDEAS TOGETHER—CAUSE AND EFFECT

List as many effects as you can of any two of the following events:

1. the baby boom
2. the spread of television throughout society
3. the fall of Communism in Eastern Europe and the Soviet Union
4. an increase in the value of the American dollar

List as many causes as you can for any two of the following events:

1. the Czech Republic winning Olympic gold in men's hockey, 1998
2. the recent rise/fall in support for the federal government
3. 20th century American interventions in Central America
4. global warming

CAUSE AND CORRELATION

What causal relationships (if any) do you think underlie the following correlations? In each case one may be the cause of the other; it may be one of the causes of the other; or there may be no causal relationship. If you think there is a causal connection, state if you think it likely to be the only cause, and if not list as many other possible contributing causes as you can think of:

1. a rise in crime/a rise in unemployment
2. a rise in violent crimes (such as rape and murder)/a rise in unemployment
3. the 1990s collapse of the cod stocks off the Newfoundland coast/large catches taken by foreign trawlers outside the 200 mile limit
4. increases in government support for the performing arts/better plays being written and performed
5. Japanese children spending far more time in school than do North Americans/higher productivity in the Japanese economy

6. a large decrease in rain in Somalia/famine in Somalia
7. record potato crops in the 1840s in Ireland/the potato famine in the 1840s in Ireland

Putting Ideas Together (447–451; 461–62)

Fill in *but, although, however, despite, because,* or *as a result.* Pay close attention to the punctuation:

1. _____ he was sick, he could not come to work yesterday.
2. _____ he was sick, he came to work yesterday.
3. He was sick yesterday. _____, he still came to work.
4. _____ his sickness, he still came to work yesterday.
5. He was sick yesterday. _____, he did not come to work.
6. He was sick yesterday, _____ he still came to work.
7. She has practised for many long hours. _____, she is now a good player.
8. She has practised for many long hours, _____ she is still not a good player.
9. She is now a good player _____ she has practised for many long hours.
10. _____ she has practised for many long hours, she is not yet a good player.
11. She has practised for many long hours. _____, she is not yet a good player.
12. _____ her long hours of practice, she is not yet a good player.

But (449)

Rephrase so that consecutive sentences do not include the word *but*:

1. There is no question that the Mariners on balance have lost run-scoring potential with the replacement of Smith, Jones, and Brown with Martinez, Womack, and White. But they have gained better defence and a more positive attitude. But it is not at first clear whether these will be enough to enable them to win the World Series championship that has so far eluded them.
2. Having the right to own private property is generally considered an important liberty in this society, but for many people there will be more interference with liberty under a system of private ownership than there will be under a system such as that of the Native peoples of North America (under which the land is held in common). But this does not show that a system of common use or common ownership is necessarily right for Western society today. But it should make us question our often unthinking allegiance to private property rights.

Joining Words (445–460)

Fill in *but, however, though, although, despite,* or *whereas*—whichever is correct:

1. There is no question that the Mariners have on balance lost run-scoring potential with the replacement of Smith, Jones, and Brown with Martinez, Womack, and White. They have gained better defence, _____ , and a more positive attitude. Whether or not these will be enough to enable them to win the World Series championship that has so far eluded them is not yet clear, most fans seem glad of the changes.

2. _____ the Mariners have on balance lost run-scoring potential with the replacement of Smith, Jones, and Brown with Martinez, Womack, and White, they have gained better defence and a more positive attitude.

3. _____ the loss of the run-scoring potential of Smith, Jones, and Brown, the Mariners should still produce a lot of runs from the bats of Martinez, Womack, and White. Moreover, they have gained better defence and a more positive attitude.

4. Some aspects of deconstruction proved easy to mock—none more so, perhaps, than its emphasis on the text rather than the author. "Do deconstructionists think the text writes itself?" sceptics sneered. _____, it may well be a worthwhile endeavor to act as if the text has no author.

5. Some aspects of deconstruction proved easy to mock—none more so, perhaps, than its emphasis on the text rather than the author. "Do deconstructionists think the text writes itself?" sceptics sneered. In fact, _____, it may be an entirely worthwhile endeavor to act as if the text has no author.

6. _____ their scepticism, those opposed to deconstruction were sometimes influenced by deconstructionist techniques of analysis.

Fill in appropriate joining words from the following list: *but, however, though, although, despite, whereas, yet, also, and, as well, indeed, in fact, further, moreover, not only ... but also*

1. Surrey has been growing enormously in recent years; _____, it now has twice the population that it had only ten years ago.

2. The opening of the Coquihalla Highway made it much easier for cars to travel from Vancouver to Kamloops; _____, it cut almost two hours off the journey. Trucks, _____, found it almost as slow as the old route via Cache Creek; _____ the very steep grades force them to slow down considerably.

3. _____ the opening of the Coquihalla Highway made it much easier for cars to travel from Vancouver to Kamloops, it was not much of a help to heavy trucks. A fully-loaded transport truck can only climb the

steep grades very slowly. _____, the toll charges levied make the journey more expensive than travel via the Trans-Canada Highway.

4. _____ is a fully-loaded transport truck unable to climb the steep grades at more than a snail's pace, _____ it must pay for the privilege.

5. Deconstructionists followed Derrida's lead in arguing that nothing but the text is deserving of study—indeed, that there is nothing but the text. They argue that to refer to an author's life is to engage in idle speculation. Surely in at least some cases, _____, what the author intended to say is of more than passing interest. Surely in at least some cases, _____, information about the author's life will help to shed life on the text.

6. Deconstruction argues in favour of a separation between the text and the world when it comes to any consideration of the author as an individual. Deconstruction is eager to show, _____, how a text is conditioned by the society in which it was created—and the dominant ideology of that society. The bias is towards the collective and the unconscious. The conscious motivations and intentions of the author are deemed to be irrelevant, _____ it is the job of the critic to reveal the unconscious motivations.

Because (461, 462)

In each of the following sentences *because* is used incorrectly. Explain why, and rephrase to correct the problem. (You may replace *because* if you wish.)

1. The compound in the red beaker is lighter than the compound in the black beaker because it weighs less.

2. Shakespeare mixes comedy with tragedy frequently because he includes comic material such as the gravediggers' scene in *Hamlet* and the Fool's banter in *King Lear*.

3. The black American family unit has broken down, because statistics show that the proportion of black American children born illegitimately has tripled over the past twenty years.

4. The fact that the proportion of black American children born illegitimately has tripled over the past twenty years does not in fact indicate any increase in the number of single parents, because two parent families are having fewer children.

Because, So, As a Result (461, 462)

Fill in *because, so,* or *as a result*:

1. _____ he writes carefully and checks his work, he usually does well.

2. He writes carefully and checks his work, _____ he usually does well.

3. He writes carefully and checks his work. _____, he usually does well.

4. I think that party has done a good job in government, _____ I will vote for it.

5. I will vote for that party, _____ I think it has done a good job governing.

6. I think that party has done a good job governing. _____, I will vote for it.

PUNCTUATION AND JOINING WORDS (451, 466)

Punctuate the following:

1. Jones was not even in the same city at the time hence he could not have committed the murder

2. The team was heavily favored to win the division three of its best pitchers however were injured for long periods hence it was unable to finish better than fourth

3. Gauthier's proviso is a general principle hence it applies both to property owners and to those whose land has been expropriated as we shall see however it is not a principle that can successfully be used as a ground on which to base private property rights

4. Mulroney was sometimes thought of as being too concerned with popularity and unwilling to lead in his actions however he frequently went against the dictates of public opinion the Free Trade Agreement and the GST for example were both opposed by a majority of Canadians should politicians in fact always follow public opinion or do they have a duty to do what they believe to be right regardless of what the majority feels if we on the left try to deny conservative governments the right to make unpopular decisions then in order to remain consistent we will also have to insist that liberal or social democratic governments only put forward legislation that is popular

FOR EXAMPLE AND SUCH AS (470, 472)

Fill in *for example* or *such as*:

1. A number of his friends, _____ Frank Jones and Joshua Smith, have criminal records.

2. A number of his friends have criminal records. Frank Jones and Joshua Smith, _____, have each spent several years in jail.

3. At several points in the play, Antonio acts cruelly. _____, he insults Shylock even when the Jew is prepared to lend him money.

4. Christian characters _____ Antonio and Gratiano act cruelly towards Jews throughout *The Merchant of Venice*.

5. Certain forms of transportation, _____ bicycles and canoes, cause no damage whatsoever to the environment.

6. Certain forms of transportation are friendly to the environment. Bicycles and canoes, _____, cause no damage whatsoever.

7. There is a connection here between literary tendencies and political ones. Just as postmodern theorists are more alive to the collective influences at work upon the creation of a text, so too they tend to be more concerned in the political sphere with collective rights than with individual ones. The collective rights of women and of minorities, _____, tend to be given more weight than the individual rights (_____ freedom of speech) that have traditionally been the concern of the British and North American tradition. This distinction lies close to the heart of the debate over "political correctness."

So That, So … That, or Such … That (474, 475)

Fill in so that, so … that, or such … that:

1. His prose is _____ convoluted _____ it is difficult to understand what he means.
2. It is _____ a convoluted prose style _____ it is difficult to understand what he means.
3. He writes in an inaccessible way _____ the reader will sense the difficulty inherent in the ideas themselves.

Comparisons (474, 475)

too   so … that   so that   such … that   very

From this list of expressions choose the one that fits into each of the sentences below:

1. After the birth of their first child they both felt _____ happy.
2. He was _____ late _____ the meeting was almost over.
3. She is now _____ a big girl _____ none of her clothes fit properly.
4. The sun is _____ bright today.
5. The sun is _____ bright today _____ you have to shield your eyes.
6. There is _____ a bright sun today you have to shield your eyes.
7. I shielded my eyes _____ I could see more clearly.
8. You should do your work now _____ you will be able to enjoy yourself this evening.
9. This table is _____ big; it will not fit through the door.
10. This table is _____ big _____ it will not fit through the door.
11. This table is _____ big to fit through the door.

That or Which (476)

Fill in that or which:

1. The essay _____ I wrote last week was eleven pages long.
2. The essay, _____ I wrote in only one night, was eleven pages long.
3. This comparison, _____ Fitzgerald first makes in the book's opening paragraph, is repeated frequently throughout the text.
4. The comparison _____ Fitzgerald makes in the book's opening paragraph is repeated frequently throughout the text.

In which of the above could *that* or *which* be omitted?

Putting Ideas Together (445–476)

In each of the following there is one mistake. Correct it:

1. He went away in the morning and he came home the same night and he told me that he had had a good trip. (456)
2. Although he has short legs, but he is a fast runner. (447)
3. Despite that the teacher marked hard, we all passed. (450)
4. Mark was sick because he stayed in bed all day. (461)
5. Because the players would not give up, so they achieved victory. (467)
6. Michipicoten Island on Lake Superior is very beautiful, but it is also very inaccessible. However, it is possible to reach it by private boat. (449)

Fill in appropriate joining words, expressions, or punctuation, choosing from those in the lists provided:

1.

as well	however
and	though
as a result	despite
; [semi-colon]	

The idea of building a canal from the Mediterranean Sea to the Red Sea is centuries old _____ it was considered even in the time of the Roman Empire. _____, it was not until the late nineteenth century that the project was actually begun. _____ many difficulties, the canal was finally completed early in this century, _____ for many years most ships bypassed the Cape of Good Hope. In the late 1960s and the 1970s, _____, ships that were too large for the canal began to be built. _____, conflict between Israel and Egypt caused the canal to be closed at various times. _____, a great deal of sea traffic now once again travels right around Africa, just as it did before the Suez Canal was built.

2.

despite	such as
and	however
although	as a result
moreover	

Uganda is again becoming one of Africa's more developed countries. _____ it has certain natural disadvantages, _____ having no sea port, it has a relatively good infrastructure _____ its agricultural sector is increasingly productive. _____, it exports more products than do most of its neighbors. _____ political difficulties with rebels in the north of the country, the government remains stable. _____, many nearby nations look to Uganda for leadership. _____, Uganda is of course much less well-off than are most European countries.

RUN-ON AND INCOMPLETE SENTENCES (477, 480)

Correct each of the following run-on or incomplete sentences:

1. "She's miniature, her hands are about the size of my thumb," he said. (*Peterborough Examiner*)
2. How much influence the book might have, how it compares to other philosophical books, how it fits in with the current trends in philosophy, these are all very hard to determine.
3. It had taken the best part of an hour to put the plan forward, it took another five minutes before I got my answer. (F.H. Winterbotham, *Ultra Secret*)
4. The informant did not lie to us, he gave us his idea of what the people believed they were doing. (Anthropology essay)
5. Another positive element is that outside firms will bring new or substantially revitalized agricultural resources into use, they will create new employment to operate the production facilities.
6. Suppose an industry which is threatened by foreign competition is one which lies at the very heart of your national defence, where are you then? (Economist W. Hewins, quoted in the *Atlantic*)
7. Hydrochloric acid is a very dangerous substance. So always handle it very carefully.
8. The rookie sidearmer didn't merely have a fine year in the team's bullpen, his campaign ranks as one of the very best seasons in baseball history.
9. In Heriot, Scotland, a run on the bank isn't a sign of financial instability, it's just the way things always have been and still are, every Thursday from 3:30 to 4:30. The only time the bank is open. The good things in life stay that way. (Advertisement)
10. The freedom fighter spun around just in time, then he fired quickly.
11. Getting the right price for your residence is not just good luck, it's getting the right agent to help you. (Advertisement)
12. At first Bauer had no trouble with the climbing. At 7.8 km he was second best, only Delgado was faster. (*The Toronto Star*)
13. A major breakthrough came in 1912, two BASF scientists made the world's first synthetic ammonia, which remains the key ingredient in most fertilizer. (*Financial Post*)

14. Jones argues that the world is overpopulated. This doesn't make sense because Jones says that the world has too many people but in some areas they don't have enough. (Sociology essay)

15. Television executives don't really care if a show is good or not, so long as it is popular, the larger the audience the better, TV is a mass medium. (Communications essay)

16. When Coca Cola altered its formula it forgot that the biggest ingredient in the brand's success was its traditional place in North American culture. They weren't just tampering with a recipe, they were changing a social institution. (*The Toronto Star*)

PUNCTUATION (477, 478, 485, 492)

Punctuate and add capitals to the following:

1. she stepped gingerly over the fallen body then she screamed
2. manning's argument then is that an elected senate would be both more representative and more effective than an appointed one
3. however old you are you can still enjoy the outdoors
4. he would like to go skiing his age and infirmity however prevent him from doing so
5. the complex plot structure that byatt employs in her novel weaves together strands from many literary traditions
6. byatts novel which employs a complex plot structure weaves together strands from many literary traditions

COLON OR SEMI-COLON

Add either a colon or a semi-colon to each of the following sentences. (see pages 172–174).

1. Images of air and sky occur repeatedly in the first three stanzas of Heaney's poem__ "the eye concedes to/Encroaching horizon," "Between the sights of the sun," "An astounding crate full of air."
2. The company is in disarray__ it filed for bankruptcy last week.
3. This was how the Prime Minister phrased it__ "If Lindros wants to choose Oshawa over Quebec City, well then I guess he knows something about Oshawa that I don't."
4. A key feature in Locke's justification of property is the famed Lockean Proviso__ the claim that property rights can arise without consent "at least where there is enough, and as good, left in common for others."

THE SEMI-COLON

The semi-colon is one of the most useful—and one of the most underused—punctuation marks (see pages 172–173). The following exercise should help to show its usefulness both as a means to more concise writing (enabling the writer to eliminate joining words or expressions) and as a way of eliminating the impression of jerkiness that short sentences create.

Rewrite each of the following, using a semi-colon in each case:

1. "Liberal" can mean many things. The *Oxford English Dictionary* lists thirty-seven definitions.
2. Great theatre companies often have humble beginnings. Stratford, Ontario's Shakespearean Festival, was held in a tent for its first few years.
3. This policy is an unwise one for the government to follow, because it would make the poor even poorer.
4. Showing that the law has not been violated during this affair establishes at best that the Minster is not a criminal, but it fails to show that he deserves to retain a place in the Cabinet.
5. The law does not require you to compensate others for their loss if you are not at fault. It only requires you to pay compensation if you have caused the damage.
6. These theories permit people to be treated as objects because of the way in which they allow people to be used as material means for the production of morally good states of affairs.

Punctuation (477–493)

Correct the punctuation mistake in each of the following:

1. Mbabane which is the capital of Swaziland, is a small town encircled by hills. (485)
2. "Why did you come here," he asked me. (488)
3. We all rode in my brothers car to Ottawa. (492)
4. Both Mandela and de Klerk believed that apartheid couldnt last much longer. (491)

Punctuate and add capitals to the following passages:

1. what did you think of the election he asked me i was surprised and disappointed that the republicans took so many seats i think they should bring in proportional representation soon he agreed
2. i just dont know what to do said don i cant seem to punctuate properly in english so i keep on writing incomplete sentences and run on sentences mary suggested several things that might help first of all she said you should read each word out loud and notice when you pause also she

added remember that the words *so* and *and* should not begin sentences also the word *because* cannot begin a main clause finally the word *that* should not be used to join two clauses together into one sentence don thanked her for this advice then he began to write a composition

Direct and Indirect Speech (494–499)

Rephrase so as to provide a grammatically correct introduction to the following quotations:

1. The Prime Minister asked if "Will the country accept double-digit inflation?"
2. Lentriccia argues: "Regardless of Byron's intention, the meaning of the text is opaque."
3. In the mid-1950s social scientists were concerned that perpetually increasing leisure time "will lead to vast social changes by the year 2000."

Jargon, Abstraction, and Doublespeak (501–504)

Translate each of the following into more easily understood English:

1. The new pen has negative vulnerability to water entry.
2. The building in which the reactor is situated was apparently constructed with a view to structural rather than containment integrity.
3. The former aide to the President tries to help clients strategize whatever their objectives may be vis-à-vis Washington, D.C., or the world.
4. Since data are central to the issue of implementation guidance we believe it is advisable to examine the data that your organization is assembling, in order to maximize the actualization of projects designated for implementation, and to preclude unintended effects.
5. With regard to the staff members' requests for supplements to the level of remuneration, management is of the opinion that it would be injudicious to advocate an increment.
6. The loss of Challenger put NASA into a temporary hiatus of shuttle flights. They regarded it as certain that they would have a shortfall in the national launch capability in the near term.
7. In considering the multiplicity of factors involved, this essay will also explore possible solutions to the parameters of the problem of the bias that is particularly strongly felt in many American Caucasian communities against ethnic heterogeneity in school transportation arrangements.

Bias in Language (505)

Rewrite each of the following so as to make it bias-free:

1. Any doctor is obliged to put his patients' concerns ahead of his own.
2. Simply increasing the number of policemen on the streets will not necessarily lead to a decrease in crime.
3. The history of mankind forms only a short chapter in the history of the planet.
4. In the 1950s most Americans worked in blue collar jobs; now the situation is reversed, with the number of white collar jobs far exceeding the number of blue collar ones.
5. In short, except for his reproductive power, a child has a fully developed capacity for love long before puberty. (Sigmund Freud, "The Sexual Enlightenment for Children")
6. In most cases the genius has reached the height of his intellectual powers by his early twenties.
7. Our Stone Age ancestors are often crudely characterized as cavemen.

Metaphors (506)

Unmix the following metaphors:

1. We don't want to throw the baby out with the bath water before we check to see if the coast is clear.
2. Unless every clause in the agreement is airtight the deal could come unglued and we'd be left up the creek without a paddle.
3. The government's scorched earth policy in response to the rebels has dampened hopes for an early settlement of the war.
4. We were all swamped by an avalanche of paperwork.

Slang and Informal English (507–517)

Rewrite each sentence to eliminate slang words or expressions:

1. She has five kids and fifteen grandchildren.
2. The work he handed in was truly awful.
3. It is kind of difficult to understand why public perceptions of John Major changed so quickly.
4. There is a bunch of reasons why the debt became so large.

Spelling (229, 528, 530)

In each sentence there are spelling errors. Correct them:

1. At the beggining of the year the commitee made its dicision. (3 errors)
2. The goverment of Malawi was long dorminated by President Banda. (2 errors)
3. A scene with over fourty charachters in it is a very unusual occurence in a Pinter play. (3 errors)

4. We have learned about garmetes, gemination, and photosinthesis. (3 errors)
5. They tried to leave serreptitiously so that the school principle would not notice their departure. (2 errors)
6. The yeild on a stock like this is likely to be non-existant; one buys it only for the capitol gain. (3 errors)

INDEX